BORN READY

The Mixed Legacy of Len Bias

by dave ungrady

Edited by: Barbara Huebner
Cover design: Shannon Sykes
Interior Design: Jeff Thoreson
Copy editor: Kevin Fay
Proofreaders: Thomas Floyd, Bridget Thoreson

Front cover photo provided by University of Maryland Athletics Media Relations
Back cover photo provided by University of Maryland archives

Library of Congress Control Number - 2011961271

ISBN: 978-1467972369

To my wife and best friend Sharon and our infant son Cayden, who inspire me every day. And to Col. Todd Hixson, my former college track teammate and roommate and beloved friend who lost his life as a U.S. Marine Corps intelligence officer while serving his country in the Iraq and Afghanistan wars.

"I'M SURPRISED THE LEN BIAS STORY IS NOT BEING TOLD ON A YEARLY BASIS WHEN NEW ATHLETES COME INTO COLLEGE, OR IN HIGH SCHOOL. THE LEN BIAS STORY IS ONE OF THE BETTER STORIES YOU CAN USE TO GET AN INDIVIDUAL OR TEAM TO DO THE RIGHT THING."

DAVE DICKERSON, MARYLAND FORWARD, 1985-1989,
TULANE UNIVERSITY HEAD COACH, 2005-2010

"YOU READY, LEONARD?"

"COACH, I WAS BORN READY."

BORN READY

The Mixed Legacy of Len Bias

SECTIONS

Foreword   11
by Maryland Poet Laureate Stanley Plumly

A Mixed Legacy   13

Born Ready   20

Maryland Athletics   46

Teammates   74

Family and Friends   108

Celtics   139

The Nation   152

Michael Leonard Bias   170

Afterword   178

Acknowledgements   182

FOREWORD

By Stanley Plumly

Maryland Poet Laureate

Professor, Director of Creative Writing at the University of Maryland

It must have been the middle of May, no more than a week or so before the end of term, when I experienced a Len Bias surprise. I know it was 1986, because I'd come to the University of Maryland the fall before in order to help start up a Master of Fine Arts Program in Creative Writing. The university was still new to me – its geography, its complexity of colleges and departments, its different levels and schedules. Of course, I knew about the fine reputation of the English Department. I knew and loved the location of the school in relation to Washington, D.C. And I knew, from a general impression, something of the reputation of the Maryland football team under Coach Bobby Ross. But second only to being aware of my own department, what I was most familiar with – from its national reputation – was Maryland's basketball team and its "colorful" coach, Lefty Driesell.

Once on the Maryland campus, I followed Driesell's team with special interest. I say "Driesell's team" when what I mean is the team of Len Bias, the All-America forward who was, by acclamation, the best basketball player in the country – a player, like the great ones, who could dominate the other team all by himself, in any number of ways. Based on the few times I'd seen Bias play – primarily on television – I remember thinking that he played like a professional: His skill and size, speed and quickness, grace and aggressiveness set him apart. Yet for all his talent, he was also a "quiet" player – no showboating, no display, all business. He was what might be called a working-class player.

About a month before the semester was over, I was asked by the Dean's office (Arts & Humanities) to introduce Gwendolyn Brooks, the national poet laureate who in 1950 became the first black poet to win the Pulitzer Prize, at an event that several campus groups had pooled resources to sponsor.

Brooks was a diminutive woman of 68. Over the years, she'd lost none of her personal fierceness or political consciousness – you could see that immediately in her demeanor and humor. I'd been in her company a couple of times: once, at a reading in Chicago, her hometown; and at a national poetry party at the Jimmy Carter White House, where there were more than a hundred poets and guests. In the moments leading up to the Maryland reading, we chatted and got introduced to various sponsors and administrators backstage. Brooks was just ending her tenure as laureate and was looking forward to returning to Chicago. I remember asking her to read one or two particular favorites of mine, one of which is her signature poem, "We Real Cool": We real cool. We Left school. We Lurk late. We Strike straight. We Sing sin. We Thin gin. We Jazz June. We Die soon.

It was, as I recall, a 7 o'clock reading. There would be a reception after. My introduction was geared toward reminding the audience of Brooks's standing in the poetry community and of her importance to her own committed communities, including American black culture and women's studies. The structure of the event called for the dean to introduce me, followed by my introduction of Brooks, who, once I'd finished, would enter from stage right to come to the podium. For a moment, Brooks and I were standing there together, when, suddenly, from the opposite side of the stage there arrives a very tall young man bearing a large bouquet of red roses.

It was Len Bias, whose presence came at the request of Joyce Ann Joyce, a professor of Afro-American Literature at Maryland. Bias took Joyce's class in the 1983 fall semester, and as Joyce explained it, "graciously" earned a D grade despite the fact he missed classes frequently and flunked the two assignments he completed. It was not her policy to flunk athletes.

Joyce developed a friendship with Bias, and considered him "sweet and thoughtful." Joyce arranged the reading by Brooks and asked Bias if he would present Brooks with a bouquet of flowers. She thought Bias's gesture would help show a link between the excellence of black basketball players and black poets and showcase the artistry of both. She had hoped that Bias's participation could translate to increased respect for poetry to the level students respect basketball players. Joyce said Bias was pleased that she respected him enough to ask him to present Brooks with the gift and that "he was as excited about the idea as I was."

The Maryland basketball banquet was being held at the same time at the Stamp Student Union about a half mile away, but that did not stop Bias from surprising Brooks and everyone else attending the event.

He shakes my hand and then embraces the diminutive Brooks and places the great flowers into her open arms. The audience goes slightly wild. I can see the tears in Brooks's eyes and everyone can see the smile on Len Bias's face. At the reception, we all talked, but who knows what about. Likely we talked about the future, notably the future of the basketball star.

The gravesite of Len Bias in July 2010. The stone was later repaired. (*by Dave Ungrady*)

Chapter 1
A Mixed Legacy

In the last half-century, scores of tragic deaths have burdened the sports world. Florence Griffith-Joyner, 38, a three-time Olympic gold medal sprinter, died in her sleep in 1998 after suffering an epileptic seizure. Golfer Payne Stewart, who won three major championships, and baseball all-stars Roberto Clemente and Thurman Munson perished in separate plane accidents while in the midst of their careers. Stewart was 42; Clemente, 38; Munson, just 32.

More recently, NFL players Corey Smith, 29, and Marquis Cooper, 26, drowned at sea in 2009 during a fishing trip off the Gulf Coast of Florida. That same year, a drunk driver who ran through a red light killed Los Angeles Angels rookie Nick Adenhart. Just hours earlier, the 22-year-old pitcher had recorded the first shutout of his career. Pat Tillman, an NFL safety, joined the Army in the aftermath of the 9/11 terrorist attacks and was killed in Afghanistan by what turned out to be friendly fire. He was 27. Steve Prefontaine, a rebellious distance runner who held multiple American records, died at the age of 24 when the sports car he was driving crashed into a rock wall.

Then there was Reggie Lewis. By the time he completed his seventh year with the Boston Celtics in 1993, Lewis had become an NBA All-Star and team captain. The 6-foot, 7-inch Lewis had endeared himself to Celtics fans beyond his success with the team, due in part to his humanitarian work and his stellar career at Boston's Northeastern University. While playing for the Huskies, Lewis was a three-time America East Conference Player of the Year. Lewis's death in

1993 of heart failure at the age of 27 while shooting baskets during an off-season workout rocked the world of the Celtics. Again.

A top international track meet in Eugene, Oregon – the Prefontaine Classic – is named after the revered distance runner, and tributes are still regularly left at the site of his death, now known as Pre's Rock, 41 years after the crash. A highway and a bridge bear Tillman's name, and some 30,000 runners took part in the 2010 Pat's Run, a 4.2-mile road race in Tempe, Arizona, which raises money for the Pat Tillman Foundation. In Boston, the Reggie Lewis Track and Athletic Center, on the campus of Roxbury Community College, is named after the late Celtics star, whose jersey hangs in tribute in the team's training center in Waltham. His banner hangs in the TD Garden, the Celtics' home arena.

By contrast, although some 11,000 people attended his memorial service, there are no statues of Len Bias. There is no Len Bias Boulevard stretching across the Columbia Park, Maryland neighborhood where he grew up, a few miles outside of Washington, D.C. There are no memorial tournaments or charity events raising money in his name for victims of cocaine-induced deaths. At least the Columbia Park Civic Association tried to honor Len's memory. According to John Ware, a longtime neighbor of the Bias family in Columbia Park, the group wanted to establish a $1,000 annual scholarship award in Len's name for someone in the neighborhood to attend college. But he says Lonise Bias, Len's mother, turned down the gesture. "She didn't tell us why," he says.

Like Tillman, the death of Bias provoked painful scrutiny of those involved – people who were supposedly on his side. Like Prefontaine, his loss dealt such a serious blow to his sport that he has become an iconic figure to a generation. But more than any athlete who has died in the last half-century, Bias still evokes a searing and confusing mix of regret and remorse, anger and sympathy, bewilderment and bitterness, and lingering sadness over the success the young athlete might have known had he not celebrated too hard, too soon.

Had Bias not died of cocaine intoxication on June 19, 1986 – less than 48 hours after being taken by the champion Boston Celtics as the No. 2 pick overall in the NBA draft – he and Lewis would likely have formed a fierce frontcourt for more than a decade, one that arguably might have been unmatched in NBA history. Had he lived, Bias would be approaching the age of 50, long-retired from what would almost surely have been a brilliant NBA career and perhaps as beloved in Boston as legends Larry Bird and Bob Cousy.

But how do you define the legacy of a universally endeared and admired All-America basketball player, one with the potential to be one of the greatest of all time, when he goes and throws it all away? How can you honor a young man whose youthful indiscretion placed the University of Maryland, the school that helped make him a star, into a tailspin that lasted for almost a decade? How can a fan or even a friend of Len Bias salute the vast achievements and joy of his brief life without also acknowledging how his choice that night wreaked havoc on the world around him, both near and far?

You want to, badly. But even 25 years later, you struggle.

Take a leisurely walk through the Comcast Center in College Park, Maryland, the epicenter of University of Maryland athletics and home venue of the men's and women's basketball teams, and you will pass a temple of Terrapins tradition and triumph known as the Maryland Walk of Fame.

Life-size photo cutouts of the best athletes ever to grace the fields, pools, tracks, mats, courts and courses in College Park spring to life. The first image you see on the left is Renaldo Nehemiah, who set his first world record in the 110-meter hurdles in 1979, as a Maryland sophomore. Nehemiah is trying to hurdle over lacrosse superstar Frank Urso, a four-time All-America who led the Terrapins to two national titles in the 1970s.

Saunter over to the middle, and you notice two of Maryland's all-time great basketball players from the early 1970s, All-Americas Len Elmore and Tom McMillen, standing side by side a few feet to the left of a large head shot of Louis "Bosey" Berger, who in 1931 became Maryland's first basketball All-America. Slide over to the right and, next to the Maryland Terrapins mascot Testudo hoisting a sign that reads "Fear the Turtle," stands Bias. He is adorned in the glowing gold Maryland jersey with the blazing red number 34, his arms raised triumphantly.

Most of the several dozen Maryland athletes or teams displayed on the wall have been selected to the Maryland Athletic Hall of Fame. Bias is not among them. The only two-time ACC Player of the Year, the All-America is considered by many to be among the top basketball talents ever to wear a Maryland uniform. None of the others left out of the Hall of Fame matches Bias's athletic impact. Only two Maryland basketball players, John Lucas in 1976 and Joe Smith in 1995, have been drafted higher than Bias in the NBA draft – and to do so, they had to be picked No. 1.

Bias's number 34 banner was first retired in Cole Field House in 1988, with no ceremony so as to avoid scrutiny. It now hangs from the rafters at Comcast Center, and Bias is recognized as one of the best basketball players in Maryland history. But a Hall of Fame bylaw stands between Bias and membership in the school's most revered athletic fraternity: Nominees must have good character and reputation, and not have been a source of embarrassment in any way to the university.

Hall of Fame committee members, however, are free to interpret the bylaw. "There's some support for him if you just looked at his athletic career," former Hall of Fame committee chairman Michael Lipitz said in 2010. "But in the context of the bylaws, there will be people who support the argument that he shouldn't be in the Hall of Fame."

Over time, the committee may see the wisdom of selecting Bias based more on his accomplishments than on a few moments of deadly indiscretion. In fact, a committee member told me that Bias's nomination might be discussed by the end of 2011. Perhaps Maryland will follow the lead of the Washington Metropolitan Basketball Hall of Fame, which plans to induct Bias at a ceremony in the spring of 2012.

And to assist their decision-making, perhaps they can defer to assessments made in various media outlets by some of the top basketball minds and observers in the country about the impact Bias's short but brilliant career had on Maryland and on the game.

> "I have said many times that the two most difficult opposing players to prepare for in my time in the ACC were Michael Jordan and Len Bias. Len was a gifted player. He was special, and our league has had a lot of great players. When I think about Len Bias now, I think of how hard he competed and how tremendously talented he was. Other than Michael Jordan, he is the player that no teams had the answer for. My feeling is that he would have been one of the top players in the NBA. He created things. I consider a playmaker as someone who can do things others can't, the way Jordan did. Bias was like that. He could invent ways to score, and there was nothing you could do about it."
>
> – *Mike Krzyzewski, Head Coach, Duke University and the USA men's basketball team*

"Lenny was a god at Maryland. Absolutely a god. He was that good and he was larger than life in every sense of the word. That body, that booming voice, he was from outer space."

– Scott Van Pelt, ESPN broadcaster and University of Maryland graduate who was a sophomore at Maryland when Bias died

"I played against Len Bias in the ACC and he was a unique power forward/small forward because he was a guy who could play with his back to the basket and he had a body by Adonis. He also had this great athleticism with a soft touch. To put him with Larry Bird and the Boston Celtics, you would think that his career would have been a 15-20 year career, NBA All-Star games and probably one of the greatest players that ever played this game if he had an opportunity to do it."

– Kenny Smith, former North Carolina player and 10-year NBA veteran; NBA analyst for Turner Sports

"I saw great players from both the ACC and Big East every night. Jordan. Ewing. Mullin. Sampson. Later on, David Robinson. But Bias was the most awesome collegiate player of that bunch. That jumper was so pure. I mean, Michael Jordan, at that time, would have killed for that jumper. And Bias was 2 1/2 inches taller."

– Michael Wilbon, former Washington Post columnist; ESPN basketball analyst

Some have discovered unique ways to memorialize Bias. In the summer of 2010 a disc jockey by the name of Len Bias performed at a nightclub in Provincetown, Massachusetts. The deejay turned out to be Eli Cohen, who grew up in Springfield, Massachusetts, as a Celtics fan. "A lot of deejays go under a stage name, names of real people," he says. "The name is an uncommon name. It has a nice ring to it. And in some ways it's a tribute. I was a fan of Len Bias. I think he was a cool guy. Also it's to get attention."

He was, however, concerned about the attention he was receiving. During an interview, he asked if the Bias family would sue him for using the name while practicing his hobby. "My father, when he first saw it, he said 'their family better not find out.' I mean no disrespect."

A group of former Maryland students who claimed to play basketball with Bias at Maryland formed the Len Bias band, but they won't talk about why. "Let sleeping dogs lie type of thing," a friend of the band members, who simply identified himself as Ed, wrote in an email.

Mike Cogburn was the manager on duty at Town Hall Liquors in College Park when Bias stopped by a few hours before he died. Cogburn remembers steering Bias to a pint of Courvoisier Cognac after he saw Bias was about to buy a type of brandy that Cogburn called "cheap booze." Cogburn thought that as a top NBA draft pick Bias could afford a better grade of liquor. He talked with Bias about the Celtics and the NBA, and Bias autographed the purchase receipt. Cogburn then walked him out to a car, where his friend Brian Tribble sat waiting.

About six months later, Cogburn was fired from Town Hall due in part, he claims, to the media attention he brought to the bar and liquor store when he did local TV interviews about seeing Bias the night he died and getting his autograph on the receipt. The bar owner, he says, was not pleased when the media calls didn't stop. Cogburn then moved to St. Croix, where he stayed until Hurricane Hugo devastated the island in 1989. After that, times got so tough that Cogburn was forced to sell the receipt for just $200.

Another College Park bar is forever linked to the Bias legacy as well. John Brown, the owner of RJ Bentley's in College Park since the mid-1970s, hung a Bias jersey in his restaurant. Brown honors dozens of Maryland athletes by hanging jerseys, some signed, on the walls: Albert King and Buck Williams, members of the 2002 national championship basketball team; football legend Boomer Esiason; and members of national championship women's field hockey and lacrosse teams among them. For a time, his wall of fame included Bias's number 34 on a back wall of a dining room. In the early 1990s, the jersey was stolen from its glass-enclosed frame.

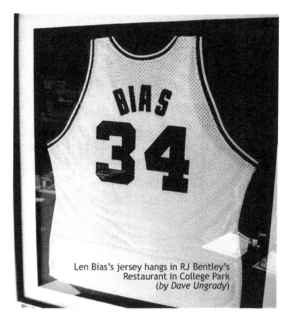

Len Bias's jersey hangs in RJ Bentley's Restaurant in College Park (by Dave Ungrady)

Brown had been offered as much as several thousand dollars for the jersey, so at first he assumed the thieves were looking to cash in. But a couple of years later, a Maryland lacrosse player told Brown that he overheard some young men at a party in Annapolis say they had something special from Maryland, and he thought they were talking about Bias's jersey. While attending a tailgate party at a Maryland football game a short time later, Brown told some Maryland lacrosse players that whoever found the jersey would receive a $150 bar tab at his restaurant. A few weeks later, on December 1, Brown received an unmarked brown envelope in the mail. Inside was Bias's jersey.

A loyal customer told Brown a couple of years ago that her brother and two of his friends stole the jersey and rotated possession of it. "They put it up wherever they were living," Brown says. "One would have it for a while, something bad would happen to him, they'd hand it to the next guy and something bad would happen to that guy. So they got fed up with it and sent it back. This could be an urban myth: the 'curse of the Bias jersey.'"

Curse or no curse, the death of the 22-year-old Bias did trigger a legacy perhaps more complicated and compelling than any athlete before him. His decision that June night in 1986 profoundly affected the lives of his friends and family; drastically changed the careers of University of Maryland administrators, coaches and athletes; dramatically altered the destiny of the Boston Celtics; and sparked a change in the way cocaine dealers and users were punished in the United States, handing out what many now view as unduly harsh prison terms under new mandatory-sentencing laws sparked by his death.

Who knows how many lives have been ruined?

But the legacy of Len Bias also resonates in the numbers that reflect a decreased use of cocaine.

A survey conducted by the National Institute on Drug Abuse in 1986 revealed the rate of cocaine use among 12th-graders at 12.7 percent. By 1992, six years after the death of Bias, the rate had fallen to 3.1 percent. "Sometimes, you need a sentinel event like this one to alert everybody," Nora D. Volkow, the director of the National Institute on Drug Abuse, said at a vigil commemorating fatal victims of drug abuse held in Arlington, Virginia, in 2006, according to a *Washington Post* report.

Thanks largely to Len's mother, who attended the vigil, the impact lives on. Lonise Bias believes her son died for a larger purpose. Within weeks of his funeral, she began what has turned into a 25-year career and campaign of public speaking against drug use and of promoting the power to overcome life's obstacles.

In the summer of 2011, Lonise Bias said in a newspaper report that she is trying to develop a 100,000-square-foot Bias Family Center in Prince George's County, Maryland, not far from where Len Bias grew up. The center would offer such community programs as mentoring and peer training and would include computer labs, boxing rings and an art gallery.

Who knows how many lives have been saved, and how many more will be for decades to come? Brian Straus had no connection to Bias other than growing up in the Washington area and watching him play on TV and was not a rabid fan of either the Terrapins or the Celtics. He was raised in white upper-middle-class suburbia. But when I told Straus, a longtime friend and an accomplished soccer journalist, that I was writing a book about the legacy of Bias, his immediate reaction surprised me.

"He was the reason I never used cocaine," Straus says. "He was exactly the reason when I was at parties in college at [the University of Pennsylvania] and saw people do cocaine and I didn't try it. He was the great traffic light, the devil on your shoulder saying don't do it. It wasn't an essay question. It was just like a punch in the gut that told you don't touch this ever."

It was a sentiment echoed time and time again. Greg Abel, who owns a communications company, is an avid University of Maryland sports fan and says he watched all the Maryland games on television while growing up in Owings Mills. He played basketball on his high-school team and vividly remembers Len Bias and his brother, Jay, putting on a dunk show for him and other boys at John Kochan's basketball camp in the summer of 1985, when Kochan was the head coach at Millersville University. Before coming to Millersville, Kochan was an assistant coach at Maryland and helped recruit Bias. The lasting impact of Bias's death was the same on Abel as it was on Straus.

"Every time I saw cocaine at a party or was offered to do it, I never did," says Abel, who has hosted pre- and post-game broadcasts of Maryland basketball games on ESPN radio in Baltimore. "I also never sought it out or hung out with people who did coke because the drug will always be linked to Bias's death in my mind."

Closer still was Keith Booth.

In April 2011, Booth talked excitedly about the day he met Bias, his hero. It happened during a promotional appearance by Bias and teammate Keith Gatlin at a sandwich shop in East Baltimore. Booth, an impressionable 10-year-old, arrived three hours early to secure a spot at the front of the line for the 11 a.m. event. When he met Bias, he told him that he would play hard and one day be a Terrapin just like his idol, and, yup, that he would at least tie Bias's scoring record.

Booth knew the owner of the sub shop and was given close access to Bias and Gatlin once the signing ended. He says the moment is recorded in a picture of him with Bias and Gatlin and several others, which hung on a wall in the shop for almost a decade.

When his older sister woke him on the morning of June 19, 1986, after hearing on the news that Bias had died, Booth grew hysterical. He cried uncontrollably as he called his mother at work to tell her the tragic news. Booth was 11 years old. He saw the kinds of people where he grew up in his East Baltimore neighborhood who used drugs. They weren't like Bias.

Before Bias died, the thought never crossed the boy's mind that elite athletes used drugs. He used Bias's death as a reminder to stay focused on basketball and his grades, and to continue a lifestyle that avoided drug use. "Once I understood what it was and how it happened that he died, it made me never want to touch a drug ever or abuse my body," he says. "It affected my life to help me become the person and man I am today."

For almost a decade, every time Booth visited the sandwich shop, the photo hanging on the wall reminded him of that happy day. When he was 17, he stopped by one day and it was gone. The owner had moved to Greece, and taken the photo with him. "Every time I tell that story, it makes me sick to my stomach," Booth says. Bias was gone and now, too, the treasured photo.

Soon after Bias died and long before the photo vanished, Booth went to a sporting-goods store and bought an autographed poster of the player to hang on a wall in his room. There it stayed until his freshman year of college, when he gave it to one of his cousins. "I'd see it every day," he says. "It reinforced the impact his death has had on me and the player I remember I fell in love with growing up."

Although he'd seen Bias play only on television, he vividly remembers him as "the first guy who played the game with such passion in college," sending blocked shots two rows deep into the stands and even slapping the hands of opposing players during pre-game introductions with intimidating force.

Those images shaped Booth's career: a Terrapin All-America in 1997, Booth spent 2005 to 2011 as an assistant men's basketball coach at Maryland. In between, he did something his idol never lived to do: Booth played for two years in the NBA, winning an NBA title with the Chicago Bulls in 1998. But, despite his banner hanging in the rafters of the Comcast Center alongside Bias's, Booth never did break his scoring record.

An inconspicuous but poignant symbol of Bias's death lay in disarray in the early summer of 2010 at the Lincoln Memorial Cemetery in Suitland, Maryland, just outside the southeast D.C. border. Part of his flat headstone was falling into the earth. The dirt had given way around the left side of a the stone. When a cemetery worker who showed me the burial site noticed the flaw, he said with no emotion, "We should probably fix that." A year later, someone had. The hole was patched up and now the stone is just like all the others.

Unlike Bias ever was in life, or ever will be in death.

Chapter 2

Born Ready

The middle-class, black community of Columbia Park sits in humble repose a few miles northeast of Washington, D.C., its rectangular street pattern a reflection of its commonality. Only a mix of colors distinguishes one tidy, box-like house from another, their front yards the size of half a basketball court, positioned neatly in parallel rows, one house segueing into the next.

In the 1970s and 1980s, young boys who wanted to develop their athletic skills flocked to the Columbia Park Community Center, reverently referred to as The Rec, spending tireless hours perfecting their skills on a small, indoor windowless court with a ceramic floor.

Johnnie Walker was one of them. He had spent his earliest years growing up in the Congress Heights section of Southeast Washington, D.C., considered one of the poorest sections of the city, about a mile from where the Anacostia River dumps into the Potomac River. There, it was difficult to ignore young adults shooting heroin and drinking liquor all hours of the day. But at 15, Walker moved to the relative comforts of Columbia Park, where life was humble and simple and drug and alcohol abuse did not become an issue until the late 1980s.

Walker played two years of varsity basketball at Northwestern High School in Hyattsville, Maryland, graduating in 1978. While putting off college for a year, he volunteered as a coach at The Rec, monitoring basketball activities for neighborhood kids and preparing his players for the center's summer league team. He taught them fundamentals and conditioning with innovative exercises, such as plyometrics, which he learned from Bob Wagner, his former coach at Northwestern. Wagner wanted to build his new program with the best available talent, so he alerted Walker to keep an eye out for Len Bias, a young player at nearby Greenbelt Middle School whom he had heard showed promising talent.

During practice one day in the winter of 1979, some kid kept peeking through the doors to the gym at The Rec, yelling to his friend Terrence Lewis. Walker scolded Lewis, telling him to ignore the kid and pay attention. The interloper finally gave up and left.

"Who was that?" Walker eventually asked out loud.

"That's Leonard Bias," someone said.

A few months later, while walking to The Rec, Walker spotted Bias riding a bike and approached the ninth-grader, saying he understood that he played for Greenbelt Middle School. Bias tried to sell himself to Walker, saying he was better than Lewis. He told Walker that his parents didn't let him leave the street much without their supervision, so Walker offered to talk with them and receive permission to serve as his guardian to, from and while he was at The Rec, if he was interested in joining the group. Walker could stop by the Bias house, he told the young man, and meet him so the two could walk to The Rec together.

"They said yes, but don't you think his dad didn't come up and check on him," says Walker.

At the time, Bias was in the midst of a critical phase in his basketball development, using a setback to fuel a fiery determination to be a great basketball player. He had been cut from the middle-school team twice, in the seventh and eighth grades. "It was one of the big shocks in my life," Bias said in a 1985 *Washington Post* article. "I remember going down the steps to look at the [team] list and my name wasn't on it. I couldn't believe it. Right then, I decided I was going to show these people that I could play the game."

"He kept saying the whole time, 'God, let me get better,' " says his middle-school and high-school teammate Reginald Gaskins in the documentary *Without Bias*. Young Leonard's biggest motivation came from the teasing, his father recalled in *Without Bias*, explaining: "He was going to be the best."

As he integrated Bias into the group at The Rec, Walker took stock of him as a tall, lanky and raw athlete and a bit of a whiner when he felt he was being fouled unfairly. Walker treated Bias like any other regular in the group, meaning he roughed him up, pushing him after he took a shot. With Walker in his path, there was no such thing as an easy layup. Walker hit Bias with elbows and muscled him away from the basket, acting like a bully a few years before the NBA's Detroit Pistons made the style fashionable in the mid-1980s.

Brian Waller, one of Bias's closest friends at The Rec and a high-school teammate, also endured Walker's tough training. "He'd give us everything that wasn't in the rule book," he says. "When you're not used to it, you whine and cry. People were fouling [Bias] all the time. No matter how much he whined, Johnnie was still killing him. On Monday and Wednesdays we'd play against the older guys in the gym; that's how they played. You either step up or you don't."

It took a while for Bias to grow into his body and develop his superior talents. "When he was young, kids used to laugh at him when he played basketball," said Lee Madkins, the director of the center during Bias's youth, in a *Washington Post* report soon after the player's death. "They never picked him on a team. Then he ended up with everyone wanting him on their team."

It took only a couple of months for Bias to adapt to the physical play, and soon he became the intimidator on Columbia Park's 16-and-under traveling team. In order to set the tone at the beginning of each game during his first summer with the team, he played a role: Columbia Park purposely let opponents win the opening tip so Bias could block or goal-tend their opening shot. As Waller remembers, it helped Columbia Park win every game that summer. Bias also showed his athleticism for his age by finishing off alley-oops. He was the only player on the team who had the leaps to complete the play. Columbia Park felt so confident that players on the bench would read the newspaper toward the end of runaway games. "At that age, we didn't think if it was embarrassing for the other team," says Waller.

Bias considered attending DeMatha Catholic High School, at the time one of the top programs in the country, but Walker steered him toward his alma mater Northwestern, which had a history of local greatness in basketball. Before the 1980s, Northwestern won three state championships and produced a few NBA players, most notably Larry Spriggs, who won an NBA title during his five seasons with the Los Angeles Lakers from 1981 to 1986. Wagner became the school's head basketball coach in 1978 after several years as an assistant.

Wagner grew up in the 1950s in the town of North Brentwood, the first African American incorporated town in Prince George's County, which included Northwestern High School and Columbia Park in its boundaries and sits close to the northeast Washington, D.C., border. He used basketball to help him attend Northwestern, a good high school, and later attended the University of Maryland, a mile north of the high school, in the late 1960s.

At The Rec, Waller witnessed Bias's dramatic evolution as a basketball player, and by the time Bias got to Northwestern, says Waller, "it was like night and day from when I first met him." Nonetheless, Wagner considered Bias a work in progress. He was growing taller as he inched toward his ultimate 6-foot, 8-inch frame, had developed a better shot and was a leaper, but Wagner knew there was more to becoming a good rebounder than having an ability to jump. He also thought Bias lacked a certain toughness and always had to open his mouth, so he encouraged him to play in men's leagues and learn from some veteran players. "Len was a crybaby, a whiner," says Wagner. "We wanted the older guys to rough him up a bit, but not hurt him. And we wanted the older guys to talk to him."

Wagner soon discovered Bias's adventurous spirit. While waiting around school for the start of the first game of the season as a sophomore, Bias discovered open access to a room that stored candy bars for the pom-pom squad. He couldn't resist the temptation to satisfy a sweet tooth, and grabbed some candy. When Wagner found out, he benched Bias for the game.

"Leonard was a handful to manage," Wagner says fondly.

Michael Jordan defends Len Bias. The two
are considered the best players to come out
of the Atlantic Coast Conference.
(*Campus Photo Services*)

At Northwestern, Bias developed his skills rapidly under Wagner, and by the end of the year had become a starter and was, according to Waller, an impact player with a decent shot who could rebound and block shots.

During the summer after his sophomore year, Bias for the first time attended the Five Star Basketball Camp. There, the top high-school basketball players in the nation gathered annually to learn from NBA or college players as well as such luminary coaches as Bobby Knight, Chuck Daly and Hubie Brown. The camp also served as a prime location for college coaches to scout the top high-school talent and is considered the precursor to the AAU programs that now serve the same purpose. The best players received free tuition at the camp, but worked off their fee as waiters. That first year, Bias paid his own way.

Waller, who also attended, says Bias's first Five Star camp experience transformed him as a player. "He either outplayed the other guys or played them evenly," he remembers. "His confidence changed after the Five Star camp. After that, there was no looking back."

One of the first people Bias met at camp was Michael Jordan, then a rising-star senior at Laney High School in Wilmington, North Carolina. As Waller remembers, Jordan had already been at the camp for a week working with Spriggs, the Northwestern alumnus and at the time a top player at Howard University, who was among the counselors that year.

"We saw Jordan sitting on a bench and Larry said he wanted to introduce him to his homeboys," says Waller. "Larry introduced me as my nickname, 'Ice.' Jordan said, 'They call me 'Black Ice.' "

With the ice broken, roommates Waller and Bias spent lots of time with Jordan and his roommate Buzz Peterson, who would later become Jordan's teammate at North Carolina. The four bonded quickly, gathering in each other's rooms at night talking about their basketball dreams. The friendship between Bias and Jordan grew stronger the following year. Waller and Bias ran into Jordan and a friend at a University of Maryland football game, and the four left the game early to play two-on-two games in Cole Field House for about an hour.

"We beat them," Waller says proudly.

At Northwestern his junior year, with his body beefing up, Bias became a more-dangerous presence against bigger boys. Wagner worked on Bias's outside game in practice to help him prepare for his college career, but saw the value of keeping him underneath the basket as much as possible. Bias felt more natural on the perimeter and often drifted away from the basket; the coach kept trying to feed him the ball in the low post. Bias soon became a force of concern for opponents. Through the first five games of his junior year, Bias averaged 22 points a game. He scored 23 to help Northwestern beat county rival Eleanor Roosevelt by 40 points and win the county AA title for the first time in more than a decade.

Even as his basketball career at Northwestern was gaining momentum, Bias had already started developing a fondness for the University of Maryland. While in middle school, Bias had worked in Cole Field House as a popcorn vendor, although Waller insists that Bias spent more time eating popcorn and watching games than actually selling the snack. During the summer, Bias attended Maryland head coach Lefty Driesell's basketball camps and also spent two summers on the Maryland campus attending Upward Bound programs. Upward Bound provides high-school students a chance to take college prep classes and work on a college campus for six weeks.

Then there was the emotional connection. Throughout high school, Bias and Waller would often walk the couple miles from Northwestern to College Park and cruise the Maryland campus, dreaming about the days they would showcase their basketball skills at Cole Field House. Maryland coaches left home game tickets for Waller and Bias. The two relished the experience, sitting near courtside behind a basket, watching their hero Ernie Graham along with future NBA players such as Buck Williams and Albert King lead Maryland to the ACC regular season title in 1980. They dreamed of wearing the Terrapins' home colors of red, white, black and gold.

Dozens of times, they met up on campus with Graham, a Terrapin from 1977 to 1981 who still holds the school record for most points in a game, with 44. "Everything Ernie did, we did," says Waller. "We'd go to his room. We'd go to a gym and play ball. We'd go play in Cole Field House. We were so blessed. We were so happy."

Waller and Bias played one-on-one games alone on the Cole Field House floor during the off-season, or pick-up games with Graham and other Maryland players. If Graham was in line to play the next game, he would often do so only if Bias and Waller could play on his team; otherwise, he would wait until the three could play together. The two high schoolers lifted weights in Cole Field House in the same rooms used by Maryland's basketball players and other athletes. After workouts, Waller and Bias ate dinner with Graham at a campus dining hall. They accompanied Graham to a party in the campus Student Union and, as Waller emphatically mentioned with a smile, mingled with the college girls. Once, Graham took the two into Maryland's basketball equipment room and outfitted them with a wide range of Terps basketball gear, including red Nike basketball shoes and National Invitation Tournament T-shirts.

Graham remembers Bias as a nice, enthusiastic kid who smiled and joked around a lot. "He would just show up and stand there at the door," says Graham. "He wouldn't want anything or say anything. He says 'I'm doing whatever you're doing.' He always had that smile, always had a joke or something funny to say. He kept everybody laughing."

Graham admits that he started smoking marijuana before he entered Maryland and started using cocaine recreationally while at the school. He says one of his teammates, John Bilney, joked about Graham's drug use by writing "$100 a gram" on Graham's door. But Graham insists he never exposed Bias to drugs.

"They never used drugs with me," says Graham, who eventually became addicted to cocaine, an ordeal that lasted until 1994. In 1996 he started Get the Message, an after-school program that teaches drug prevention and life skills. His program recently became affiliated with the Cal Ripken, Sr. Foundation and he speaks up to a three times a month for the group. "The smell of marijuana would be in our dorm room but we would turn the fan on and let it get out of there. But I'm not saying they didn't smell it on the walls. I would never light a bong or smoke a joint in front of them. I wanted to hide that from them. I wanted them to respect me. I wanted them not to look at drugs."

All that time spent playing basketball helped Bias eventually thrive as a high-school player, and he showcased his talent often against other top area players. Waller remembers how during preseason games against top D.C. high-school teams, Bias more than held his own against such players as Johnnie Dawkins of Mackin High School, who later was a star at Duke, and Billy Martin of McKinley Tech and Anthony Jones of Dunbar, both top recruits for Georgetown in 1981. All three went on to play in the NBA.

"Every time we played those guys, Len outplayed them," says Waller. "He always shined against the other big-time players."

By the summer after his junior year, Bias had reached the heralded Five Star camp status of waiter, which allowed him free tuition. Howard Garfinkel, who started the camp in 1966 and ran it for 42 years, says that after his second year at the camp Bias received a 5-plus rating – the highest a player can receive – signifying "super" potential to dominate college at the Division 1 level. He also won the Most Outstanding Player award that year over such future NBA players as Dawkins and Billy Thompson, who helped Louisville win the NCAA in 1986.

"He was one of the top 10 or 15 best ever at our camp," says Garfinkel. "He was an extra-terrestrial athlete and a great scorer. And he was a great person, very likable."

Back at Northwestern, much was expected of Bias and the team during his senior season. But the Wildcats started off slowly, winning just one of their first five games. This was due in part to Wagner benching Bias for two weeks. First, Bias had approached him in tears, wilting under the pressure of choosing a college. Then, Wagner heard from teachers that Bias's grades were slipping. The coach felt a break would help Bias regroup and even considered not letting Bias play the entire season. He wanted to ensure that Bias, whom he calls "a smart kid," had not forgotten about the importance of academics and told the young man that when the teacher said he was again focused on doing his work in class, he could play.

Such disciplinary measures helped define Wagner's coaching style, which he developed from watching some of the top college coaches of the time. He traveled to Pittsburgh to watch a clinic put on by Bobby Knight, who won his first national title at Indiana in 1976, and remembers sitting in on sessions by Rick Pitino and Rick Majerus, two other top college coaches, learning subtle ways to get the most out of each player. He labels DeMatha coach Morgan Wootten, one of the most revered high school basketball coaches of all time, as a positive influence, as well.

Wagner tried to push each player to his breaking point and claims that graduates of his program never had a harder practice in college than they endured under him in high school, but he also often praised the player who made the pass leading to a basket more than the one who scored the points. He used plyometric exercises he learned from University of Maryland track coach Frank Costello to enhance his players' strength and agility. He tried to develop warriors who fought hard and always defended the concept of team. In practice he hardly ever blew a whistle, teaching his team to play through unfair calls and "no calls." In Wagner's system, a warrior wanted to be fouled, go to the foul line, make the shot and say nothing, then run down court and defend.

Wagner wanted to minimize fear in his players. "When you have fear, you have violence," he says. "Most people strike out in violence when they're afraid. My goal as a coach and a teacher was that there was never a situation in a game that we did not go over in practice. And we respected everybody and feared no one."

Wagner's philosophy was part Patton, part Zen. Early was on time and on time was late. If you arrived late to practice, you didn't practice and if you didn't practice, you didn't play. Players had to wear a jacket and tie to games, and had to remain at school after class the days of games to reduce the chance they might arrive late or miss the game completely. "If I didn't, they'd go somewhere with their girlfriends and they'd come late," he says, and then he would have to deal with the issues of whether they would start, or even play.

- - - - - - - - - -

By his senior year, Bias had also learned to control his outbursts. No longer did he slam the ball in frustration after a bad play or yell at a referee for what he thought was an unfair call. He instead channeled his frustration and aggression into his play.

To Wagner, Bias epitomized the warrior mentality he tried to instill in his troops. He was a battler, and he learned, as true warriors do, how to gain the upper hand without hurting his team. Wagner remembers the time Bias was taking a beating in the first half of a game in Boston against a small Catholic school. But Wagner and Bias both understood the rule of retaliation, which says the referee often misses a first physical violation but calls a foul, or worse, on the act of retribution. So, don't retaliate right away. Instead, wait for a more subtle moment to send the message. That's the way it's done on the playground.

At the start of the second half, Wagner suddenly noticed that one of the players who beat up on Bias earlier was doubled over in so much pain that he had to leave the court. Wagner didn't see what Bias had done, but he understood its impact. Bias had sent the player a message without hurting his team and, as Wagner remembers, was not called for the foul.

With Bias back on the team, Northwestern won 19 consecutive games and advanced to the state championship final. Down by eight after one period, Northwestern fought back to tie the game with one second remaining. Vernon Butler of High Point High School, who later played at the Naval Academy, scored the winning basket at the buzzer from about 25 feet as Bias, careful to avoid a foul, leaned slightly into the shooter and raised his arms in a futile attempt to divert Butler's focus. Bias scored 18 points and had 13 rebounds in the final and ended the season with equally impressive numbers, averaging 19 points and 12 rebounds a game.

During his senior year, Bias made the usual recruiting rounds, visiting a handful of schools that included Oregon State, the University of San Francisco and North Carolina State in addition to Maryland. Wagner, a good friend of Driesell, worked closely with Bias to choose a school but insists the player never asked him which college to choose.

Wagner set up a system that allowed dozens of recruiters to speak with Bias in an office at the Northwestern gym during summer league games for only 15 minutes, which, he admits, did not please all the coaches. He encouraged Bias to consider a school that would cater to his academic

and social needs in case basketball for some reason did not work out so that his chances of graduating would improve. In those days, coaches faced fewer restrictions on the number of visits they
could make to a recruit. After Driesell spotted Bias sitting out front of Northwestern High School
one day when he drove by the school, he stopped by to say hello. As he approached, he saw that
Bias was drawing an impressive sketch of the school. "I said, 'You're an artist better than you are
a basketball player,' " Driesell recalls.

Still, basketball was Bias's main focus when picking a college, and recruiters would have to
work hard to convince him not to attend a school that was just a few miles from his home that featured his college basketball idol in Graham and was the scene of many fond memories throughout
high school.

Wagner encouraged Bias to visit Oregon State because he wanted the player, who grew up in a
strong African American community, to visit a school where he was a racial minority. Waller says
Oregon freshman A.C. Green, a four-year starter at the school who later played 17 seasons in the
NBA, escorted Bias around the Oregon campus. Waller says Bias was impressed that Green had
access to a Lincoln Town Car, but that was not enough for Bias to seriously consider playing college
basketball in the Pacific Northwest. While Bias was visiting the University of San Francisco, he
watched senior Quintin Dailey of the home team battle Dominique Wilkins of Georgia and came
home raving about Wilkins's jumping ability and dramatic dunks. He commented to Waller about
how Wilkins had legs like a thoroughbred horse.

"All of a sudden he started lifting weights with his legs," says Waller. Wilkins would go on to
become a nine-time NBA All-Star.

Dailey, who later played 10 years in the NBA in a career that was plagued by drug abuse, remembers Bias as a good kid who smiled a lot. After he watched Dailey stage a fierce battle with a
teammate in practice, Bias asked Dailey why he worked so hard and made so many mistakes. "I
told him you have to make your mistakes in practice so you can do what you can do in games,"
says Dailey. "We wanted him bad, but he said he had to go to Maryland. I told him that I'm from
Baltimore and I came out here, why can't you? We also had some power forwards who were young,
so he had to go where he could best fit in."

If any school stood a good chance of stealing Bias away from the Terps, it was ACC rival N.C.
State. At the time, the Wolfpack featured Dereck Whittenburg and Sidney Lowe, teammates at De-
Matha High School who were Bias's good friends, as well as local basketball rivals.

"By the end of the visit, I knew I wanted to go to State," Bias said in a *Washington Post* story in
1985. "That's the last thing I told Coach Valvano when I left."

Those words from Bias to Valvano as he said goodbye to the coach left Valvano in a dreamy
state. His decision would have been a major upset in the recruiting wars between Maryland and
N.C. State. "Are you kidding? I remember him hugging me at the airport and saying he was coming," Valvano said in the *Post* story. "I said, 'Don't tell me that. I'll get too excited.' If we had gotten
that kid ..."

If it had been up to Bias alone, Valvano very well might have. Walker claims that despite Bias's deep connections to Maryland, N.C. State was his first choice, based in part on an enjoyable campus visit. "N.C. State did a lot of things down there for him," says Walker, who refused to elaborate other than to add, "He had a good time. They lived well down there."

It turned out, however, that no college could compete with the passion Bias felt for Maryland combined with the influence James Bias had on his son. The elder Bias liked the fact that it would be easy for Len's three younger siblings to watch their big brother play so close to home. "He had great respect for his father," says Walker. "The fact is, his father wanted him to stay home and go to Maryland. Len didn't make the decision to go to Maryland."

Driesell, for one, felt little concern that Bias might attend another school. "He wasn't like Tom McMillen and had everyone recruiting him," says Driesell, referring to the former Maryland player, eventual All-America and Rhodes Scholar who was the top high-school recruit in the country in 1970. "I felt good that he liked Maryland. He hung out there all the time."

To the surprise of few, Bias signed with Maryland in mid-April 1982.

Any thoughts that Bias possessed about developing an imposing game as a freshman were quickly quieted by the reality of adjusting to the college game. Maryland had finished 16-13 the previous year and 5-9 in the ACC, its worst conference finish in four seasons. It may have been a team ripe for a change, but Bias didn't start a game until after the New Year.

Bias did show flashes of brilliance that season. In one highlight, he hit a 17-foot jump shot with two seconds remaining that helped unranked Maryland upset 15th-ranked Tennessee-Chattanooga by one point in the first round of the NCAA tournament. Bias ended up starting 13 games for Maryland and averaging 7.1 points per game, the best of any Terrapins freshman.

But Bias was far from content with his first year at Maryland. Walker says that after a loss to UCLA in late December, Bias asked him to contact Valvano about transferring to N.C. State. Bias was unhappy after Driesell subbed him out of the game after he took a shot, and felt that Driesell wanted him to focus more on defense than offense. Bias was often asked to defend such players as Virginia's 7-foot, 4-inch center Ralph Sampson and Houston's Clyde Drexler. Sampson would become a three-time college player of the year, and Drexler, a 1983 All-America.

Bias was frustrated at being unable to showcase his offensive talents, says Walker. "He would say they're trying to change his shot, and that every time he tried to shoot the ball, they have something to say to him and they'd take him out of the game. He finally got tired of it. Here's a guy who's been a scorer and you're asking him to not shoot the ball?" Walker asks rhetorically. "[Scoring] is all he's done, and now don't do that?"

Driesell was working to persuade Bias to change his shot by releasing the ball at the height of his jump, to take advantage of his superior leaping ability, and Bias admitted that it took him a while to adjust. It wasn't until late in his junior year, he told the *Washington Post* that March, that he finally felt comfortable with his new technique: "Now when I go up to shoot, I don't expect anybody to block me."

After that upsetting UCLA game, Waller remembers standing near Bias and overhearing an animated conversation in the tunnel area of Cole Field House when N.C. State stars Whittenburg and

Lowe – wearing flashy clothes and jewelry, bragging about owning nice cars, and on their way to winning the NCAA championship that season – tried to convince Bias to transfer.

Walker says Driesell called him shortly after the UCLA game to discuss Bias's concerns and ask if Valvano initiated the contact with Bias, which would have been an NCAA violation. Walker says he talked bluntly with Driesell, saying Bias didn't like the fact that he had to focus so much on defense and was clearly unhappy with what he felt were Driesell's attempts to break him down and control him. He said Bias felt that he wasn't supposed to take shots. Before the end of the season, Driesell met with Bias and worked out the problems.

"After that, Leonard said everything was OK," says Driesell.

After his freshman year, Bias realized he needed to work on his main weakness – dribbling the basketball – if he wanted to be a dominant force in the NBA, so he asked incoming freshman guard Keith Gatlin for help. Gatlin and Bias worked together all that summer, playing one-on-one in Cole Field House, with Bias wearing special dribble glasses that didn't allow him to look down at the ball. At times, they started their sessions near midnight after getting back from a movie.

With improved ball-handling skills and a renewed sense of purpose, Bias would help Maryland to one of its most rewarding seasons. Maryland began the season ranked No. 8 in the country. By the time the Terrapins met top-ranked North Carolina on January 12, they were 10-1 and had moved up to No. 5. Thanks in large part to Bias, who scored a career-high 24 points while helping to hold Michael Jordan to 21, Maryland trailed by just one point with about two minutes remaining before Jordan and fellow All-America Sam Perkins led Carolina to a 12-point victory. It was one of Bias's best games of the season.

In early February his role increased after Maryland's junior guard Adrian Branch, who was averaging 12 points a game, was suspended from the team for about two weeks after being arrested for misdemeanor possession of $10 of marijuana. Gatlin, the freshman guard who replaced Branch in the starting lineup, says that even though the team lost its next three games, the time without Branch helped Bias and the team become more balanced.

"Lefty and the coaches felt it would be good to go inside-out," says Gatlin. "Lenny could get it off the rim and post up and shoot it. We started going inside with Lenny and Ben Coleman and Mark Fothergill, and then send it out for Jeff Adkins or me to shoot. We went from a perimeter team to an inside team and pushed the ball out. That's how we played the rest of the year. When Adrian came back, we had another dangerous shooter from the outside."

The Terrapins ended the season at 24-8, finishing second in the ACC regular season standings with a 9-5 conference record. Despite his impressive numbers – he finished the year second on the team in points (15.2) per game and third in rebounds (4.5) per game – Bias was not selected for the all-ACC team when it was announced in early March. The snub provided added motivation. Waller remembers receiving a phone call from Bias: "You see the paper today? I didn't even make the second team. You see the dudes they got in front of me? That's alright, I'm gonna go down to the ACC and win the MVP of the tournament."

Maryland made it to the Sweet 16 in the NCAA tournament after winning the ACC tournament title for only the second time up to that point and the first since 1958. In the ACC tourney, Bias had 15 points and 7 rebounds in a first-round, six-point win over N.C. State, and scored 15 points, including 10 in the first half, in a two-point semi-final win over Wake Forest that saw him make a free throw with one second remaining. In the final game, against Duke, Bias scored 26 points, converting 12 of 17 field goals – 10 of which came on a 24-3 run that erased an eight-point Duke lead early in the second half. It was enough to convince voters to name him the tournament MVP, just as he had proclaimed.

It was the way Bias played in the ACC final against Duke that helped build his legend. He slammed down dunks, hit turn-around jumpers that frustrated defenders and soared so high on jumpers from the baseline that the outstretched arms of the defenders must have felt no more annoying than a mosquito flyby. When a lame alley-oop pass from Jeff Adkins seemed destined for an opponent's ready hands, Bias showed his pure athleticism by leaping from the baseline and swatting the ball with his left hand toward the rim before the Duke defender Dan Meagher could take the ball away.

- - - - - - - - - -

Maryland's senior center, Ben Coleman, told the *Washington Post* midway through the season that one reason Bias improved as a player was because he'd become a better listener. "You couldn't talk to Lenny his freshman year," Coleman said. "Criticism or advice would go in one ear and out the other. I would try and tell him that the players who wanted to get better would sit and shoot the breeze with other guys, listen to what peers had to say. But he didn't take advice very well. But that's changed as he's gotten older."

Walker often pressed Bias to work harder, telling him that if he would only dedicate himself more to the sport, his potential was limitless. By the end of his strong sophomore season, with his confidence boosted, Bias had gotten the message. Bias admitted that he worked hard on his game for the first time during the summer after his freshman year. "I could always shoot and I could always play inside," he said in the *Post* story. "But I was never really worried about the specifics of what I did. I never did the things to make myself better, like repetition of certain drills. In the past, if I was supposed to work on something, I would do it once a week and be happy I did it at all."

"His work habits changed," says Waller. "He began to take things more seriously."

The following summer, Bias started working out in the weight room with Maryland's football players. He spent a lot of time following the lead of Maryland tight end Ferrell Edmunds, a rising sophomore who later played seven seasons in the NFL and made two Pro Bowl teams. Edmunds remembers that college basketball players back then mostly avoided strength training, instead opting for extra work on a treadmill or an exercise bicycle. Bias preferred the strength work, at times performing high repetitions of the bench press with 225 pounds.

"He would do a lot of reps, not a lot of weight, for endurance," says Edmunds. "It was foreign then to see a basketball player working out with the football players. He would challenge us. If you did 15 reps, and he thought he could do it, he'd try and beat you. He loved competition. He was challenged by everybody."

Costello was Maryland's strength and conditioning coach at the time. He says the only other athlete he worked with during his 15 or so years at Maryland who compared to Bias in overall athletic ability was Renaldo Nehemiah, who set a world record in the 110-meter hurdles while he was a Maryland sophomore and won the made-for-television *Superstars* competitions four times in the 1980s.

"He had it all," says Costello, who was also Maryland's head track and field coach from 1974 to 1980, of Bias. "He was off the charts in everything. He was fast, he was agile, his vertical jump was on another level – definitely over 40 inches. When we did agility work, he made everything look so easy. He was a perfect guy to train. He tried hard. He didn't miss workouts. He was always on time and did everything he was asked to do. You remember these things. Some guys are like pulling teeth to work out. Not Len. He was a pleasure to work with. And he was a funny guy, had a good sense of humor."

During a three-game stretch in early January of his junior year that included four ACC games against teams ranked among the top 20 in the country – including No. 2 Duke and No. 5 North Carolina – Bias started to show why he would be named the top player in the ACC that season. He led Maryland in scoring in a two-point win over 17th-ranked N.C. State (17 points), a one-point loss to North Carolina (23 points), and in its next game five days later, a two-point overtime win over Duke (24 points). Against Duke, Bias scored 16 second-half points to erase a 14-point deficit, causing Duke coach Mike Krzyzewski to lament afterward how many of Bias's shots bounced around the rim before sliding through the net. Krzyzewski thought Bias was a lucky shooter until he reviewed the game tape and realized that Len's soft touch helped him make the shots.

Two weeks after the Duke game, Bias scored 30 points in a three-point win over 14th-ranked Villanova, the eventual national champion. In late January, he scored 24 points in a win over Old Dominion, and converted Maryland's last two free throws in the final seconds of the Terrapins' one-point win over N.C. State in late February.

At the end of the regular season, Bias led the ACC in scoring with 19 points per game on 53 percent shooting from the field and led Maryland with an average of 6.8 rebounds. In a *Washington Post* feature about Bias the day before Maryland was to meet Duke in the first round of the ACC tournament, Indiana Pacers personnel director Tom Newell said: "Len Bias has a chance to become one of the best players to ever play his position. I don't mean one of the best now, I mean one of the best ever. He's replaced Newton's theory of gravity with Michael Jordan's theory of gravity – which is that there is none. He just climbs up there and hangs."

Despite Bias's team-leading 22 points, Maryland lost to Duke. But the season wasn't finished, and neither was Bias. In the NCAA tournament, he was Maryland's leading scorer with 25 points in a one-point, first-round overtime win over Miami of Ohio. In the second round, against the Naval Academy, Bias led Maryland with 20 points in the 64-59 win, but perhaps more importantly, showed how much his defense had improved since his freshman year when Driesell in the second half assigned him to defend 6-foot, 11-inch All-America center David Robinson with Navy leading by 11 points. Robinson then almost immediately scored what would be his last basket of the game – with more than 16 minutes remaining – and Maryland fought back for the win.

A loss to Villanova in the Sweet 16 showed the effect of a poor performance by Bias. Double-teamed much of the game, he scored a season-low eight points on 4-of-13 shooting, failing to score in double figures for the first time in 53 games. Maryland lost by three points, ending a season in which Bias established himself as a bona fide pro prospect.

Bias enjoyed a trio of post-season accolades: He was voted ACC Player of the Year, all-ACC and a third-team All-America, offering sweet redemption for not being named all-ACC the previous season and creating a swirl of speculation that he might enter the NBA draft the following summer.

But on May 2, Bias settled the uneasy nerves of Maryland fans and coaches by saying he would indeed stay in College Park for another year. His decision came after Driesell requested that his good friend Red Auerbach talk to Bias. Auerbach dined with Bias and his parents and all agreed that he would return to Maryland. Auerbach, of course, had told Bias after the previous summer that would do everything he could to make him a Celtic, but the Celtics had the 20th pick of the 1985 draft, and certainly Auerbach must have known the chances were slim that Bias, as the ACC Player of the Year whose upside still featured plenty of positive growth potential, would still be available.

In a *Boston Globe* story published the day after Bias died, Auerbach detailed his dinner discussion with Bias. "I told Lefty when he set the dinner up I would tell the kid the truth, and not to expect me to tell the kid to go back to Maryland for his final year if I did not think he had anything to gain by going back as a senior. When we met, I told Len how I felt. I told them that if he came out in the draft, he would not be drafted in the top 10. I thought he would go around 15th. I told him, on the other hand, if he stayed in school for another year, he would be one of the top choices in the draft, certainly in the top seven, putting him in the lottery, and that we might have a chance to get him. He told me he would love that. He would love to play for the Celtics."

Perhaps no one was more pleased about Bias staying than Driesell. After a chilly start to their coach-player relationship, the pair seemed to grow fond of each other. Bias had learned to filter out some of Driesell's heated rants in order to tap into the wisdom of a coach who had developed a couple dozen NBA draft picks in his 16 years as head coach.

Driesell, in turn, learned to appreciate a player who had come to him with seemingly limitless but raw potential. The first time Driesell saw Bias play in high school, the player threw the ball at an official and drew a technical foul. "A lot of people told me he's a hothead, you're crazy for re-cruiting him," says Driesell. "I knew he was a hothead and a great competitor. I knew he was going to be good. But I didn't think he was going to be that good."

Driesell, a devout Christian, was also impressed that Bias became a born-again Christian at Maryland and resumed attending church services. The coach remembers the time he saw Bias sitting alone in Cole Field House reading a Bible. Sue Tyler, a former coach and associate athletic director at Maryland, recalled seeing Bias reading a Bible while leaning against a wall in Cole Field House.

Driesell relished Bias's fun-loving personality and his modest, but passionate, approach to the game. The coach fondly remembers a typical interaction with Bias when the team would be on the road getting ready to leave a hotel or depart a bus on the way to an arena.

"You ready, Leonard?"

"Coach, I was born ready."

"I don't think he thought of himself as a great player," says Driesell. "He never went around

Len Bias and Derrick Lewis, right, enjoy a victory. (*Maryland Media, Inc.*)

beating his chest. He enjoyed basketball and had fun with it."

Bias may have been having fun off the court in a way that would have shocked those who knew him closely. Derrick Lewis was a teammate of Celtics star Reggie Lewis at Dunbar High School in Baltimore in the early 1980s. In the spring of 1995, nearly two years after Reggie Lewis died of a heart attack, Derrick Lewis (not the Derrick Lewis who was Bias's teammate) told the *Boston Globe* of snorting cocaine with Bias and Reggie Lewis at a McDonald's restaurant during the summer of 1985 in the Boston area. Here's how he described the night at McDonald's: "It was real late, so nobody was there. Len went into the bathroom, took a toot, then me, then Reggie, then the next guy. We'd make sure nobody was coming. Then we went and had a couple of beers at another place and got real toasted. Then we went home. After that, we never talked about it."

He told the *Baltimore Sun* about a week later that his comments in the *Globe* were exaggerated and taken out of context. Graham says he flew up to Boston with Bias to take part in a Celtics mini-camp that summer at the invitation of Auerbach as a tryout. Graham, who was addicted to cocaine at the time, remembered spending time with Reggie Lewis, Derrick Lewis and Bias during the camp but says he could not "clarify" that Bias used drugs at the camp and did not explain further. "Don't see the need for it," he adds.

As Bias began his senior season, Maryland returned three starters from its NCAA Sweet 16 team and was ranked No. 19 in the country. But, ominously, Bias sprained an ankle in a pickup game in late October and missed a few days of practice.

In a season-opening win against Northeastern, Bias fouled out, but came back emphatically the next game with a career-best 33 points in a one-point win over George Mason. He scored 29 points in a seven-point win over Hawaii Pacific in late December and, after he scored 28 in a loss to No. 3-ranked Duke in early January, he had tallied at least 20 points in 10 of Maryland's 12 games.

But while Branch as a senior the previous season could rely on Bias to pick up the scoring slack if he had a bad night, Bias had no such support. He commented in a *Washington Post* report that a lack of scoring balance was becoming a concern. "Everyone isn't looking for their shot," he said. "They're depending too much on one person."

Bias took charge again with 26 points in a one-point loss to No. 5 Georgia Tech. By the time Maryland faced No. 1 North Carolina on January 14, they were 10-4 and 0-2 in the ACC. Bias was the leading scorer with 20 against the Tar Heels, but Maryland lost by four.

Against North Carolina, according to Driesell, Maryland played like the best team in the country for 35 of the game's 40 minutes. That would not be the case in its next three games, all losses to ACC opponents. In a 12-point loss to Duke, Bias scored a career-best 41 points. After the game, Duke forward Mark Alarie commented that focusing too much on Bias may have been hurting the team. "When [Bias] has the ball one on one, you can't stop him," he said. "But the rest of the time it's hard for the other players to get into the flow of the offense, because the basis of it is to get the ball to him."

With the Duke loss, Maryland dropped its first six conference games of the season, tying its worst conference start in history. In early February, with Maryland sporting a disappointing 11-10 overall record and 1-6 in the ACC, attention turned to Bias's life off the court. After all, how often can the media write about his accomplishments on the court before fans might lose interest? It was the same old story: Maryland struggles, but Bias dominates.

A feature in the *Washington Post* focused on Bias's talents as a graphic artist and a fashion fanatic. "I'd like to play basketball, model clothes and draw, in that order," Bias said in the story. Bias proudly wore a new piece of outerwear thought to be a fur coat, but his friends knew it was faux fur. Walker claims Bias bought the coat at a cheap store in Georgetown, where the two ventured frequently to satisfy Bias's need for stylish clothing.

"He liked silk shirts," says Walker. "We used to get the silk shirts by the boatload. He was a clothes horse. He liked being stylish. Leonard wanted to be fashionable. He loved the ladies."

Jeff Adkins, a Maryland player from 1981 to 1985 who shared a suite with Bias for two years, remembers Bias as a "neat freak. He always ironed his jeans and his room was spotless." Bias's dapper style extended to game time. "On the court he always kept his hair cut and shaped up," says Waller. "He always tried to look nice."

Jim Spiro's duties as manager of the men's basketball team at times extended to driving Bias to a barber shop in Landover near his house. Spiro says he drove Bias about a dozen times to get haircuts before Bias got his own car. "I'd ask Lenny where he was going [at night] and he'd say, 'I'm going to the go-go, to see Chuck Brown, or Trouble Funk.' He'd go to the Chapter III nightclub."

Bias's senior season was showing flashes of brilliance on the court, but he at times felt frustrated with the pressures of becoming one of the top college players in the nation. Myriam Leger, a college friend with whom Bias often talked about their mutually strong interest in Christianity, remembers noticing that as he approached his senior year, he wasn't as happy-go-lucky as he once was. "He didn't say hi the same way," she recalls. "He seemed burdened."

Media reports referred to a more-surly Bias in his dealing with the press. Bias addressed the pressures in a *Washington Post* story in March 1986. "People are always talking about my attitude, but they never put themselves in my place," he said. "A lot of players are doing the same things I am. It's just more magnified because I'm an All-America. And the publicity gets hard. It makes me uncomfortable and I feel bad for my teammates, who are helping us win as much as I am. "

Throughout his college career, Bias stopped by Northwestern High School to visit Wagner, who noticed Bias becoming more concerned about the pressures during his senior year. "We'd walk the halls and not talk about basketball," Wagner says. "I just let him talk. The media and other people started to absorb his time and attention."

"The one thing Len valued was his privacy," Wagner said in the *Post* story. "You know: 'I want to be myself.' Some reporters said he didn't want to talk to the press. But people had to realize he wasn't a good loser. If he didn't have a good game, he didn't want to talk about how this happened or how that happened."

Walker, Bias's mentor, recalled that Bias struggled to find joy during the season, due in part to some interest in turning pro after his junior year. "He didn't want to stay his senior year," says Walker. "They weren't as good as his junior year. He just pretty much wanted it to be over. That team didn't pan out like they were supposed to."

Things seemed to be on the upswing when Maryland beat Clemson to win its second consecutive ACC game, then traveled to Raleigh to play N. C. State. Bias scored a team-high 21 points and made two free throws with about a minute and a half left that helped clinch the one-point win for Maryland. Having now won three consecutive ACC games, Maryland was on a bit of a roll. But that momentum fizzled after Driesell suspended Bias and teammates Jeff Baxter and John Johnson for violating a team curfew after the N.C. State game.

Media reports said the three players returned at about 4 a.m. to Maryland's hotel after watching a replay of the game at a friend's room on the N.C. State campus, but that's not what happened. Baxter admits that the three were actually at an off-campus party with an N.C. State player whose name he declined to make public. He insists that neither he, Bias nor Johnson drank alcohol or took drugs. The party included what Johnson calls a "Freak Momma" contest set up to select the most attractive female. "We were just dancing. And we had a ball," Baxter says with a laugh. "We were pumped up that we won the game. I still remember to this day how much fun that was."

Baxter added that they returned to the hotel by about 1 a.m. and were greeted by Maryland's assistant coaches and Driesell, who asked, as Baxter delicately put it, " 'Where the bleep, bleep have you been?' We knew we weren't supposed to be out, but we didn't think the impact would be anything big. For me, it was, OK, we didn't do anything. We didn't think it was a big deal."

Driesell benched Bias, Baxter and Johnson for the next game, a loss to Clemson. They returned for the following game, and the team earned a comfortable victory over the University of Maryland Eastern Shore.

Needing to win three of its last four ACC games for a chance at an NCAA tournament bid, Maryland next traveled to Chapel Hill to meet top-ranked North Carolina. For a team trying to recover from its worst conference start in history and a recent suspension to its star player, nothing could seem more daunting a task than beating the top team in the country on their court.

Against North Carolina, Bias showed why a basketball guru such as Auerbach promised he would try to make him a member of his Celtics team. With Maryland down by nine with just under three minutes remaining in regulation, Bias hit a medium-range jumper, then converted a dunk after stealing the inbounds pass. With Maryland ahead by one and about 15 seconds remaining in overtime, he helped secure the win by blocking a driving jump shot in the lane by Kenny Smith.

Bias finished with 35 points, leading Maryland to a 77-72 win in overtime. It was the signature game of his college career: winning a game few thought Maryland could win, against the best team in the country, in front of more than 21,000 people in the "Dean Dome," the most daunting arena in the conference – one named after its then-head coach, Dean Smith, no less. "God was with us tonight and God means Len Bias," Gatlin said at the time. Gatlin scored Maryland's last four points in the game after Bias's block.

The spiritual basketball powers of Bias, even aided by a game-leading 30-point performance, couldn't help Maryland avoid a loss to Georgia Tech in its next game. Before the 1986 season, 7-foot Georgia Tech center John Salley was considered a candidate for the top player in the country, but even he conceded otherwise after the game. "Len Bias is the best player in the country," said Salley, who guarded him. "I concentrated as hard as I could, trying to outdo Bias."

Bias again topped the scoring sheet, with 22 points in a win over Virginia, to close out his Cole Field House career in his last home game. After its rocky start, Maryland won six of its last 8 regular season games to gather momentum for an NCAA tournament bid, and fitting that unpredictable seasonal narrative, Maryland clinched an NCAA bid with another win against North Carolina, this time in the first round of the ACC tournament. Compared to the previous win over North Carolina, Bias's performance was more steady than dramatic: 20 points and a career-high 13 rebounds. Still, he reached a much-anticipated milestone and became Maryland's all-time leading scorer with 2,072 points.

In the ACC tournament semi-final the next night against Georgia Tech, Bias hit a soft 12-foot jumper to tie the game at 62 with 12 seconds remaining, putting his points total at a game-high 20. After Maryland stole the ball from Georgia Tech on its next possession, it designed a play to get the ball to Bias as quickly as possible. There were five seconds remaining. With the ball in Bias's hands, the Terrapins stood a solid chance to advance to their second ACC tournament championship game in two years. It would be a fitting tribute for Bias to score the game winner. But the ball never reached his hands. Georgia Tech stole the inbounds pass and scored with one second left for a two-point victory.

His team wasn't playing, but Bias nonetheless suffered another setback during the ACC tournament final the next day. When the winner of the John R. Wooden Award was announced at halftime, boos echoed through the Greensboro Coliseum. The award, honoring the top college player of the year in the nation, went to Walter Berry of St. John's University. Bias had finished third in the voting, behind Berry and runner-up Johnny Dawkins of Duke. Three days later, however, Bias beat out Dawkins and the other top ACC players to be named ACC Player of the Year for the second consecutive season. He was also named first-team All-America along with Dawkins and became Maryland's first consensus All-America since John Lucas in 1976.

Maryland's players were beaming with contagious confidence and fully expected to make a strong run in the NCAA tournament. In Maryland's first-round game against Pepperdine, a five-point win, Bias hit another milestone. His 26 points left him with 712 points for the season, breaking the record he set the year before. Two of those points came from the foul line with 37 seconds remaining and Maryland clinging to a two-point lead.

In its next game, Maryland faced the University of Nevada, Las Vegas, which boasted a No. 11 national ranking and a 33-4 record. Bias played a bullish offensive game, scoring 19 of Maryland's last 21 points and its last four from the foul line to pull the Terrapins within one point. But Maryland fell short, 70-64. Bias ended with 31 points, but he fouled out with three seconds remaining. It was a fitting final Maryland performance for Bias during a season in which he carried a young team on his broad shoulders: another stellar individual performance diluted by team disappointment. Understandably, Bias lingered in front of his locker after the game, a towel draped over his head, his face buried in his hands. "I feel like we could have gone a lot further," he said.

With his college basketball career over, experts expected Bias to be among the first few selected in the NBA draft in June. All Bias wanted was to be selected by the Boston Celtics. As a surprise to some, Bias still wanted to earn his college degree. With a lucrative and promising professional career looming, Bias for all practical purposes did not need to graduate by the end of his senior year. He could have earned some credits during the summer and finished his degree during the off-season, as former Maryland star Len Elmore did. Earning a degree on time would only prove that he could indeed conquer any challenge.

But early in the spring semester, Bias reiterated his commitment. "One thing I really want is a degree," he said in a *Washington Post* story. "I didn't used to want it that much. But now I do, badly. I'm not the greatest student, but I could be if I paid attention to it. I want people to know I went to Maryland and that I left with something. So they'll say 'that's the school where Len Bias graduated from.' That's an accomplishment."

Driesell says an academic adviser told him Bias was struggling that semester and that Bias should consider dropping his classes to avoid receiving flunking grades. Driesell asked Bias if he could pass his classes, telling him he could drop them if that's what he wanted to do.

"No, Coach," he says Bias told him. "I can pass them."

"He had confidence," says Driesell. "It's the kind of guy he was."

Bias's confidence in graduating was peculiar considering he had for the most part ignored his academics during part of his senior year. Wendy Whittemore was an academic adviser for the men's basketball team for one year starting in May 1985 and worked with Bias. She said in a *Washington Post* story shortly after Bias died that he had a difficult time dealing with the fact he was failing classes. In a 2010 interview, Whittemore said Bias stopped attending classes after the fall semester. She added that Bias was not the type to "take the easy way out. Len had a sense of dignity. He was intelligent. He knew it and I knew it." Whittemore did not say what grades Bias received while she worked with him.

Bias did end up dropping two courses, but received F's in three others and fell 21 credits short of graduating. Whittemore said in a *Washington Post* story that the pressures of being a basketball star with a bright NBA future made it hard for Bias to concentrate on his studies during his last semester. "It was difficult for him to be anywhere on campus without students wanting to spend time with him. Imagine yourself in a situation where you go from place to place and everybody just wants a little time: 'Can I talk to you about this? Wasn't that great? What are you going to do next?' I don't think he was ever able to get away from that. I had no question whatsoever about his abilities under normal circumstances. But last season it seemed like every ACC game that we had that was away happened to fall on a Thursday, so all of the guys missed a good number of classes during the season. Could any student have finished his course work under the circumstances? I think not."

Dick Dull, Maryland's athletic director at the time, said in the same story that it was unrealistic to think that Bias would complete his five courses. "Len was under an incredible pressure that was totally inconsistent with studying and finishing his degree. All of a sudden, Lenny Bias had become a star, and he had to deal with the pressures of NBA teams calling him, taking physicals, making public appearances, talking to the news media and selecting an agent. That not only takes a lot of time, it was also a very tiring, stressful existence."

Still, about a week before he died, Bias showed interest in working toward a degree to satisfy his mother's wishes. In a meeting with an academic coordinator, Bias made plans for summer school. He also was interested in making some money and having some fun after Maryland's season ended, and that took him even further away from his academic ambitions. In early April, Bias started talking with Walker about being part of the ACC Barnstorming Tour, an annual series of games that pit the top conference players who are planning to enter the upcoming NBA draft against teams of top high-school players or other local all-stars.

The games, which were played in North Carolina, were not meant to be as competitive as an ACC contest. Mike Sumner, who has been organizing the games since 1979, compared them to a

Harlem Globetrotters event, where play is loose and bending the rules is common. Games at that time benefited the Muscular Dystrophy Association. Other players who took part in the tour included Dawkins and Alarie of Duke and Brad Daugherty of North Carolina. All were later selected in the first round of the 1986 NBA draft.

Sumner marveled at Bias's generosity. The player stayed willingly after games to sign autographs, and during one game wheeled a young boy with muscular dystrophy onto the court, passed him the ball, and slammed a dunk from the return pass. "He always went out of his way to be good to the fans," says Sumner, who hosted Bias in his home during the trip. "He would sit and talk with the kids with muscular dystrophy. He went to schools and talked to kids about life as a prominent basketball player. He was just a prince of a fellow, a wonderful individual."

Bias, according to Chris Washburn, also found time on the trip to use cocaine. Washburn, then a sophomore at N.C. State, met Bias during the Wolfpack's trip to play Maryland in College Park in late January. He had never played against Bias, but had watched him develop into a superstar and vividly remembered a dunk Bias slammed over Daugherty about 10 days earlier in Maryland's four-point loss to the No. 1-ranked Tar Heels in Chapel Hill. Washburn was so excited to meet Bias that he says he stopped by one of his classes during the trip to College Park to introduce himself before the game. He says they became good friends.

Some three months later, Washburn claims, Bias introduced him to cocaine. Washburn says he was back at school after N.C. State's loss to Kansas in the NCAA tournament's Elite Eight and was planning to go to class the next day when he was awakened by a knock on his door at 3 a.m. It was Bias, who was in the area while on the Barnstorming Tour, and Charles Logan, a former basketball coach at St. Augustine College in Raleigh, North Carolina.

"Usually I didn't wake up at 3 a.m. but it was Len Bias coming into my room," he says. "I didn't use cocaine until that time. But I didn't want to be the only one not trying it. It was a big part of it that Len asked me to try it. I liked that it was something different, made you feel like you were on top of the world."

Washburn never made it to class. "Funny thing about that night," he says. "To this day, [of the three] I'm the only one that's still alive." Washburn says Logan later became addicted to cocaine. An obituary in the *Newark Star-Ledger* says he changed his name to Abdus-Salaam Logan and overcame his addictions in 1999. He died of pancreatic cancer in January 2006.

Washburn's NBA career would be short-lived. After he became addicted to cocaine during his rookie season with Golden State, he played only two seasons, with three different teams, and received a lifetime suspension from the league in 1989 after failing a drug test three times. From 1991 to 1994, Washburn spent time in prison for drug-related offenses. He later played professional basketball in Europe and Puerto Rico as well as the Continental Basketball Association and the United States Basketball League, while still addicted to cocaine. Washburn stopped using cocaine in 2000 and now speaks to youth about the perils of drugs.

Brad Daugherty, the No. 1 pick of the 1986 NBA draft by the Cleveland Cavaliers, said in a June 2011 interview on Cleveland.com that he was certain Bias did not use drugs before the day he died.

"I just know 100 percent that was the first time he'd ever done that," says Daugherty, who played for the University of North Carolina. "We did some barnstorming our senior year, and I remember he wouldn't even drink a beer. Here we were, all college seniors, graduating and playing ball. We'd stop to have a couple beers and he didn't touch it. I just thought that was really amazing."

Daugherty recalls a congenial moment with Bias as the two sat on a round couch in a hotel lobby in New York City the night of the draft. "We were sitting there laughing and he asked me, 'Man, what kind of car are you going to buy?' I'll never forget that. I said, 'Shoot. Len, I'm a country boy. I'll probably get a new pickup truck.' He started laughing. He said, 'Man, I'm going to buy myself the biggest Mercedes you've ever seen. That thing's going to be longer than a train.'"

John Brown, the owner of RJ Bentley's restaurant in the small downtown of College Park, was well aware of cocaine use in the 1980s, but says he never heard of Bias using it. Brown has developed comfortable friendships with top Maryland athletes since opening the restaurant in 1978 on the main commercial strip along Route 1. It's common for prominent sports broadcasters Jimmy Roberts, Bonnie Bernstein and Scott Van Pelt, all Maryland graduates, to drop by Bentley's to say hello to Brown when they're in town.

Bias, along with Walker, often stopped in for lunch at Bentley's during his junior and senior years, and Brown eagerly welcomed the superstar and Walker into his restaurant. A couple of times, Bias volunteered to take part in charity events at Bentley's, including one in which he, Gatlin and Maryland football player Azizuddin Abdur-Ra'oof were picked up by campus police, handcuffed and taken to the restaurant, where they were placed in a fake jail for a sorority benefit. Patrons made bids on the athletes to release them from their brief prison sentences.

Brown remembers Bias acting with class in his bar. "He was not a bar hanger, one of those guys who came in every night and was hitting on chicks," says Brown. "He would stand around, have a beer or two with his friends. And then Len would say, 'Alright, guys, we've got stuff to do, let's go.'"

Bias also started spending more time with Brian Tribble, whom Bias got to know during pickup basketball games on the Maryland campus. Their friendship grew quickly and perplexed some of those who knew Bias well. Wagner says he first heard of Tribble after Bias died and was surprised the two were friends. Walker and Waller say they met Tribble just once before Bias died. Gatlin remembers Tribble as a good guy, but one with whom he had little contact.

When Waller would ask about Tribble, Bias would defend him. "He's my friend, he likes workin' out, he likes playin' ball, likes lifting weights, that's my man, OK?" recalls Waller.

Walker says he first met Tribble when he stopped by to visit Bias in the Leonardtown dorms. Another time Walker stopped at Leonardtown for a planned meeting with Bias and discovered that he was at Tribble's apartment a couple miles north of the Maryland campus. When he got there, Walker asked Bias what there was to do at the apartment. Bias said they were working out. "Tribble had some weight machines there," he says. "I said, 'Why would you have to come up to his apartment to work out when you can work out anytime you want (on campus) in a room full of workout equipment? I don't understand it.'"

A couple of days after Bias died, Walker sought out Tribble to try and make sense of his friend's death, saying he wasn't "satisfied with it all." He says Tribble told him then that he and Bias were using cocaine the day he stopped by the apartment looking for Bias and that he thought Walker had found out then that Bias was using cocaine.

Another time Walker stopped by to visit Bias in Leonardtown he noticed the herb Goldenseal in his room. For a time, Goldenseal was considered a way to help mask the presence of drugs during a drug test. "I asked him, 'Why you have that here?' He said, 'You know, that ain't mine. That's Terry Long's.' I said, 'Why is it in your room if it's Terry Long's?' He said, 'Oh, you know, he was in here talking about something and he just left it there before he left.' I didn't pay attention to things that were going on. I wanted to believe everything he was telling me."

Shortly before the NBA draft, Bias stopped by to say hello to Brown, and the two enjoyed a lunch together. After the meal, Bias asked to borrow money. Brown was taken aback. Soon after his eligibility had expired in late March, Bias had secured a loan of about $20,000 from a local bank where his mother, Lonise, worked in anticipation of signing a lucrative NBA contract. Bias had used the money to lease a Nissan 300 SX, replacing a 1977 Oldsmobile Cutlass that Bias had called his "gray four-door Porsche." A story in the *Washington Post* in August 1986 told of Bias's shopping sprees the previous spring for a 14K gold chain worth $1,300, nameplates for a friend and himself for $550 and jewelry for many of his female friends. The report claimed that he bought suits and purchased two $1 million disability insurance policies.

Brown was surprised that Bias needed more money: "I said 'Len, what happened to all your up-front money?' He said 'I just don't have it.'" Brown knew Bias wouldn't have to pay his travel expenses to attend the draft in New York City, but Bias said he needed what he called "airport money," if he wanted to buy a magazine or a newspaper or some gum.

Brown told Bias that he would give him money, but only if he worked for it. Bias agreed, so Brown directed Bias to water some shrubs that had just been planted on property Brown owned behind the restaurant. Neighbors noticed Bias's peculiar work detail and called Brown to wonder if all was well with the soon-to-be high NBA draft pick. He assured them there was nothing to worry about. After Bias had worked for about 90 minutes, Brown wrote him a check for $37, which he cashed at the bar before he left.

According to Walker, Bias also received money and gifts from fans, violating NCAA rules. He recalled the time one summer when Bias called someone on the phone saying he needed money, after which he got in the car. "He'd throw out a random number," says Walker. "I rode with him. I sat in the car while he talked to the guy, who gave him all crisp $100 bills. We would go from there to spend money on clothes. He had no problem spending up to $500, $600, $700 on clothes. If he was spending money, he'd never say it was drugs. It was clothes."

Walker recalled free lunches in College Park with Bias and the time they walked into a Circuit City store to buy a stereo and walked out with a receiver, speakers, cassette deck and turntable, for free. But there was a catch. "The guy comes up, says 'Hey man, you Len Bias?'" he says. "'Hey man, give me some tickets to the Carolina game and I'll give you the stereo. Pull around to the loading dock and we'll load up your car.' Whether he took care of the tickets, I don't know. He was a free spirit. We had a lot of good times."

Baxter remembers Bias being generous with his money. "I do know he always had cash," he says. "I don't know where he would get it from, if it was boosters-related or not. If I needed something, he would get it for me."

According to a *Washington Post* story, Bias on the Monday before the draft spent the day in New York with his father, James, attending draft-related events. Bias spent at least part of the night in his hotel room, watching television.

Washburn claims that Bias was high on cocaine during the draft, during which he says the two sat next to each other. He says Bias never told him he had used cocaine that night, but he was certain Bias was on the drug when he told Washburn "I'm alright," which Washburn claims is a colloquial reference for being high on cocaine. "We knew each other had done [cocaine]," he says. "We both came in late. He didn't have to tell me."

Bias stayed in Boston the following day to meet with representatives of Reebok and the Boston media. The following description of how Bias's last night evolved is based on testimony by Long at the trial of Tribble, according to reports, and from portions of the documentary *Without Bias*.

Bias returned to his dormitory suite at Washington Hall after 10:30 p.m. with a bag full of Reebok shoes and Boston Celtics jerseys. David Gregg, a freshman basketball player, and Maryland football players Brian (Keeta) Covington and Ben Jefferson were there eating crabs. Bias wanted them to have a party, Long testified. "We're going to celebrate," Bias said to Gregg, Covington and Jefferson. About 20 minutes later, Bias left the suite at about 11:30 p.m. with Madelyne Woods, a friend of Bias's who stopped by to visit. Bias said he had to "go drain his lizard." "We knew what he meant," Long said. "He said he hadn't been with a girl in three days."

Long and Gregg walked to a nearby convenience store to buy soft drinks and went to sleep when they returned. At around 2:30 a.m., Bias, who was with Tribble, knocked on Long's bedroom door and said "Wake the [expletive] up. We're gonna celebrate."

Bias then woke up Gregg and told Gregg and Long to get some beer from a nearby refrigerator. Long and Gregg saw a mound of cocaine on a mirror on the desk when they returned to Long's room. After Gregg asked Bias and Tribble where the cocaine came from, Long said, "Tribble said something about getting it from the bottom of a stash and they planned to get a kilo the next day." Long, Gregg, Bias and Tribble started snorting the cocaine through cut straws until about 3 a.m. when Jeff Baxter knocked on Long's door. Long told Tribble to put the cocaine away when Baxter knocked because the players knew Baxter did not use drugs. Baxter stayed for about 15 minutes.

The others then resumed snorting cocaine. Tribble went to the bathroom, stumbled back to Long's room and said, "We're all [expletive] up." Long added that they all felt much the same way. They snorted cocaine until sometime after 6 a.m. Bias then rested on Long's bed for about five minutes before struggling to go to the bathroom because he was wobbly. Bias then suffered a seizure. Long placed a pair of scissors in Bias's mouth to prevent him from biting his tongue while Gregg held Bias's feet. Tribble called his mother who told him to call the county emergency number for an ambulance. Tribble made the emergency call at 6:32 a.m.

911: P.G. County Emergency

Tribble: Yes, I'd like to have an ambulance come; (to someone else) what, what room? What room?

(Answer from the background: Washington Hall)

Tribble: What? Eleven-oh-three Washington Hall. It's an emergency. It's Len Bias and he just went to Boston and he needs some assistance.

911: What are you talking about?

Tribble: Huh?

911: What are you talking about?

Tribble: I'm talking about, uh, someone needs, Len Bias needs help.

911: Well, it doesn't matter what his name is, what's the problem?

Tribble: He's not breathing right.

911: What's the address?

Tribble: Eleven-oh-three Washington Hall on Maryland University's campus.

911: Washington Hall?

Tribble: Yes, sir.

911: What's your name?

Tribble: My name is Brian.

911: Brian what?

Tribble: Tribble.

911: Tribble?

Tribble: Yes, sir.

911: What's your phone number, Brian?

Tribble: I'm, I'm in Len Bias's room. I don't know the phone number there.

911: What's the room number?

Tribble: Eleven-oh-three.

911: Eleven-oh-three?

Tribble: Yes, sir.

911: OK. What's, it's just Washington Hall, what's the address of Washington Hall?

Tribble: It's, uh, I don't know, it's no address. It's just Washington Hall. Come up by Hungry Herman's and go straight up there and it's on the right-hand side, so please come as soon as you can. It's no joke.

911: OK, Washington Hall apartment number eleven-oh-three?

Tribble: Yes, they're giving him mouth-to-mouth. You can hear it now. Hear 'em? This is Len Bias. You have to get him back to life. There's no way he can die. Seriously, sir, please come quick.

911: OK, Washington Hall and apartment, uh room number, eleven-oh-three.

Tribble: Uh-huh.

911: That's one thousand, one hundred and three?

Tribble: Uh-huh. Eleven-oh-three. One thousand, one hundred and three.

911: All right. We'll have an ambulance out, all right?

Tribble: Excuse me?

911: We'll have an ambulance out.

Tribble: OK.

911: Thank you.

Tribble: Yeah.

After the ambulance took Bias to the hospital, Long cleaned the empty beer bottles and cut straws from his room and emptied them into a dumpster behind the dormitory. Bias was pronounced dead at the hospital at 8:55 a.m. Cocaine intoxication was later determined to be the cause.

Chapter 3

Maryland Athletics

Not all families react the same way to the unexpected death of a beloved son. Most come together and mourn, placing the passing in quiet perspective and relishing fond memories of an enriching life. Others are destroyed by shock and finger-pointing, never getting over the tragedy and crumbling right down to their foundations. After the death of Len Bias, the University of Maryland family fell somewhere in the middle; fueled by infighting and resentment, it plunged into a profound depression, losing its sense of purpose and perspective before fighting its way back to a rebirth.

For close to a century, right up until the death of Bias, the Maryland athletic department existed mostly in a state of domestic bliss. Mixed in with more than a dozen national titles were moments of distrust and dissension, but the Terrapins relied on familial fondness to thrive and prosper.

Almost from the beginning, the school turned often to its own blood to build its athletic department. Harry "Curley" Byrd started playing football at Maryland in 1905 and is one of the best athletes in the school's history. He served as head football coach and became the school's first athletic director in 1914, a position he held until 1936. He later became the school's president. Millard Tydings, a 1910 graduate of the school and later a U.S. Senator, called Byrd the father of the University of Maryland.

Geary Eppley, a football and track-and-field star at Maryland, succeeded Byrd as athletic director

from 1938 to 1942. Many former Maryland athletes stayed in College Park as coaches and administrators.

If Curley Byrd was the athletic department's father, Jim Kehoe was its favorite son. A Southern
Conference middle-distance running champion at Maryland in 1940, Kehoe started coaching the
track-and-field team in 1947 and won 48 conference titles in track and cross-country through 1969.

Only in 1955 did Maryland fail to win a conference title in indoor or outdoor track with Kehoe as
coach. That year, North Carolina beat Maryland by 1.5 points indoors and 1 point outdoors. When I
visited Kehoe in 2003 to talk with him for my first book on Maryland athletics, *Tales from the Maryland Terrapins*, he spent a good hour proudly paging through press clippings and other documents
that displayed his impressive record. When he mentioned the conference losses in 1955, a stubborn
look of regret rolled across his face. "Dammit, I'll never get over that," says Kehoe. He was 85 years
old at the time.

That competitive fire typified Kehoe's approach toward athletics. A former Marine, he expected
excellence and accepted no excuses. Kehoe added to his lofty legacy as a University of Maryland
sports heavyweight during his role as athletic director from 1969 to 1978. One of his first, and most
significant, moves was to go out of the Maryland family to hire the charismatic and crafty basketball
coach, Lefty Driesell, away from Davidson College, which Driesell had twice led to the Elite Eight
at the NCAA Tournament. Such success made it easier to forget that Driesell had played basketball
for Duke, a main Maryland rival.

When Kehoe took over as athletic director, he pronounced the department in deep trouble. Kehoe
initially focused on rebuilding the floundering football and basketball programs to help raise athletic
department revenue, which had dropped considerably. He invigorated the marketing and fund-raising
departments with fresh, Maryland-familiar blood. He recruited his Marine buddy and Maryland track
teammate, Tom Fields, to lead the fund-raising effort, and by the end of the decade the department
was dug out of a lingering debt. Russ Potts, a graduate of Maryland's school of journalism, directed
the marketing and promotions department through a period of clever innovations that included radio
and television network broadcasts of its football and basketball teams. Close to half of the coaches
on staff were former athletes at Maryland.

In Kehoe's first two years in office, basketball season ticket sales increased from 225 to 3,000
and football season tickets increased about 50 percent, to 7,500. In 1972 Kehoe hired football coach
Jerry Claiborne, another Maryland outsider, who returned the team to national attention after more
than a decade of underachieving seasons. From 1956 to 1971, the Terrapins compiled a record of
50–100–1 and had only three winning seasons. Under Claiborne, Maryland football won ACC titles
from 1974 to 1976, and, before resigning in 1981 to take the head coach's job at the University of
Kentucky, he led the Terrapins to seven bowl games.

Kehoe showed loyalty to former Terrapin athletes, whom he integrated into many athletic-depart-
ment positions. He hired one of his best pupils, All-America high jumper Frank Costello, as Maryland's head track coach in 1974. Costello continued the Terrapins' string of ACC titles and led
Maryland to its highest national ranking in history.

One of Costello's favorite teammates at Maryland was Dick Dull, a javelin thrower. In the mid-
1970s, Dull was suffering through what he described as a "misdirected" period of his young adult
life and found himself jobless after having worked as an attorney for several years. "It was the tur-

bulent '70s, and I needed to right my life," he says, without offering details. Kehoe helped redirect Dull's personal path, hiring him as an assistant track coach and the department's business manager in 1975. He later served as an assistant athletic director in charge of nonrevenue sports.

In 1978, Kehoe departed from his position as athletic director with the department in the financial black. However, Carl James, his successor, soon put it back in the red, accumulating a $400,000 deficit in just two years, so Kehoe returned on an interim basis to try to right the ship. He backed Dull as his long-term successor, and Dull took over as athletic director in June 1981. In the family hierarchy of Maryland athletics, Dull could be classified as a younger sibling who found his way with the help of his surrogate father – Kehoe.

When he took over as athletic director at age 35 for an annual salary of $48,000, Dull's stated priorities were to increase season football ticket sales and to improve the academic performance of Maryland athletes. Of his Maryland family ties, he said at a press conference on June 19, 1981, "By being associated with the university, I felt I knew the problems better than the other candidates."

"I wanted the job simply out of being competitive," Dull told me in 2002. "I used to say there's only one side of the desk to sit on, and that's the director's job." Little did Dull know in 1981 that five years to the day after he was hired, Len Bias's death would create problems that his nearly two decades of experience as a Maryland athlete and administrator and an esteemed member of the Maryland athletic family could not help him resolve.

- - - - - - - - - -

Dull did not talk with me for this book, but he did discuss Bias with me when I wrote *Tales from the Maryland Terrapins*. He was a state champion javelin thrower out of Biglerville High School, located a few miles north of his hometown of Gettysburg, Pennsylvania, when Kehoe recruited him and others with an innocent, Rockwellian style. "Coach Kehoe took everybody for a ride in a horrible red jeep, and we all ended up at a Dairy Queen for an ice-cream cone," he says. "I came away so enthralled with the man that I wanted to go. He was honest. He did not hold grudges. He was a remarkable person in his ability to forgive and go on."

In 1966, Dull won the Championship of America javelin competition at the Penn Relays in a driving rainstorm in Philadelphia, about a two-hour drive from his hometown. One season, it took him and about a dozen teammates five days to drive across country to California in red, state-issued station wagons to compete at the outdoor national championships. He enjoyed the camaraderie and the occasional juvenile antics. "We would look for a hotel and a track for practice," he says. "We would put six or eight people in a room, some sleeping on mattresses and others on box springs. It was a fraternity that you never had to join."

Dull served a year in the Army after earning his undergraduate degree and completed his law degree from Maryland in 1971. He practiced law before returning to Maryland in 1975 as an assistant coach working with the javelin throwers.

I have been a friend of Dull since the late 1970s when I was a member of the Maryland track team and Dull was an assistant coach. We considered Dull to be a trusted confidant and we tagged him with the nickname "Smooth" because of his casual, unflappable demeanor and his dapper style. "That's because I was the only one who knew how to dress, according to the black guys [on the team]," he says with a laugh.

Bob Nelligan, the women's gymnastics head coach from 1979 to 2009, remembers Dull as a people person who showed interest in all sports. Most athletic directors of that era focused their time on the revenue-producing sports of basketball and football and regularly traveled to away football and basketball games. Rarely did they attend nonrevenue sports events, especially on the road, but Nelligan recalls Dull attending away gymnastics meets with Chancellor John Slaughter. Dull occasionally even showed up at gymnastics practice, watching the team from a distance as he stood by the entrance to the workout room.

"I don't know anybody in the department who didn't like his demeanor," says Nelligan. "He said hi to secretaries, the guys who were cleaning the top of Cole Field House. He was very comfortable with the athletes. He was one of the few athletic directors who would show up at your office and see how you were doing. He was just one of those people who you wanted desperately to see succeed."

Nothing less than success was expected, especially from Kehoe. Dull realized early that the men's basketball and football teams needed to succeed, calling them the "bread and butter" needed for Maryland athletics to thrive. The men's basketball program had gained momentum, competing in a postseason tournament for three consecutive seasons after a three-year absence. But in 1981 the football team recorded its first losing season in nine years. Four months into his job, Dull needed to hire a football coach after Claiborne resigned to take the head-coaching job at Kentucky. Under command from university chancellor Robert Gluckstern, Dull became a search committee of one. "He said 'You're going to pick the coach and I'm going to approve it,' " Dull recalled.

He chose Bobby Ross, whose only head-coaching job had been at the Citadel from 1973 to 1977, where he posted a 24-31 record. After leaving the Citadel, Ross had been an assistant coach for the Kansas City Chiefs for four years before taking the Maryland job. During Ross's five years at Maryland, the team played compelling football, winning three ACC titles, playing in four bowl games and earning a top-10 national ranking. Attendance increased. At three games staged in Baltimore's Memorial Stadium, Maryland football attracted at least 58,000 fans. More than 50,000 fans attended four other games in Byrd Stadium. Also during Dull's reign, the men's basketball team won the ACC tournament championship in 1984, the first time it won a conference title since 1958. The football team also won an ACC title in 1984 – the first time in history both teams took the titles in the same year.

Dull was considered a young, rising star as an athletic administrator. Two other Division I athletic programs, Ohio State and Southern California, wanted him as their athletic director. He vividly remembers the reaction of Duke Athletic Director Tom Butters, who was sitting in a section directly opposite him, after the basketball conference tournament win in 1984. "He gave me a thumbs-up," says Dull, whose good fortune continued for two more years, due to the success of the football team and, in smaller part, the emerging talents of Bias. He even started discussions with Slaughter about a multiyear contract extension. But when Bias died on June 19, 1986, Dull's promising future fell harder than a quarterback suffering a Randy White blind-side tackle.

On the morning of June 19 Dull was home when Maryland Assistant Vice President John Bielec called to inform him of Bias's death. Dull immediately called Jeff Hathaway, an assistant athletic director, to go to Leland Memorial Hospital in nearby Riverdale and confirm the news. The tragedy turned Dull's world upside down. "I was in shell shock for about six weeks," he says. "You go from being the fair-haired boy to people calling for you to leave. It was difficult for me to handle. It was unlike anything I had ever seen."

Dull says he felt as if he were one of the main characters in what he called "a Greek tragedy" in which there were no winners. "I can remember walking out of my office to go to the bathroom, and someone would be following me down the hallway. It was like that every day."

Scrutiny of the Maryland athletic department streamed in from many directions. The media criticized the academic philosophy of Maryland's basketball team, claiming that too few players graduated. Some members of the Maryland faculty saw a public platform to voice their displeasure with what they claimed were special privileges afforded the athletes so they could remain eligible. Dull says the worst legacy of Bias's death for the university was the tattered relationship between the school's faculty and the athletic department. "We had worked so hard to make something we were proud of. The relationship went south. When you lose the confidence of the faculty, things get difficult."

Within weeks of Bias's death, Slaughter appointed J. Robert Dorfman, a university physics professor, to serve as the chairman of a task force to review the academic practices of the athletic department. He disagrees with Dull's assertion that Bias's death disrupted the relationship between athletics and academics. Rather, he says, it made such big headlines that it drew the whole university community together to focus on academics and athletics. "Many faculty came up to me afterward and told me they had learned a great deal from the reporting and the television interviews. They had a better understanding of what was going on in the athletic department."

Dull, along with Slaughter and Driesell, testified in front of a grand jury called by the prosecutor for Prince George's County, Arthur Marshall, to investigate the cause of Bias's death as well as drug use at Maryland. Dull remembers police officers letting him out the back door of a courtroom to help avoid the throng of media covering the story. When Dull publicly stated that Driesell should keep his job despite the fact that he was part of the grand jury investigation, he sensed his own job was in jeopardy. It was a move that helped convince Slaughter that a change was needed. "Dr. Slaughter told me 'I wish you hadn't said that.' He felt he had to make a decision about Driesell," Dull says. "I painted myself in a corner because of my support for Lefty. We agreed that the situation was not going to go away unless I stepped away. I don't have regrets."

Slaughter says Dull was very supportive of the decision. "He felt I would be able to accomplish what I needed to do if he stepped aside. He and I sort of reached an agreement that it was the best thing to do. He was helpful to me, and I admired his courage."

Dull resigned on October 7, 1986. On the way to the press conference announcing his resignation, according to a report in the *Washington Post*, Dull told Slaughter, "I might recite Martin Luther King's words: 'Free at last.' " It turns out that Dull, in the second year of a four-year contract, had long been thinking about leaving when it expired. At the press conference, according to reports, he said there was more to life than "slaving away trying to manage an intercollegiate athletic program. It was about a year and a half ago that I realized I no longer had a personal or private life, that I didn't do anything I enjoyed, like fishing, playing golf or photography."

Dull's ties to Maryland were not completely severed. He says Slaughter kept him on as a consultant for the length of his contract, some 22 months, so he could retain his salary. Dull added that Slaughter is still a good friend, and that he has used him as a top reference for jobs. Dull admitted he was haunted by the Bias death and its aftermath for about a decade and sought professional help. "The stain of being at Maryland …" he said in a *York Daily Record* story in 2008. "I could not get a job interview [in athletics] for 10 years." Dull dabbled in real estate and worked for a travel agency and a few years after Bias died worked as an administrator at University College, a night school on the College Park campus. He worked as a consultant and for a while lived off his savings. He dropped away from anything connected to Maryland.

Dull's friends talk uncomfortably about how Bias's death affected him. "He went from a guy who was always upbeat and positive to someone sullen and sad," says Sue Tyler, who worked at Maryland for over 20 years through the mid-1990s as a coach and associate athletic director before moving on to become the athletic director at the University of Maine.

"Dick always was a sensitive guy," says Costello, one of Dull's closest friends, who served as Maryland's first strength and conditioning coach in the 1980s. "Anybody who is a sensitive guy and who sees tragedy, it affects them more than others."

Dull's professional fortunes turned around in 1995 when he accepted a job as athletic director at the University of Nebraska Kearney, a Division II school. Slaughter helped him get the job. Dull stayed at Nebraska until February 1998 before taking the same position at Moravian College, a Division III school in Bethlehem, Pennsylvania, near his hometown of Gettysburg. He returned to Division I sports when he became athletic director at Cal State Northridge in Los Angeles in May 1999.

Even as he revived his career as a high-level athletics administrator, Dull could not avoid his past connections to the Bias death. According to a report in the *Los Angeles Times*, when Dull appeared before a public forum on the Northridge campus while being considered for the University of California job, he admitted during opening remarks to missteps regarding special admissions of athletes. "The scrutiny brought attention to mistakes I made," he said. "I was encouraged to admit student-athletes who had little chance to succeed academically. My role in encouraging these admissions was a mistake."

And a year into his job at the school, a *Times* reporter asked Dull if Northridge had seen the end of negative publicity that plagued it due to "misadventures" before Dull took the job. His reply: "Oh, I think that kind of time bomb can go off any time. I would never suggest that intercollegiate athletics, because of its interest in the media, is ever going to be immune from a student-athlete getting into trouble, or a coach or an administrator doing something wrong. What we're trying to do is put in place, as much as we can, systems that will give us a greater percentage of not having things happen. We just need to be forthright and honest and we don't need to be engaged in deceit and dishonesty in dealing with our constituents and with the media."

Dull worked at Northridge until 2007, when he moved back east to take the athletic director's job at Belmont Abbey College, a Division III school near Charlotte, North Carolina. He held the job through the summer of 2008. Through the summer of 2010, Dull had not seen a Maryland basketball game in College Park since he resigned as athletic director, but he has seen the team play elsewhere. When the Terrapins played in the NCAA Elite Eight at Stanford University in 2001, then-Maryland Athletic Director Debbie Yow gave Dull tickets to the game. He says he enjoyed seeing old friends, such as broadcaster Johnny Holliday and former Sports Information Director Jack Zane. "You reach a point where you hold resentment and you hurt yourself," he explains. "I'm a stronger person now because of it. I look at the horizon, and say 'It can't get any worse than that.' "

Interestingly, Dull tried to return to Maryland as an athletics administrator in 2008 when he interviewed for the position of executive director of the M-Club. Nelligan, the long-time women's gymnastics coach, served on the search committee. "Everybody loved his presentation," says Nelligan. "He had been an athletic director, he had been at small schools where he knew the importance of shaking hands, which really wasn't Dick's strong point when he was athletic director at Maryland. And I thought he would have been a very strong candidate to unite that part of the department. But I also felt that he would always have to answer questions about Lenny. His legacy will always be tied to that."

Dull was not selected.

After giving his presentation, Dull stopped by Nelligan's office and the two old friends talked for about an hour. Dull wanted to know how Nelligan was doing personally and asked for updates on mutual friends. A short time later, Dull sent a letter to Nelligan, thanking him for a tour of Comcast Center and making sure his buddy was OK with the fact that he didn't get the job.

"He's had to live with this Bias thing for a long time," Nelligan says. "He does deserve to live with some closure."

Dick Dull, left with his former Maryland track teammate Frank Costello in April 2011. (by Chip Zimmer)

For Dull, closure – oddly enough – could come in the form of proximity to his dramatic days in College Park. During a string of conversations we had about his taking part in this book, Dull mentioned several times that he would like to move back to the College Park area. During one conversation in May 2010, Dull mentioned he had begun slowly packing books into boxes, anticipating a move, perhaps by the fall, back closer to a place that provided so many good memories as a young adult, a place that was the backdrop for a life-changing episode as a young and promising athletic director, a place that once seemed like family.

"I miss it," he says.

By the end of the following summer, Dull had returned closer to his athletic-director roots with the help of the extended Maryland athletic family. In August 2010, he accepted a position as a project manager in the athletic department at Hood College in Frederick, Maryland, about 45 minutes from College Park, where he helps raise funds for new athletic facilities at the school. The man who hired him, Hood athletic director Gib Romaine, was the defensive coordinator for Ross at Maryland and was later a fundraiser at Maryland.

In April 2011, Dull attended a reunion of former Maryland athletic department employees, some of whom had worked under him in the 1980s. It marked the first time I had seen Dull in about a quarter century. Typically, he mingled mostly in the background, quietly chatting with old friends. And typically, he offered comfort when I asked him if he was OK with me moving forward with this book. He encouraged me to complete the project. We talked little else about it, preferring to focus instead on positive memories from his days at Maryland.

LEFTY DRIESELL

Fighting through tears during a press conference on June 20, the day after Bias died, Maryland head basketball coach Lefty Driesell said, "He's in a better position right now than we are. He's at home with the Lord. I really sincerely believe that. I'm sad but not worried because I know where Leonard is, I know he's in heaven. We'll miss him. I love you, Leonard, and I miss you. I'll see you in heaven one day."

During the immediate months that followed Bias's death, Driesell – a born-again Christian – must have felt he was living in a hell on earth. His reputation as a pioneer among college basketball coaches was transformed into one of a coach who was, at worst, indifferent to his athletes' academic needs and at best blind to their off-court shenanigans.

No University of Maryland sports personality symbolized the transformative days of the school's athletic program during the 1970s as profoundly as Driesell. He stormed into College Park in 1969, leaving behind a Davidson program he had coached for nine years. Davidson finished the previous season with a 27-3 record and advanced to the NCAA Tournament's Elite Eight. He left for a Maryland program that had finished 8-18 the previous year, its third consecutive losing season.

Driesell's audacious and affable style on the floor coupled with his strong persuasive ability as a recruiter helped create a product that dramatically increased attendance in Cole Field House. By the early 1970s, sell-out crowds were the norm in the 14,500-seat arena, far from the peak of 5,000 fans a few years before Driesell arrived, and they were coming to see such impact players as Tom McMillen, Len Elmore and John Lucas, each of them All-Americas who would go on to forge strong NBA careers.

Driesell converted Maryland basketball into both a respected commodity and a commercial sports brand. During his first year, he renovated the locker room, the training room and offices. He was the main attraction during a new weekly television show and all games were broadcast on the radio. The next season, seven home games were televised. He had floor seats installed in Cole Field House to enhance the team's intimacy with fans. The pep bands played "Hail to the Chief" as he walked onto the floor.

Driesell posted a winning record in just his second season. To start off his third, he staged a Midnight Mile to kick off the first day of practice. Some thought it was a publicity stunt to promote a team that had earned a No. 6 preseason national ranking with such players as Elmore and McMillen, both of whom would become All-Americas. But Driesell claims a practical purpose.

"I did that to get a jump on people," he says. "We were going to be the first ones to go to work and the last ones to play that season. And having the mile at the beginning of [the later] practice used to screw it up. The guys were too tired to practice." Driesell's innovation bred the Midnight Madness promotion common among NCAA teams today.

In a sense, the Terrapins *were* the last to play during the 1971-72 season, but not in the NCAA tournament. Maryland finished second in the ACC tournament that year, but at that time only one team per conference advanced to the NCAAs so the Terps headed to the NIT, which was considered a respectable junior achievement to winning the NCAA, and won. In 1973, Driesell led the team to the NCAA Elite Eight for the first time; in 1975 he did it again.

As if his success on the court was not enough, in 1974 Driesell received the first NCAA Award of Valor for helping clear residents from a burning townhouse complex in Bethany Beach, Delaware, after noticing the blaze while fishing on the beach with a friend. He firmly denied rumors that he pulled people from the burning building, saying that he knocked on doors and warned people, including about a dozen children, to flee the scene. True to form, Driesell found humor in the incident. "I was banging on people's doors, hollering for them to get out," he says. "One lady said 'Get out of my house, I'm gonna call the police.' I said, 'Lady, *you* better get out.'"

Former Maryland coach Lefty Driesell flashes his trademark victory sign as he walks on to the Cole Field House court. (*Campus Photo Services*)

But after the death of Bias, Driesell fell from Maryland's good graces more rapidly than he had brought fame to the Terrapins. Some consider him a scapegoat. J. J. Bush has been an athletic trainer at Maryland since 1971, and during his early years on the job was assigned to Driesell's teams. No one has been as close as Bush to the inner workings of the department over the last half-century, and Bush believes that Driesell was treated unfairly.

"I think the buck should have stopped with Lenny," he says.

Tyler was a member of a task force set up to study academic issues within the athletic department after Bias died. "Nobody wanted to be the problem, so they found something and pointed at Lefty and Dick Dull and Jim Dietsch," says Tyler referring also to Maryland's athletic director and academic adviser, respectively, at the time of Bias's death. Both departed their positions within four months of the tragedy. Of the three, Driesell faced the most private and public scrutiny, mostly because of reports that he played a part in instructing someone to clean the room in which Bias died before police arrived.

Privately, some scrutiny also came from the Bias family. Bob Wagner, Len's high-school coach and a friend of Driesell, remembers a moment of hostility from Len's father. Wagner and Driesell had driven together to the wake. Once there, Driesell and Wagner walked over to James Bias to offer condolences. "I know Mr. Bias was still hurt and upset," says Wagner, who was close to the Bias family. "He says [to Driesell], 'You stay away from me. You killed my son.'"

It wasn't the only time Len Bias's father directed his anger at Driesell. James Bias told the *Washington Post* in the early months after Len's death that Maryland exploited its athletes by suggesting they take easy courses and emphasizing athletics over academics. He claimed the university used his son to make money. "Any statement I could make would be tantamount to a grain of sand compared to what [Driesell] can find examining himself."

Publicly, Marshall, the Prince George's County prosecutor, set up a grand jury to investigate possible drug use on the basketball team and whether Driesell was involved in hiding evidence from the scene of Bias's death. Driesell admitted in a *Sports Illustrated* report in November 1986 that he instructed assistant coach Oliver Purnell to clean up the suite where Bias lived with several teammates at the behest of Lee Fentress, the agent for both himself and Bias. Fentress, an attorney, confirmed the account in a news report, but claimed that his command came during an emotional moment without considering the implications. He declined an interview for this book. In any event, Purnell did not clean up the room, and the grand jury chose not to indict Driesell. Jeff Adkins, a former Maryland player, was a first-year graduate assistant coach in 1986. He says Purnell asked him to help clean up the room, but when they reached the Washington Hall dorm where Bias's suite was located, police would not let them past the secured area.

"I did absolutely nothing wrong," says Driesell.

Driesell was never accused of violating NCAA rules, but his recruiting of some marginally academic athletes and his monitoring of their academic efforts were questioned after Bias's death. The same *Sports Illustrated* report revealed that 15 of the 19 freshmen Driesell brought in from 1980 to 1985 failed to satisfy the school's minimum admissions standards. Their combined SAT average of 670 was 100 points below that of Terrapin football recruits and some 355 points under the university-wide average.

Wendy Whittemore, the basketball team's academic adviser, quit within a couple weeks of Bias's death. She told the *Washington Post* that players generally missed 35 to 40 percent of their classes during the season. And the *Sports Illustrated* report claims that Whittemore's predecessor, Larry Roper, quit partly in frustration over Driesell's approach to academics and that another ex-counselor complained "there weren't any guidelines when it came to academics."

Dave Dickerson was entering his freshman season when Bias died and stayed with the program through his graduation. He served as an assistant coach for Driesell at James Madison and at Maryland for nine years before accepting the head coaching position at Tulane, where he stayed through the 2010 season. He says Whittemore's assessment "is closer to the truth than not true," but that basketball players travel more than other athletes and on commercial flights, which prolongs the time away from school. And, he added, the team at times traveled with tutors. How much the players used them is another matter.

Dickerson defends Driesell's approach to academics. "Coach Driesell has been vilified throughout this process," says Dickerson. "Coach Driesell was very in tune with his players' academic success, and he wanted to see his players be successful; at least that's the way he was toward me. I never saw him throughout my year of playing with him, coaching with him at Madison, never heard him or saw him put academics on the back burner. And I never saw him sacrifice a kid's academic progression for his athletic gain."

Tyler recalls seeing Driesell pressure his assistant coaches to make sure his players were attending class. "He said 'We've got to get their butts to class,' " she says, explaining that he was concerned about players attending classes in the morning but skipping them in the afternoon, or cutting their morning classes after coming back from a road trip. Through all the scrutiny, Driesell remained defiant. He said shortly after he resigned that a secret poll he gave to his players revealed a vote of confidence and that a campus newspaper poll supported him.

Driesell's public campaign to preserve his integrity and save his job clashed with the university's renewed mission toward athletic and academic excellence. Slaughter decided to release Driesell from his coaching duties due in part to his concerns that Driesell had not provided the leadership needed by the team at the time. "My conclusion was we were not going to turn that around unless a change was made," Slaughter says. "I thought we needed to change coaches for a variety of reasons. I could come up with a whole lot of reasons, but I consider that a closed chapter. I don't want to open it anymore."

Slaughter made those comments in 2003 during interviews for the book *Tales from the Maryland Terrapins*. He said then that he had not had any direct contact with Driesell since the coach stepped down, although he did write a letter congratulating Driesell on advancing to the NCAA tournament in 1994 while he was coaching at James Madison University.

"I like Lefty a great deal," Slaughter says. "I'm not sure it's reciprocated at the moment."

When asked about his feelings toward Slaughter, Driesell says, "No comment. I have a lot of feelings about Slaughter but I'd rather not say."

Driesell claims he was asked to remain as coach for one more year and then resign with nine years left on his contract. "My lawyer said, 'We can fight this thing, and you can keep your job,' but I'd be working for free because his fees would be so big," he says. "I said 'Let's settle.' It was a great 17 years at Maryland except for my last year."

Driesell held an emotional press conference on October 29, 1986, to announce that he would step down as head coach. One of the more poignant scenes in Driesell's Maryland career is a picture of the coach leaving the press conference with his arms wrapped around the shoulders of his wife and children as he walked one last time through a tunnel that led from the locker room to the court. In his glory days, the coach passed through the same tunnel on the way to climactic conquests. This time, he left behind perhaps the most storied and compelling tale in Maryland athletic history.

Driesell's misery was tempered by an arrangement he had made as part of his departure as head coach. He transitioned to an assistant athletic director position charged with overseeing the department's sports information and marketing departments as well as the Maryland Educational Foundation, which raised money for scholarships and other department needs. He was paid $120,000 a year for nine years – the remainder of his 10-year coaching contract – and could continue his basketball camps at the school for the same length of time. Driesell says he collected the full salary even after he left Maryland.

When asked in 2010 what the athletic department wanted him to do in his new role, he pauses for a couple moments, laughs, and then says "Hide." He largely did just that, if not by choice. Once the public figurehead of the athletic department, the fiery Driesell morphed into an inconspicuous rank-and-file employee. He worked in a comfortable three-room office in Cole Field House, bringing his long-time basketball secretary along with him for comfort and continuity. Driesell says part of his job was to convince the elderly to place their life insurance policy in their will and make the athletic department the beneficiary when they died.

"I was getting ready to do that, but never got that much involved," says Driesell. "When I took the job, [then athletic director Lew] Perkins said just come on over when you want to and do what you want."

While a senior at Maryland, I worked as an intern in the athletics promotions office. I remember vividly how Driesell walked the office halls and concourse level in Cole Field House as if he were the king of a thriving empire. His sturdy stride supported a tall, confident man and reflected a constant sense of purpose. His blunt style prompted feelings of both fear and respect. Once, while I worked with other interns preparing basketball game-day programs, Driesell pushed open the door to our office and wanted to know why the programs weren't ready. He did not buffer his bullish entrance with a greeting. After we quickly offered an explanation that appeared to not satisfy the coach, he left just as abruptly as he had entered.

For reasons I cannot recollect, I stopped by to see Driesell a couple of months into his new job at Maryland. I do remember sensing while we walked along the concourse at Cole Field House that he clearly was not his former ebullient self. He seemed a humbled and transformed man, once vibrant and boisterous, now walking deliberately and seeming lethargic and uninspired. In late May 1987, Driesell stepped out from his new obscurity as a fundraiser when he was called to testify for the prosecution in the trial of Brian Tribble, who was the only person charged with a crime in connection to the death of Bias.

In an artist's rendering, Lefty Driesell, facing forward, testifies in the trial of Brian Tribble, sitting far left. Prosecutor Jeffrey Harding is far right. *(provided by Jeffrey Harding)*

Driesell had never before talked under oath in public about the events of the tragedy. Describing the scene of Long and Gregg at his house shortly after Bias died, Driesell testified: "David kept saying, 'Terry, tell Coach what happened!' Long said Bias came in real late and he and Brian came in together or maybe Brian came later and that Brian brought in the coke and that Leonard took it and Brian said, 'Don't put your head back when you snort, you'll get a header,' but Leonard said, 'I'm tough,' and he threw his head back and had a seizure and then it happened again and Long administered CPR and they called the paramedics."

Driesell's testimony that Tribble "brought in" the cocaine stunned Thomas Morrow, Tribble's attorney, who felt he was misled by the prosecution for not knowing that Driesell might claim that Tribble provided the cocaine. Morrow asked the judge to drop the conspiracy charge against Tribble and to declare a mistrial based on Driesell's comments as hearsay. The judge instructed the jury to ignore those comments by Driesell, striking the only testimony that suggested Tribble had provided the drugs that killed Bias. Tribble was acquitted on all charges.

Jeffrey Harding, the State's Attorney who prosecuted the case, calls Driesell's testimony at Tribble's trial "important evidence" because it appeared to indicate that Tribble provided the cocaine that killed Bias. But he also claims that no amount of evidence the prosecutors presented against Tribble would have resulted in a guilty conviction. To support his theory, he recalls indifferent expressions from the jury as he gave his opening remarks.

"I had 15 people sitting in that box and not one of them looked at me," he says. "I already knew what was going to happen. There was a long grand jury investigation that brought the University of Maryland to its knees. The jury felt that we were going after their son, Len Bias. They wanted us to stop, let it go. Bias did the cocaine. He's responsible. The evidence really didn't matter."

Driesell left Maryland in 1988 to become head basketball coach at James Madison University. In 1994, the Dukes won the Colonial Athletic Association conference tournament title and advanced to the NCAA tournament for the first since 1983. Driesell departed James Madison in 1996 to become the head coach at Georgia State, where he stayed through 2003. He retired as the fourth most-winning coach in Division I history with 786 victories.

In the summer of 2002, Driesell returned to Maryland's College Park campus for the first time since departing for James Madison, to attend his induction ceremony into Maryland's Athletic Hall of Fame. He returned the next winter, on January 20, 2003, when the Terrapins honored his retirement from coaching at halftime of a game against N.C. State at the Comcast Center, Maryland's new basketball arena that opened at the beginning of that season. The crowd roared as Driesell walked onto the court and flashed the familiar victory sign with his right hand, pointing to the rafters. For two minutes, they stood and cheered. It must have felt as if he were back in Cole Field House, in the building where he helped develop Maryland basketball into a nationally respected program, ready to lead his Maryland team to another of its many victories. And it provided a bit of consolation for the coach, who had not been invited to Maryland's final game at Cole Field House the previous season. An athletic department spokesman explained the absence of an invitation by saying they focused on individual players, the first ACC championship team in 1958 and the first team to play in Cole.

John Lucas, who played for Driesell from 1972 to 1976, departed Maryland as a three-time All-America and was the top pick in the 1976 NBA draft. He offered perhaps the most balanced assessment of Driesell's personality, which endeared many and irritated others at Maryland. "Coach was genuine to a fault," he says. "What you saw was what you got. He doesn't have any gray areas."

"He was the nicest guy," says Len Elmore, a 1974 All-America at Maryland under Driesell. "His selflessness [made him] very self-effacing. Some people used to bristle at how humble he came off, and some of it was an act. But he had a plan. He took a lot of heat on himself to take it away from us."

Driesell bore the most public scorn of any University of Maryland athletic figure directly related to the fallout from the death of Len Bias. But in a style that was his trademark, Driesell – determined, defiant and perhaps a bit deceptive – soldiered on and reinvented himself as a contender wherever he coached. Driesell's college basketball legacy was further entrenched when he was elected to the NCAA Basketball Hall of Fame in 2007.

Driesell reluctantly agreed to talk about Bias in the summer of 2010, but not without apparent angst. When asked by phone to meet and discuss his memories of Bias, he initially refused but later in the same discussion agreed and asked to set up the details later. During several follow-up calls he vacillated until finally agreeing to a phone interview.

He praised Bias's work ethic in practice. "I used to have to take him out of practices because he would dominate, score all the time and get all the rebounds," he says. "I had to ask him, 'Sit down, will you?' He was a great kid to coach, very coachable. When I recruited him, I didn't think he'd be that good. He was everything you want in a player. He never got hurt, was never late, always worked hard."

Before Bias's death, Driesell insists, there was no indication the player even drank alcohol much less used drugs. To support his claim, Driesell recounts the time Slaughter called him to say he saw Bias walk across the Maryland campus with a six-pack of beer. When he confronted Bias about it, Driesell discovered it was a six-pack: of root beer.

Driesell also tells a story about a recruit whom Bias guided around campus a couple of weeks before he died. While still in mourning, Driesell asked the recruit if he saw Bias use drugs or alcohol. "He said, 'We went into two or three clubs, and he wouldn't even drink a beer. Coach, I'm telling you, he wouldn't even drink a beer.' I would have bet every penny I had that he would be the last player to use cocaine. I had some other guys that maybe they did, but I would never have thought of Leonard. I still think it was the first time he tried it, and he didn't know what he was doing."

Driesell remembers how Fentress, the agent he shared with Bias, warned the player to stay away from anything connected to drugs. "I was sitting right there when Lee Fentress said, 'He got tested by every NBA team he went to.' Fentress told him, 'I don't care if you're in a car and you're smelling a joint, get out and take a cab.'"

Driesell had dealt with the death of players before. In 1976, Owen Brown and Chris Patton both died of heart problems while playing basketball. Patton fell to Marfan syndrome and Brown, an NBA draft pick that year, was a victim of hypertrophic cardiomyopathy. But Driesell called the resulting fallout from Bias's death the most traumatic.

"I loved Leonard," he says. "He was like a son [to me]."

If Driesell defends Bias as someone who didn't drink or do drugs, he also defends him academically. The coach still believes that Bias, who failed to earn one passing grade his final semester at Maryland, earned an unfair reputation as a student. "A lot of people say he was a bad student," he says. "But he was a darn good student. The only time he didn't go to class was during his senior year.

And Driesell counters aggressively the thought that Bias, in his words, "set Maryland back." Bias was the reason Walt Williams, a Washington, D.C., native who grew up watching Bias play, enrolled at Maryland two years after the star died. Williams, who helped keep Maryland basketball viable during the down years following Bias's death, confirmed Driesell's theory. "I was a very big Len Bias fan," says the man who would break Bias's Maryland single-season scoring record. "It was a big thing for me to go to Maryland and follow in his footsteps. That was a part of me staying at Maryland. Maryland had gone through so many things with [the death of] Bias. People forget all the good he did. He made me feel like I can do well in basketball because I saw him do it."

Keith Booth, a Baltimore native who attended Maryland in the mid-1990s, also chose the school because of Bias. Booth's years at Maryland helped the school return to national prominence. Driesell finds further solace in a story he recently told with gusto. During the early summer of 2010, a man approached Driesell as they walked out of church near Driesell's home in Virginia Beach.

"Someone said, 'Aren't you Lefty Driesell? I was always a big Maryland fan, and Leonard was one of my favorite players,' " says Driesell. The man explained that shortly before Bias's death, he had reached a personal low, losing his job and his family due to a cocaine addiction. When friends told the man that Bias had died, he immediately stopped abusing cocaine.

Says Driesell: "He said Leonard saved his life."

BOBBY ROSS

As Lefty Driesell's celebrated career was dissolving in the fall of 1986, Maryland football head coach Bobby Ross was trying to make the best of what was becoming a trying season. The Terrapins entered the 1986 season looking for their fourth-consecutive ACC championship, and they started off with three wins, two of them on the road. But injuries and distractions during the season began to create an environment too challenging to overcome.

For one thing, Ross personally had to endure the departures of his close friends Dull and Driesell. Then, it didn't help that the football team played its first game just 10 weeks after the tragedy. School administrators told him that his players had to talk to the media, Ross says, but they were bombarded with questions that had nothing to do with the next game or opponent and everything to do with Bias. "Guys would constantly come up to me and ask what they should say," says Ross. "I told them to tell the truth. It was a big distraction."

Although the Terrapins were unranked going into the 1986 season, the team started with expectations "probably equal" to any other team he coached at Maryland, Ross says. Injuries soon intervened. Among the key players lost was wide receiver Azizuddin Abdur-Ra'oof, who tore an Achilles tendon during the fourth game against N.C. State.

Abdur-Ra'oof, recently the executive director of Maryland's M-Club before moving in 2011 to become the Director of Student Welfare & Career Development in Maryland's athletic department, recalled how athletes felt unappreciated and disrespected after Bias died. "It was like a gray cloud followed you around all the time," he says. "It was a weird year. You didn't want to be seen. You became reclusive. At the end of the year, there was a lot of uncertainty. We didn't know where we stood being an athlete at the time. The rest of the student body looked at you differently."

Ross's reaction to a win in the last game, against Virginia in Charlottesville, typified the feelings of that season. On the first half of his car ride home, he traveled north on Virginia Route 29, a rolling four-lane highway that passes through the bucolic Shenandoah Valley of central Virginia. Such a drive normally prompts peaceful and reflective thoughts. But despite the Terrapins' commanding 42-10 win, the mood on the ride back for Ross, his wife and four of his five children was far from either serene or celebratory. It was during that 2 1/2-hour ride that the Ross family had a long talk about Dad's future. They decided that he would step down as Maryland's head coach. Maryland finished the season 5-5-1. It was the worst record in Ross's five year Maryland career.

Not long before that ride, Ross had met with acting Athletic Director Charles Sturtz to discuss the university's admissions policy and how it might affect the future of Maryland athletics. This was a big step for Ross, who tried to avoid discussing admissions with athletic administrators because he thought it might build up resentment among professors and other school officials. "I don't think that was my job as a football coach," he says.

In the meeting, Ross sought clarification about Maryland's admissions policy, which was being scrutinized following Bias's death. He was told it could be as long as three or four years before it would all be settled. "That's when I started to think about it," says Ross. "Not having a defined direction and all the other distractions, I felt it was time to move on."

Ross resigned on December 1, 1986, and says he told his players he was leaving because he felt "at that time, they needed a change, and I needed a change. The media talked a lot about poor facilities being a big deal. I would have liked better facilities, but that wasn't the reason. There was no athletic director who was going to give me better answers for the long range and short term."

Two months after resigning from Maryland, Ross accepted the job as head coach at Georgia Tech. The Yellow Jackets would go on to share the 1990 national title with Colorado. After leaving Tech, Ross coached five years with the San Diego Chargers, taking them to the Super Bowl, and five more years with the Detroit Lions. He now resides in a small, rural western Virginia town about a four-hour drive from Driesell's house in Virginia Beach.

In the spring of 2010, Driesell called Ross to ask for some insight about the Citadel, where Ross was the head coach in the 1970s. Driesell's son Chuck was named head basketball coach at the school shortly after the two former Maryland coaches talked.

"Lefty and I are good friends," Ross says. "We see a lot of each other. Sometimes there can be a jealousy between coaches in major sports. But not between us. We would talk to each other's recruits and send each other notes before big games. Our wives were very close. I remember seeing Lefty and his wife walk out the [Cole Field House] tunnel after his press conference when he said he was leaving Maryland. I said, 'There goes a legend, someone very special. There goes Maryland basketball.' It was kind of an empty feeling."

BOB WADE

Bobby Ross's December 1 resignation meant that within two months, the school had lost a powerful triumvirate: its top athletic administrator, Dick Dull, and its two most high-profile coaches, Ross and Driesell. But the transition was far from complete, When Sturtz, the vice chancellor for administrative affairs, took over as interim athletic director on November 2, 1986, it was with plans to recommend changes to the department. By the time he completed his duties in April 1987, 17 staff members had been fired, and the bureaucratic hierarchy had been greatly simplified.

"The rest of the university hated us," Tyler says of the athletic department. "Not just the men's basketball team had a problem. Coaches were down and out, saddened deeply by what occurred. The rest of the university started looking at us like we were bringing them down. We felt the whole university was looking at us like we had bad kids. We had good kids. My students told me that some of their professors would make sarcastic remarks, 'Oh, you're an athlete, you'll want special things.'"

Into that challenging environment stepped Bob Wade, whose transition from the comfort and stability of a top national high-school program at Dunbar High School in Baltimore to the ruins of a devastated

Division I college program was both swift and difficult.

According to press reports, Slaughter picked Wade over former Maryland star Gene Shue, De-Matha High School coach Morgan Wootten and Maryland assistant coach Ron Bradley. Wootten says he had no discussions with anyone at Maryland about succeeding Driesell and Slaughter said the only coach he interviewed for the position was Wade. The school held a press conference on October 30, one day after Driesell resigned, announcing Wade as the new coach. He signed a five-year contract. But in a move that foretold the closed culture that would be created within the basketball program during Wade's three years at Maryland, he stayed only a few minutes and made but a brief statement, saying he needed to hurry back to Dunbar to coach the school's football team as it prepared for a postseason game.

Wade's reputation as a strict academic disciplinarian preceded him. "He had a record of making certain that his students studied; otherwise, they couldn't play," Slaughter says. According to a report in the *Washington Post*, Wade's academic adviser at Dunbar, Geraldine West, had an office next to the basketball court and had the authority to remove a player from practice to review his schoolwork.

Slaughter also liked Wade's connection to, and success in, Baltimore. Maryland had never established a strong pipeline to the wealth of basketball talent developing in that city. "We needed greater access to Baltimore," he says. "And he was clearly a person who had shown great skills as a coach. I talked to a number of conference coaches about him – Dean Smith, Terry Holland, Bobby Cremins, Jim Valvano – as well as John Thompson. To a person, they had nothing but quality things to say. Some had coached with him at summer camps. Valvano's and Bob's wife were close friends. It was not a spur-of-the-moment decision."

Wade's record of success on the field and in the arena at the high-school level was admirable. A former defensive back who played for four NFL teams, he established a superior program at Dunbar, where he was the athletic director as well as football and basketball coach. In 10 years, his basketball teams lost only 25 games, winning 341. Three of his teams earned No. 1 national rankings. Three dozen of Wade's players had gone on to play college basketball, including Ernie Graham at Maryland and David Wingate and Reggie Williams at Georgetown.

Maryland struggled during its first year under Wade, but it's difficult to blame a coach for a team's problems when he accepts the job only two months before the first game – and that was with a delayed start to the season. To give the players more time to recover from Bias's death and to allow them to adjust to a new coach, the Terrapins didn't play their first game until December 27, about a month later than normal.

Wade faced a daunting rebuilding task. Only five players – sophomores John Johnson, Dave Dickerson, Greg Nared and Phil Nevin and junior Derrick Lewis – returned from the previous year's roster. Keith Gatlin, a junior, was forced to miss the season after improperly registering for classes, and sophomore Tony Massenburg missed the year due to academic probation. Six players were new to the roster.

Maryland won its first two games against Winthrop and Fairleigh Dickinson, but finished the season 9-17, matching its previous worst record from the 1963-64 season. And for the first time since the 1940-41 season, Maryland failed to win a conference game.

If it seemed as if Maryland's players were stuck in a prolonged wake during Wade's first year, his second season signaled a revival of their spirits and good fortunes. It helped that all five starters returned for the 1987-88 season, and Wade fashioned a strong recruiting class, including freshman Brian Williams and junior-college transfer Rudy Archer. Also, Massenburg and Gatlin rejoined the team.

"The year off was actually pleasant," Gatlin told the *Washington Post* after his first game back, in which he led Maryland with 17 points in a loss to Missouri on January 6. "I got to go home for a while at Thanksgiving and Christmas to see my family. Emotionally, I wasn't ready to play last year, anyway. The way Lenny died and every day a different story about us … I think I aged 10 years."

In that second season, Maryland's biggest win came in mid-January over seventh-ranked Duke in Durham. A dunk by Lewis, who would lead the team in points and rebounds that year, sealed a three-point win over the Blue Devils. Maryland ended the season 18-13 overall and fifth in the conference with a 6-8 record. An 84-67 win over 18th-ranked Georgia Tech at home in its last game of the year helped Maryland advance to the NCAA tournament, where it lost in the second round by nine points to sixth-ranked Kentucky. The players discovered that advancing to the second round in the NCAA tournament helped change the attitude toward the team that had prevailed on the campus the previous season. "Winning cures a lot of things," says Dickerson.

Wade's third year started to fall apart well before Maryland bounced the first basketball in practice. Williams, who averaged 12 points and six rebounds as a freshman, transferred that May to Arizona, blaming communication problems in the program and saying that he could not improve sufficiently under Wade. Two other players later transferred, most notably guard Steve Hood, who ended up at James Madison with Driesell, the new coach.

In addition, Archer was ruled academically ineligible and sophomore guard Teyon McCoy decided to redshirt the season. Altogether, eight players failed to return from the previous season's roster. It was disastrous: Maryland endured a nine-game losing streak and won just one ACC game for the second-worst conference record in history, finishing 9-20 overall.

Maryland did manage one magical moment in the first round of the ACC tournament. Taking advantage of N. C. State's 30-percent shooting from the field, the Terrapins upset them, the tournament's top seed, in the first round, 71-49, despite being limited to its five starters for most of the game.

In a cruel bit of irony, Wade was not able to coach his last official game with Maryland. Shortly after giving the post-game press conference after the win over N. C. State, he suffered cramps and dehydration and was taken to a hospital, where he stayed for tests on his heart through Maryland's next game, against North Carolina, the following night. With assistant coach Ron Bradley running the team, the exhausted and distracted Terrapins lost by 30 points.

If Wade was feeling extra pressure, it was understandable. During the last week of the season, he had admitted that his staff had violated NCAA rules by providing Archer with rides from his home to classes at Prince George's Community College and at Maryland's University College while he was being recruited, although Wade said he did not authorize the rides.

Jeff Baxter, who graduated the year before Wade started as Maryland coach, claims an assistant coach on Wade's staff told him that it was one of the coaches who told a Maryland athletic administrator that Wade had driven Archer to class. He did not name the coach. "The worst thing you can do is keep anyone from a previous administration on a staff," says Baxter. "Because if anything happened, the coaches would be quick to run back to the administration and say this is going on and this is going on."

Wade not only felt uneasy with his coaching staff, but also with the fact that Driesell still had an office nearby. "If I had to do it again, I would insist on bringing in my own people," he said in a *Boston Globe* story in 1996. "I wanted my own assistants, but I was told by the administration that they didn't have the money. I had to keep Lefty's guys Ron Bradley and Oliver Purnell. One minute they are loyal to him, and the next they have to be loyal to me? It just doesn't work that way. I never felt comfortable. I didn't trust them. Lefty's office was close to mine. I'd tell guys to do something one way. Lefty would tell them something else. I heard he would ask the guys, 'What's he running? What's he running?' It was tough being there after Len Bias. I would do it again, just a lot differently."

It didn't help when Slaughter, who picked Wade for the job, resigned in 1988 to become president of Occidental College. Slaughter had been Wade's biggest fan, and Wade's supporters complained toward the end of his last season that Lew Perkins, the new athletic director, did not support him strongly enough. It also didn't help Wade that he appeared to have stifled Driesell's recruiting efforts in Baltimore. According to the book *Lenny, Lefty and the Chancellor*, Wade had told other coaches not to talk to Driesell because Wade, then the head coach of Dunbar High School in Baltimore, felt Driesell did not abide by his recruiting rules. Wade also was unhappy with Driesell, according to the book, because Graham, who played for Wade at Dunbar, did not earn a degree. Graham says he does not remember that his failing to graduate created a rift between Driesell and Wade, neither of whom would comment.

In May 1988 the school's Campus Faculty Senate passed a resolution supporting Wade, noting that two of Maryland's rostered players – Massenburg and McCoy – had made the dean's list. Still, Wade resigned on May 12, 1989, and received a settlement that included $120,000 in cash over two years. He did not attend the press conference announcing his departure. He instead lay in a hospital bed, recovering from back surgery. Wade departed Maryland with a 36-50 record. In 1989, the NCAA – citing a number of major violations under Wade in addition to the Archer incident – imposed sanctions on the team that included no post-season play for two years and three years' probation.

In fairness to Wade, any coach called in to succeed the gregarious and endearing Driesell faced an unenviable task. Still, some within the athletic department felt that Wade appeared aloof and indifferent and isolated himself from his coworkers, which contributed to a lack of support. Tyler claims she never got to know Wade well. "He'd come in and quickly go to his own office," Tyler says. "He didn't interact much with the other coaches. He did his own thing. He had other folks do his business activities. He was such an enigma."

Chuck Walsh worked in the Maryland athletics media-relations office during Wade's time as coach. He once set up an interview for me with Wade when I was working as a sports reporter for a local cable television channel. Wade never showed up, and Walsh was unable to offer an explanation. Walsh can't recall Wade skipping other interviews but remembers the coach often giving reporters what Walsh felt was inadequate time.

"He didn't let anybody get to know him," says Walsh, now an associate sports-information director at Florida State University. "He thought from day one that everybody was against him. If you looked around our athletic department, almost everyone was a white male. I hope it wasn't a racial thing." Wade had not only been Maryland's first African American head basketball coach, but the first in the conference.

Tyler echoed those thoughts. "I think when he first got hired, everybody really tried to give him overtures and open up to him," she says. "But he kept to himself and seemed not to want to be around us. Maybe he felt he had enough to do; he was under siege and had so much going on he didn't have time."

As for the lack of support from the University Maryland sports community, Walsh feels it worked both ways. "They didn't rally around him the same way he didn't rally around them," he says. "It probably had a lot to do with the fact that he replaced Lefty on a bad note. If Lefty had retired or gone on to a different job, then Wade comes in and it might have been different."

Wade's inexperience in college basketball also appeared to contribute to his struggles. Walsh claims that several people within Maryland's athletic department told him that Wade began breaking NCAA violations beginning with his first day on the job. As Walsh sees it, Wade didn't intend to break the rules. He just didn't know enough about the rules to avoid violating them. "He was not prepared to take that job," says Walsh. "You don't come out of high school and go right to coaching in the ACC. Maybe you can go to a Division III program, but not the ACC."

"We wished he would ask more questions, then we would know what he didn't know," says Tyler. "He thought he could handle it and do whatever he could do to be successful."

John Brown, the owner of RJ Bentley's, developed a strong friendship with Wade, who brought the team into his restaurant for meals. Brown even occasionally supplied some of the food when Wade's wife, Carolyn, cooked team meals at the coach's house. "He taught them how to be men and gentlemen," says Brown, sitting behind a desk in his office above the restaurant. "They'd sit upright, they learned to have pride. He did a lot of things that might not have been correct but he did a lot of things that he won't get credit for that were wonderful. Bob was a proud man and he was strong and he was good. He was a high-school coach who mopped floors. He had no business being a college coach without support. And no one in this school was giving him support."

Few business operators in College Park have been as connected to the Maryland athletic department as Brown. He was a member of the Terrapin Club's board of directors when Wade was Maryland's coach and has worked closely with the coaches at Maryland to promote the teams and the players. Brown felt Wade received little support from the Terrapin Club. "Lines within the Terrapin Club were clearly drawn with resentment for how Bob Wade was hired and who he was," says Brown. "Support for him was minimal."

Brown recalled the time the Terrapin Club called a meeting attended by Maryland's coaches. Wade was not among them, however – he wasn't invited. Carolyn Wade called Brown the next day and asked if he would talk to her husband. After a brief phone conversation, Brown went over to Wade's house and found him distraught. " 'John, why won't they include me?' he asked. And he just shook, a great powerful man, shook and trembled," says Brown. "He was crying, his head down, and I said, 'Bob, I don't know. Obviously, they should.' "

Brown admits that Wade's stubbornness didn't help his cause at Maryland. "It seemed to go more and more like that, his bullheadedness, him not doing what they wanted. Bob made it difficult. If you didn't know him, he could be aloof. It was a divide. They hung him out to dry when NCAA violations came up."

Adkins was an assistant coach for Wade for three years and is still a good friend. He enjoyed working with Wade, saying he had a big heart and liked to help people. But he talks frankly about

Wade's weaknesses as a coach. "He wanted everybody to agree with him," he says. "And he was very cynical and thought everybody was out to get him."

Asked if Wade trusted anyone in the athletic department, Adkins flatly said, "No."

Although Slaughter had selected Wade in large part for the coach's attention to academic excellence, Gerald Gurney, Maryland's director of academic support from 1987 to 1992, felt Wade was a disappointment. "I didn't feel he was very adamant at all either for the quality of the recruits or the insistence upon academic achievement," says Gurney. "There is a very large learning curve for a transition from high-school programs to college. Wade was not particularly experienced enough or ready for that position."

"In all fairness, Slaughter did a terrible thing bringing Wade in," says Brown. "He should not have been hired to start off with. He wasn't qualified."

Gurney called Wade a "player's coach" who was a father figure to many of the young men on his team. Still, he felt Wade was uncomfortable as Maryland's head coach. "He felt that the world was against him, or the 'Terp Nation' was against him, that he wasn't welcome there. Lefty was a very imposing figure, and anyone following him would have had some difficulty with that. When you feel insecure in your position, I can understand why he wouldn't want to be open and touchy feely to everyone. He had a friend and supporter in John Slaughter; beyond that he was distant with everyone around him. It was hard to get close to him.

"And he wasn't the golden boy," continues Gurney. "He wasn't a Maryland product. It seemed as if he was imposing upon the Maryland program."

Regardless of his qualifications for the job, Wade can relish this fact: three of the players he inherited from a troubled program – Dickerson, Massenburg and Greg Nared – all went on to achieve high-profile professional success.

Wade's legacy at Maryland is mixed. His NCAA violations will be remembered for setting back the basketball program for years. Wade called the group of men's basketball coaches in the conference an "old boy's network" in a *Charlotte Observer* report and added that his time in the ACC was difficult. But as the first black head coach of a men's basketball team in the conference he can be considered a cultural pioneer, despite appearing uncomfortable in that role.

Even Slaughter, who hired Wade, ultimately questioned the wisdom of the move. "In retrospect, it might have been an impossible situation for Bob," he told the *Washington Post* in January 1990. "Bob followed a coaching legend. He was black. He was appointed by a black chancellor. He's from a high school. He's hired one day before practice begins. And the players had gone through hell after Leonard's death. Throwing Bob in the middle of that was like throwing a piece of raw meat to a pack of lions. You're going to get chewed up if you don't do things perfectly. I don't think Bob got the support he needed from many people. There were people within the athletic department as well as outside the department who did not want him to succeed."

Wade's legacy as a beloved high-school basketball coach, however, continues to grow. In 2008 some of Wade's former players at Dunbar honored the coach at a roast in Greenbelt, Maryland, a town about five miles from College Park. Those attending included former NBA player Muggsy Bogues and former Maryland star Graham. As of the fall of 2011 Wade worked as the athletic director with Baltimore City Public Schools.

"He loved all of us," Graham said in a *Baltimore Sun* report promoting the event. "He cared about us. He made a difference in the lives of a lot of young men in more ways than just coaching basketball."

DEPARTMENT CHANGES

When Lew Perkins took over as athletic director at the University of Maryland in May 1987, less than a year after Bias died, he appeared to be a good fit. For the previous four years, he had served in the same role at Wichita State University, which was enduring two years of NCAA probation when he started in 1983 after the NCAA cited the school's basketball team for recruiting violations. But Perkins helped the school recover from its problems. Before he departed Wichita State for College Park, the NCAA had cited the Kansas school for having an exemplary program.

From the day he took office, Perkins sought to percolate change. During a press conference on May 12, 1987, at which he was introduced as Maryland's new athletic director, Perkins said he planned to institute an extensive policy manual for coaches to read and sign. Tyler remembers that Perkins asked each coach to attend a group meeting and sign the manual as an agreement that they understood its content. "The key elements were accountability and to make sure your kids went to classes," she says. "Before the manual, the NCAA had what they called a satisfactory progress rule to make sure the athletes were moving to their degree. He wanted to make sure we were looking at our kids as performing well academically and getting their degrees. It reinforced what we knew needed to be done."

The manual was one of many changes instituted at Maryland during Perkins's time as athletic director. Slaughter initiated two task forces: one to review academic achievements of student athletes and another to examine the school's policies related to education and drug-abuse prevention. Further, Slaughter asked University of Michigan Athletic Director Don Canham to lead a group to review the athletic department's structure and efficiency. That review stated the department was overstaffed and disorganized, leading to the release of more than a dozen staff members in January 1987. The academic-achievement task force released its report on September 30, 1986. It recommended a number of reforms, some of which were implemented as early as the winter of 1987.

Athletes classified as individual admits were also known as special admission exceptions or at-risk students. In 1986 their number reached an all-time high of 48, with the men's basketball team claiming four individual admits. The task force suggested no more than 27 individual admits for the 1987-88 academic year, with men's basketball receiving two. Individual admits would be reduced to 18 in 1988. It suggested reducing those numbers further in future years.

The department instituted three classes of admission for athletes: preferred, for students with at least a 3.0 high-school grade-point average on a 4.0 scale and at least a 1,000 combined score on the SAT; regular, allowing a higher grade-point average to offset a lower SAT score, or vice versa; and individual exceptions to the standards, decided on a case-by-case basis.

- - - - - - - - - -

A disrupted athletic department was nothing new to Gurney. Before he accepted the job of associate athletics director for academic support at Maryland in late 1987, he had served as an assistant athletics director for academic affairs at Southern Methodist University while the football team endured three years' probation for recruiting violations. Toward the end of his stay at SMU, Gurney witnessed the team receiving the death penalty, which canceled the 1987 season. The team did not compete in 1988.

"I knew I was going into a situation that would be under a microscope," says Gurney. "I understood the Maryland area being surrounded by Baltimore and D.C. and the *Washington Post* and the *Baltimore Sun*; I knew it would be a challenge. I was confident and excited."

Gurney instituted a series of policies suggested by the task force that signaled a sea change in the way Maryland athletics administered its academic program. "The goal was not to create a culture on the team that would not be academic," he says. "If you limit the number of specially admitted students per team, then the culture would improve. That was a worthy goal and had a lot of merit to it."

Before Bias died, former Terrapins head soccer coach Jim Dietsch had led the academic support staff in Maryland athletics with the help of a small crew of academic advisers, including five academic coordinators providing support for 405 athletes, according to the task force. Gurney described it as a "one- or two-man" shop. By comparison, in 2011 Maryland athletics listed more than one dozen staff members in its Academic Support and Career Development Unit.

In September 1986, in the wake of the Bias death, Dull asked Dietsch to leave his post to become the department's ticket manager. Dietsch did not publicly object to the move at the time, saying in a press report that he agreed it would not be good to continue the current system with those who were perceived to be responsible for the athletic department's academic problems. Still, some who worked in the department felt that Dietsch, also an assistant lacrosse coach at the time, was wrongly blamed. Tyler did not agree with the decision.

"They tried to pin the academic problems on him," says Tyler. "The task force determined he was not qualified to do his job. It said it wasn't Bias's fault, but the way Jim ran the department. That was completely untrue. There was nobody who worked harder or did more for the students. He was working 18 hours a day, six or seven days a week, coaching and trying to get the academic support unit going. If a student had a class or schedule problem, he had to fix it. He was sincere, trustworthy. Jim was the least liable of anybody."

Tyler added that Dietsch acted as more than an academic adviser; he was an adviser on personal issues to a lot of the students. "It didn't matter what team you were on, you always talked to Coach Dietsch about your parents splitting up, or some other problem. Students loved him."

Dietsch, a Baltimore native, was another member of the Maryland athletic family. He played lacrosse at Maryland from 1967 to 1969 and was an assistant coach for Maryland teams that won national titles in 1973 and 1975. He took over as head coach of the men's soccer team in 1975. I made the soccer team as a walk-on in 1976, playing only through the preseason due to injury, but I quickly developed a strong affinity toward Dietsch. Although I couldn't help the team on the field, he invited me to many team trips and functions, including team dinners at the Ponderosa Steak House in College Park the night before games, and he often invited players to his house for barbecues.

While soccer coach, Dietsch helped manage an NCAA-sponsored program that matched students as mentors with local teenagers in the area, and I was proud to be part of that program under his direction. Some players who didn't agree with his coaching style at times showed their disfavor to him on the field, but it was difficult to not like Dietsch as a person. He made you feel like you were part of his family.

Tyler, who participated in many NCAA tournaments as the Terrapins field hockey coach, remembers the somber mood of other coaches after Dietsch was reassigned. "They were astounded," she says. "And they thought 'If it could happen to Jim, what would happen to us?'"

After eventually being fired by Maryland as a result of the efficiency-review study, Dietsch returned to coaching as an assistant lacrosse coach at Catonsville Community College from 1987 to 2005 and later at Limestone College, an NCAA Division II Final Four participant in 2007. From 2008 through July 2011 he was the head lacrosse coach at Division III Belmont Abbey College, earning Conference Carolinas Coach of the Year honors in 2008 after leading the team to its first winning record at 9-4. It was Dick Dull, the athletic director at Belmont Abbey from 2007-2009, who hired Dietsch.

- - - - - - - - - -

The academic achievement task force also suggested tightening eligibility standards. To stay eligible before the changes were proposed, an athlete needed to be enrolled as a full-time student taking at least 12 credits per semester, pass 24 credits a year toward a specific major (an NCAA requirement), and not to have been academically dismissed.

The athletic department enacted the following requirements from the task force recommendations. To be eligible, athletes needed to maintain the following grade-point averages based on a 4.0 scale: freshmen, 1.7; sophomores 1.85; juniors and seniors, 2.0. Those standards have become a bit stricter. As of the summer of 2010, eligible sophomores must have completed 24 applicable credits and have maintained a 1.8 average; after a second year, 1.9 and 48 credits; after junior year, 2.0 and 72 credits. If athletes did not satisfy those requirements, they would be ineligible for the following semester.

Gurney was responsible for enforcing the changes recommended by the task force. He feels the most profound change involved limiting the number of special admissions for football players. Many athletes satisfied the NCAA standards but not those instituted at Maryland. Prior to the changes, the total number of new scholarships for special admission football players could not exceed 30 annually. That number was reduced to 10.

Joe Krivak, who took over the football team following the departure of Ross and was a Ross assistant for four years, felt the sting of academic restructuring. The 1987 season began one of the worst stretches in the 119-year history of Maryland football, with the Terrapins recording a winning record just once in eight seasons. The new academic restrictions were clearly affecting the quality of players Maryland could recruit. "A lot of people in admissions got really uptight," says Krivak. "It certainly had an effect."

Krivak had to provide a list of names of his recruits and pursued them only after he received word that the players satisfied the department's standards. Or so he thought. "They would give us a green light, then 10 days or a week before the national signing day, we'd be told we couldn't recruit the players. You were given a green light, and the light turned red."

Krivak, who runs camps for quarterbacks and receivers in the mid-Atlantic area, spoke calmly and proudly of his five years as head coach, expressing frustration but no regret. He recalled one incident that typified the challenges he faced in keeping players who were admitted on the field. As Maryland prepared to play Penn State in early November 1991 during Krivak's final year as head coach, the Terrapins had a 2-6 record. Krivak discovered by the Monday prior to the Penn State game that a few of his players had not maintained the grade-point average minimum and were ruled ineligible. Krivak appealed to athletic director Andy Geiger, who replaced Perkins in 1990.

"I asked him, 'What are we doing this for? It doesn't violate any NCAA rules,'" says Krivak. "He said, 'Coach, you just have to live with it.' But he didn't have to play the game on Saturday." Maryland suffered its worst loss of the season to the ninth-ranked Nittany Lions, 47-7, and then lost its last two games to finish 2-9, Krivak's worst record as head coach.

Tyler says the incident symbolizes how things had changed. "That epitomized the kind of treatment [Krivak] got from the department. In the past, we would try to figure out a way to keep them playing. A coach goes to an athletic director and wants to hear about ways to strategize, and figure out a way to fix the problem. He didn't get the response he deserved to make him feel supported. That's just the way the culture was at the time."

By the early 1990s, that culture was one of discomfort and uncertainty. A big reason was perhaps the most significant move made by Perkins, toward the end of his three years at Maryland. On May 16, 1990, he announced that varsity teams would be restructured into four tiers. That day, he also said the school would eliminate athletic scholarships in eight of its 23 varsity sports and would reduce scholarship money by 70 percent in five others. Perkins said a budget crisis made worse by NCAA sanctions against the men's basketball team prompted the moves.

Six sports – football, men's and women's basketball, men's lacrosse, women's volleyball and women's field hockey – were placed in the first tier. Those sports, which had a history of competing for NCAA national honors, received $1.5 million of the $1.871 million available for scholarships.

In the second tier, four sports – women's lacrosse, men's wrestling, and men's and women's soccer – each received $64,000 in scholarship money, representing a 15% cut in aid. These sports were expected to contend for ACC championships. Third-tier sports would have their scholarship aid reduced by 70 percent: baseball, men's and women's swimming, and men's and women's cross-country would each receive $25,000 in scholarship money and compete regionally.

Men's and women's indoor and outdoor track, men's golf, women's gymnastics, and men's and women's tennis were placed in the lowest level and would operate without scholarships. They would compete locally except for ACC competitions.

The immediate aftermath appeared devastating to the sports consigned to the lowest level – but there was a twist. Take women's gymnastics as an example. In the years just after Bias died, the women's gymnastics team posted a string of winning seasons, including a 20-11-1 record in 1989 – the best season Nelligan had put together since he started as the Terrapins coach in 1979. But two years after Perkins eliminated new scholarships for the team, the gymnasts suffered through three consecutive losing seasons for the first time, including its second-worst season in Nelligan's 31 years as head coach.

A few years after Debbie Yow became athletic director in 1994, she reinstated some scholarships, but the gymnastics team did not return to its full allotment of 12 until 2001. "It changed the way we did things," says Nelligan. "It put us at a disadvantage and put a chip on our shoulders. We weren't able to recruit the blue-chip athletes, but we were recruiting the athletes that made Maryland what it is today. The kids that came in had a passion to learn and to compete. In some ways, it was a very opportune time to reevaluate. We went back to teaching. We would take an athlete that might have been raw and put our energies into them, and we grew together."

Another unexpected plus: The budget also allowed Nelligan more togetherness on the home front. "I spent more time with my family because I didn't have to go off campus to recruit," he says. "When you have $1,000 in your recruiting budget, you don't have to go too far."

During the time of cutbacks in the department, Nelligan was forced to find creative ways to raise and save money. The team worked as a clean-up crew following basketball games in Cole Field House. They parked cars at football games for a few hundred dollars. When Nelligan heard that extra windbreakers from the football team's appearance in the Cherry Bowl in 1985 were packed in a box, he grabbed them to use as the team's "away" jackets. Nelligan bought Maryland athletic logo patches at the school store and sewed them over the Cherry Bowl logo. "We were willing to do whatever it took to keep our program going in the right direction," he says.

Bonnie Bernstein was an Academic All-America in gymnastics all four years at Maryland, from 1988 to 1992. She developed into a nationally known sports radio and television broadcaster for ESPN and CBS and in November 2010 launched TerpVision, a multimedia series that focuses on stories about the University of Maryland. She remembers her time at Maryland as the "dark days of Maryland athletics. I don't think anyone realized the impact his death would have on Maryland athletics."

Bernstein says it took nearly two decades, when men's basketball won its first national title in 2002 with former Terps player Gary Williams as coach, for Maryland basketball to fully recover. "If you look at the proverbial light at the end of the tunnel, we were at the beginning of the tunnel," says Bernstein, referring to her generation of athletes. "The '02 championship was not just a national championship. It was the closing of a very difficult chapter of a very difficult period of Maryland basketball because of Bias and Bob Wade. Gary was given the opportunity to rebuild a program. It takes something of that magnitude to put that much negativity behind the school."

Even such prominent programs as women's basketball, then often among the top 20 teams in the country, needed to find creative ways to augment their budgets. But not all players supported the idea of selling game-day programs at football games to raise money for the team. The move convinced a couple of Maryland's top players to transfer after their freshman year because, as then-coach Chris Weller remembers, they felt the work "was beneath them. They thought we were being funded like a Division III program. That's an exact quote from their parents."

The players who did stay used the fallout from Bias's death as a vehicle to show their loyalty to the Maryland program. And the team bonded well, winning ACC tournament titles in 1988 and 1989. Also in 1989, Maryland, led by All-Americas Vicky Bullett and Deanna Tate, advanced to the NCAA Final Four for the first time since 1982. The players called themselves "The Survivors."

"They took great pride in the fact that they stayed loyal to Maryland, and they were a little resentful of the two superstars who left," says Weller. "It wasn't their goal to show them [that they could win], but they showed them."

Considering its past success, the sport that suffered the most was track and field. Maryland track was the dominant team in the Atlantic Coast Conference in the 1960s and 1970s, winning 48 conference titles in cross country, indoor track and outdoor track. The team has not won a conference title since 1981.

Bill Goodman, an ACC champion for Maryland in the long jump and triple jump in the early

1970s, took over the men's and women's teams in 1988 and retired in the spring of 2003. "It was a real struggle and was real depressing," he says. "When [the loss of scholarships] first happened to the men, it was like someone in your family died. As a coach, I was trying to keep our heads up, trying to get everybody to deal with it. I had no control over it."

Matters were made worse for the track teams when improvements in 1991 to Byrd Stadium, the home football field, forced the removal of the school's only outdoor track. For about two years, the team traveled a couple miles to train at a local high school until a new track opened in 1994. "It was almost like an excuse not to have a track team anymore," says Goodman.

As a result of the task force recommendations, Goodman witnessed the complete loss of his 12 scholarships for men and eight for women. He says that during discussions on how to restructure the athletic department, the Maryland Athletic Council initially planned to dissolve the men's and women's track teams entirely. But Goodman appealed aggressively to Geiger, Perkins's successor, defending the teams' high graduation rates and saying that cutting the teams would greatly affect the school's minority representation.

"At that time, track and field had 40 percent of minority athletes in nonrevenue sports at the school," says Goodman. "I had to form the best argument as to why they had to keep us." Goodman says the track-and-field teams received scholarships again in 1994. The men started with three and now can allocate $234,000 for scholarships. The women started with six and now can allocate $635,000 for scholarships.

Perkins indicated that the scholarship cuts and reductions in the operating budget would save Maryland up to $900,000 in fiscal year 1991. Press reports estimated that the athletic department budget deficit would reach $3.5 million by the end of that year, in large part due to $2.7 million in lost revenue because of NCAA sanctions on the men's basketball team under Wade.

During the lean financial times and the restructuring, the mood of the coaches was a stark departure from earlier eras, and it reflected the mental state of the department. Jack Jackson, Maryland's baseball coach for some three decades, had a meeting with Perkins soon after he took over as athletic director. "We started talking about loyalty," says Jackson. "He said there ain't such a thing as loyalty any more. He said anybody who stays at a job more than five years is lazy. I said 'How about the guy who likes his job, what does he do?' You walked down the halls and people never talked to you." Jackson retired as coach in 1990.

The wrestling program failed to win the ACC title only once from 1954 to 1974, and was starting to again show signs of prominence shortly after Bias died. The 1987 team featured All-Americas Steve Peperak, Tom Reese and Curt Scovel. "We were finally rolling and able to recruit the big-time guys," says John McHugh, a former Maryland wrestler who was head coach from 1978 until his retirement in 2003. "Then all of a sudden they cut our legs out from under us. For three years, I didn't sign anybody."

Still, the team managed to avoid a losing record in the early 1990s and finished second in the conference in 1993 and 1995.

Despite all the alterations and adjustments that have taken place in Maryland's athletic department since the death of Bias, the family dynamic remained strong through the summer of 2010. The few athletic directors that have led the Terrapins family since 1987 may have no direct familial ties to the program, but many in the department still provide a strong lineage to Maryland's lifeblood. As of the summer of 2010, more than a quarter of its coaches, seven in all, were graduates of the university. They included football coach Ralph Friedgen and men's basketball coach Gary Williams, Friedgen ended his 10-year run at Maryland in late 2010. Williams retired from coaching in 2011 after 22 seasons in College Park but stays on as a special assistant to the athletic director. Further, seven of Maryland's 18 athletic department senior staff were graduates of the university, including former tennis player Michael Lipitz, former football player Ra'oof and former All-America football player Kevin Glover. Lipitz moved on to N.C. State in the spring of 2011.

The restructured Maryland athletic family has worked through a traumatic time and has thrived in recent years, with 15 NCAA championships won in the 21st century, due in large part to the continued influence of former Maryland athletes who work within its athletic department. It's enough to prompt Terps legends Curley Byrd and Jim Kehoe to belt out the Maryland fight song from their final resting places, which are no doubt adorned in Maryland red and white.

Chapter 4

Teammates

By most measures, the 1985-86 Maryland basketball season was a disappointment. Returning four starters, including ACC Player of the Year Len Bias, the Terrapins had hoped to go even further than they had in 1984-85, when they advanced to the NCAA Sweet 16 before losing by three points to Villanova, the eventual NCAA champion. But Maryland struggled, finishing 19-14 and barely qualifying for the NCAA tournament before losing in the second round. As they walked off the floor after losing that last game of the season, the returning players – already eagerly looking forward to the 1986-87 season – couldn't know that within three months they would also lose their innocence.

The death of Bias transformed his teammates into adults overnight. They were thrown into a world of lawyers and depositions, blame and recrimination, finger-pointing and firings, on top of their own, unfamiliar grief. Its fallout twisted their lives like a mid-summer tornado in Nebraska. Some managed to not only weather the storm but forge lives wiser and sturdier than they might have been without the tragedy. Others never completely escaped the wreckage.

Dave Dickerson, Derrick Lewis, Keith Gatlin and Bryan Palmer not only pulled through but, through teaching and coaching, they've managed to pass along lessons they learned in that tumultuous time. Tony Massenburg overcame a stop-and-start college career to become an NBA champion. John Johnson has lived a quiet life, with little taste for basketball but still idolizing his friend. Jeff Baxter is philosophical, and Speedy Jones turned to God. David Gregg and Terry Long, who perhaps had the most to lose, have fought hard to put the stigma of their roles in Bias's death behind them, with varying degrees of success. Greg Nared went on to work with such superstars as Tiger Woods and Michelle Wie as a marketing and management representative for Nike, and Phil Nevin says he's long ago put it all behind him.

Teammates all, each with his own story.

DAVE DICKERSON

As Dave Dickerson recalls it, the escalating culture of drug abuse that swept the country in the 1970s and 1980s hadn't reached Olar, South Carolina, by the time he graduated high school in 1985. Dickerson, the youngest and only boy amid seven siblings, admittedly lived a sheltered life steeped in Pentecostal faith in rural Olar, a town of a few hundred people. A year later, Dickerson saw firsthand how drugs can not only kill a person, but cause severe collateral damage to everyone around him. He also learned lessons about fortitude and perseverance that some 20 years later helped him lead a tattered basketball team at Tulane University as it battled to recover from devastation of another kind: Hurricane Katrina.

Dickerson, an all-state player out of South Carolina, chose Maryland in part due to its proximity to Washington, D.C., the political capital of the world. Dickerson wanted someday to be mayor of his hometown. At the end of his freshman season, during which he played in 15 games and averaged 2.1 points, Dickerson had no reason not to feel positive about the next year. With forwards Bias and Speedy Jones ending their eligibility in 1986, Dickerson was expecting more playing time the following season. But then Bias died and, as for all his teammates, chaos became the new normal.

Dickerson admits he was a "green" freshman whose sheltered background would have prevented him from noticing the signs of a drug user. "I never experienced anyone losing their life from drugs," says Dickerson, who insists he never so much as saw Bias drink alcohol let alone use drugs. "I was shocked at how Len died." In the weeks that followed, Dickerson considered transferring – as did many of his teammates – but chose to stay at Maryland. "There was a big risk in transferring," he says. "And Maryland was my choice coming out of high school." Dickerson also feared that if he left Maryland he would suffer the wrath of his father, whom he called "an old-school guy. If you start something, you finish it," he says. "I was scared of my father."

In a profound understatement, Dickerson says that playing for the Terrapins that first season after Bias died was not fun. "We were viewed in a different light than any other athlete on campus," he says. "The perception of that team and the players on it was that we were drug abusers, we all didn't go to class and that we all were all part of what happened that night. There were stares, people being standoffish. There weren't a lot of people reaching out and hugging you. It was a life-altering experience."

Dickerson ended his career at Maryland as a part-time starter. He was the team captain his senior season in 1989 and earned his government and politics degree in 1990. But his most cherished moment took place after his junior season, in 1988, when he met his future wife, Laurette, a 1991 graduate of Maryland. "I'm at peace with everything that happened," he says. "I don't look back and say coulda, woulda."

Dickerson left Maryland with a reputation for helping maintain calm amid chaos, a trait that would help him in his post-college career. He never became mayor of Olar and did not pursue a career in politics; instead, he became a basketball coach. From 1990 to 1996, Dickerson worked as an assistant coach at three programs, including one season at James Madison University for his former Maryland coach, Lefty Driesell. In 1996, he began what would be a nine-year career as an assistant at Maryland, where he helped the Terrapins win a national title in 2002. While there, he recruited such All-Americas and future pro players as Steve Francis, Chris Wilcox, Steve Blake and Juan Dixon.

After the 2005 season, Dickerson was one of about 80 candidates who applied for the head coach's job at Tulane University in New Orleans. He was chosen in part, says athletic director Rick Dickson, for how he handled himself at Maryland after Bias died. A letter from former Maryland chancellor John Slaughter to Dickson boasted of Dickerson as a "pillar of calm during their storm and a national spokesperson not just for basketball but for the university," Dickson said in the *Washington Post* in 2005.

When Dickerson took over as head coach at Tulane in April 2005, he knew that he faced a challenge in rebuilding a program that had recorded just one winning season in its previous five and was coming off a 10-18 season. He had no idea how tough the challenge would be. When Hurricane Katrina hit New Orleans on August 29, it rendered the Tulane campus unusable, sending the men's basketball squad and five other school teams to the campus of Texas A&M University in College Station. Dickerson and his staff worked out of their apartments in College Station until they could set up an office in an old room in the football stadium. Once Dickerson had his team together again, he had to think of ways to keep their minds focused on playing basketball rather than on their personal hardships. He quickly told them the Bias story.

"When I got them together for the first time [in College Station], I told them the story about sticking with the University of Maryland and not transferring and weathering the storm, and look where it got me," he says. "I'm surprised the Len Bias story is not being told on a yearly basis when new athletes come into college, or in high school. I think the Len Bias story is one of the better stories you can use to get an individual or team to do the right thing.

"Without that story, I think I would have lost half my team. They had to remain loyal to a coach who hadn't recruited anyone on that team. I just told them what happened and what type of player Bias was. I told them, to this day he was the best player I played with or against, or saw during my coaching career. I compared him to Michael Jordan and [Karl] Malone and [Larry] Bird. I talked to them about what happened the morning of June 19, 1986; I went through that step-by-step. The Len Bias story was the catch to get their attention, to get guys to be loyal, maintaining the course and yes, there will be some ups and downs, tragedies here and there. We needed to continue to work and stick together. I told them: At the end of the day, you will benefit from it."

When Tulane finally played its first game under Dickerson, in College Station, it won 77-66. The team would go on to finish 12-17 in that dislocated season, followed by records of 17-13 and 17-15 – the first consecutive winning seasons in 11 years. But the program struggled with losing records the next two years, and after the 2010 season, which Tulane finished 8-22, Dickerson re-signed on March 31, 2010, never having led Tulane to a post-season tournament.

True to form, Dickerson rebounded quickly. Ohio State hired him as an assistant coach three weeks later. He soon discovered that the legacy of Len Bias stretched further than he thought.

Dickerson recalls players and coaches asking him about Bias: " 'Was he really that good? What kind of person was he? Did you know what he was doing in that room that night?' I get those questions from my 10-year-old son, who doesn't fully understand the scope of what happened. I talk to him about what's right and wrong, about making good decisions, and the consequences of making bad decisions. To this day, I still consider Len Bias a role model. Role models don't always make the right decisions. When you make a bad decision, sometimes you can pay for it with your life. Len Bias taught me more about life in the one year I spent with him than any other person outside of my family."

DERRICK LEWIS

Derrick Lewis walked through the wide, well-lit halls of Archbishop Spalding High School in Severn, Maryland, with a calm sense of purpose. Students there are required to wear uniforms of tan bottoms and white tops, and Lewis, the head boys' basketball coach and a health teacher, noticed that a few of them wore the wrong type of shoes. "They can get five demerits for that," he says, matter-of-factly. Lewis later stopped and spoke quietly with a female student wearing a forbidden blue sweatshirt. Despite his dress-code patrol, he clearly commanded respect from the students as he walked the halls, some walking past him in seeming awe, smiling sheepishly and saying "Good morning, Mr. Lewis," or "Hi, Mr. Lewis."

At 6 feet, 7 inches, his lean frame towered above the students, but they seemed reassured rather than intimidated by his height and his ease in taking charge of a situation. So it was a natural de-velopment when the former all-ACC forward from the University of Maryland accepted the job as the boys' head coach at Archbishop Spalding in 2009. When he became the school's fourth head coach in five years, Lewis knew attitudes needed to change. At the first team meeting, he laid down unfamiliar rules. Every player rode the bus home after away games. Parents were welcome to attend practices but they lost the privilege of talking to him about playing time for their children if they missed just one. "I'm no-nonsense," he says. "I'm from a different era. They need to see what's going on in practice every day to understand why their son doesn't play."

The team won eight games during Lewis's first year, but that was two more than the previous year, and he says the reaction was so positive you would have thought they'd won a championship. The team showed even more progress during the 2010-11 season, finishing with an 11-18 record.

Lewis played for the University of Maryland from 1984 to 1988 and used lessons learned from that time to forge a 17-year professional career in Europe. He formulated a philosophy that stresses proper management of players after watching his coaches at Maryland, Lefty Driesell and Bob Wade, and he uses Bias's story to teach his students ways to avoid being a victim of harmful circumstances.

At around 7:20 a.m. on June 19, 1986, Lewis remembers walking pell-mell across the University of Maryland campus to take a calculus test, not noticing the commotion at the dormitory building next door. He had departed his dorm room within a half hour of Bias suffering the seizure in Washington Hall that led to his death, but didn't notice the nearby mayhem. He had stayed up until 3 a.m. studying for the test, and so had been unable to join Bias's draft celebration.

Suddenly, Lewis spotted teammate John Johnson sprinting toward him. He's crazy for working out this early, Lewis thought. But the freshman was bringing bad news: Something was wrong with Bias, and Lewis should head to the hospital right away. Lewis was a bit annoyed that such a distraction could affect his chance to take the test. But, he also wondered, was Bias hurt? Did he tear an ACL? Was Len's basketball career over?

With little sense of urgency, Lewis drove to Leland Memorial Hospital. But he knew from the chaotic scene greeting him that Bias had suffered far more than a busted knee. Keith Gatlin was disoriented. Assistant coach Jeff Adkins and teammates Terry Long, David Gregg and Jeff Baxter milled around in varying states of distress. Baxter, knowing that Gregg had been with Bias when he died, was yelling at Gregg, "You need to tell them what's wrong, what happened!" Why was he saying that? What did that mean? After he found out that Bias wasn't breathing, Lewis thought he'd suffered a heart attack, but he still wasn't grasping the situation. Even after Lonise Bias came out of the room where her son's body lay and said that he was gone, Lewis wondered, gone where? It wasn't until teammate Tony Massenburg told him plainly that Bias was dead that he finally understood.

Motivated in part by the fact that both his parents were teachers, Lewis made up the test he missed, and earned a C in the calculus class. But the post-Bias hysteria took its toll. He couldn't grasp why Driesell was being blamed, and he was angry that Bias had been so careless with his drug use. Watching the scene of Driesell walking away from the press conference announcing his departure from the school nearly convinced Lewis to transfer, but a chat with new coach Bob Wade convinced him to stay in College Park. It helped that Wade had coached him on a McDonald's All-America team in 1984.

"He made me realize that stuff happens, and you have to deal with it," says Lewis. "Don't throw away something that you know you want to do by making a hasty decision. He said 'If you want to leave, we'll help you, but we'd love for you to stay' and he said 'You'll heal. It's gonna get better. I know it's tough now. I can't say if I was in your shoes I would have a different feeling than you do. But don't make a hasty decision and regret it later.' "

Lewis was born and grew up in Tarboro, North Carolina, and moved to Temple Hills, Maryland, some 10 miles from Bias's hometown of Columbia Park, when he was 5 years old. He earned McDonald's and Academic All-America honors at Archbishop Carroll High School in Washington,

D.C., and grew up a fan, not of Maryland, but of its ACC rival, North Carolina. Lewis says Dean Smith recruited him to Carolina, but that he didn't visit the school because the coach told him that, with Michael Jordan there, he would have to sit for two years.

Lewis wanted to attend a college far from home, so he strongly considered offers from Notre Dame, Michigan, Villanova and Virginia. Maryland was at the bottom of the list, but he says Driesell offered powerful selling points – not the least of which was the assurance, in writing, that he would have a fifth year if needed to complete his degree in engineering. As a freshman in 1984-85, the 195-lb. forward left a strong mark, finishing the season second in rebounding at 6.5 a game, behind only Bias's 6.8. His 6 points a game was fifth on the team. Lewis started all of Maryland's 34 games.

Lewis and Bias were roommates on the first team trip of the 1984-85 season at the Alaska Shootout, where Lewis witnessed the spontaneous side of his new teammate. He remembers one night when a restless Bias was itching to go out and socialize, but he – neither a drinker nor much of a partier – persuaded Bias to stay in the room. Lewis says he still has goofy pictures that they took of each other that night. Bias, known to wear fashionable clothing, posed wearing a dickie, no shirt and rolled-up jeans. After the photo shoot, they stayed in and played Nintendo. Lewis learned early in their friendship that despite being two years younger than Bias, he had some influence on him. He feels that if he had been with Bias in his dorm room that night, Bias might still be alive.

"If I had gone over there I don't think he would have ..." says Lewis, his thoughts trailing off as he sat talking for two hours in an

Derrick Lewis stands on the home court where he coaches the boys' varsity team at Archbishop Spalding High School. *(by Dave Ungrady)*

Odenton, Maryland, restaurant late in the winter of 2011. "I don't think he would have ever gone out [to party]. My relationship with Lenny was different than Jeff [Baxter] and the other players. I was a guy who didn't go out all the time and didn't do stuff. And I was one to say I could have gone over there and told Lenny, 'Man, don't go out, don't do this and just go on and go to bed, go to sleep.' I was the voice of reason."

Lewis lived with that thought as he continued his career at Maryland. He put together an impressive junior season on a devastated team that lost four players as a result of Bias's death. Lewis led Maryland in scoring (19.6) and rebounds (7.6) and was selected to the all-ACC second team. Playing basketball was a pleasant diversion for Lewis from the fallout due to Bias's death.

Lewis led the team in average scoring (15 points) and rebounding (7.6) during his senior year and again earned all-ACC second team honors. The Chicago Bulls made him a third-round pick in the 1988 NBA draft and Lewis, the first Maryland player from the 1986 team other than Bias drafted into the NBA, felt confident enough about his chances that he says he signed a two-year deal that would be in effect only if he made the team. When Lewis got to training camp, he says, at least a quarter of the questions Bulls staff asked him during an interview dealt with Bias. They asked him how close he was to Bias, and if they were roommates, both at school and on the road. They asked Lewis if they went out together and if he saw him do "anything. I was just happy to be there and I was getting grilled about Len Bias and how close we were," he says. "I was a little shocked."

If the Bias connection wasn't problem enough, on only the second day of camp, Lewis says, he contracted food poisoning from eating tuna fish. He recovered in a couple of days, but the vomiting prevented him from keeping his blood-pressure medication down. He sat out a full week and missed the team's first summer-league trip. When he was able to take the medication again, it slowed him down and made him feel groggy. "[The food poisoning] probably hurt as much as my association with Maryland at that time, maybe more," he acknowledges.

Lewis was one of the last two players cut from the 1988-89 team that advanced to the NBA Eastern Conference finals and featured emerging star Michael Jordan. During camp, Lewis, playing the 2, 3 and 4 positions, said he defended against Jordan almost every day, which he thought would help his cause. Head coach Doug Collins apparently felt differently.

"Collins told me, 'We like you; you're a good player but we're gonna send you down to Rockford [of the Continental Basketball Association]. Right now you have a problem guarding players at your position in practice.' And I said, 'Doug, with all due respect, I guard Michael Jordan in practice every day, twice a day for two hours and 30 minutes.' And he said, 'We just want you to get some experience, and we'll bring you back up.' "

Some team members, including Jordan, expressed disbelief when they found out he had been cut, Lewis says. He remembers walking toward the locker room as several team members, including Jordan, were walking the other way. "Practice was about to start and Jordan said, 'Mr. Maryland, where ya going ... if you're not out there, you know what's gonna happen.' I said, 'They cut me; I'm going home.' He said 'OK, keep playing games. When practice starts, we're gonna kick your ass.' They thought I was joking. Horace [Grant] thought I was joking. They said, 'You see that clock; you only have a couple minutes left.' And I said, 'OK, see you guys later.' And that's the last time I saw those guys."

Lewis says the Bulls never mentioned his history with Bias as a reason for not making the team but he says: "You always wonder."

Not ready to give up on a professional career, Lewis joined the Rockford (Illinois) Lightning and along with Dwayne McClain, who helped Villanova win the 1985 NCAA tournament title, guided the team to the CBA championship series, where the Tulsa Fastbreakers won in a four-game sweep. "I didn't like it a lot at the beginning, but the people I was playing with made it fun," Lewis says.

Lewis made about $10,000 playing for the Lightning in 1988-89, compared to the $400,000 he had expected to make with the Bulls. He opted to play for Reims in the top French pro league the following season, where he made about $120,000 including bonuses. He considered another try at the NBA after the Los Angeles Lakers offered what he called a "partial guarantee" worth $70,000 even if he was demoted again to the CBA. It wasn't enough to lure Lewis back stateside. "If I don't make the team, I'm back in the CBA, and it would be too late to go back to Europe," he says. Lewis stayed with Reims for three seasons and played for four more teams during his 15 years in France's pro league. He retired in 2004 and returned to the U.S.

Lewis and his wife, Kelli, used their savings to help start ArchivaSports, which provides a web-based video-archive system and social-networking tools for athletic teams. Lewis owns a quarter of the company. He also started a business renting moon bounces for parties but sold it in 2010. In 2008, Lewis started working with Archbishop Spalding's basketball program as a varsity assistant and the junior varsity head coach.

Lewis earned an undergraduate degree in criminal justice and did not plan to become a teacher. His parents are retired teachers and his mother suggested he try teaching. As a health education instructor, Lewis talks to the students about the dangers of drug and alcohol abuse. The topic of Bias arose after some of Lewis's students saw a picture of Lewis along with some Maryland teammates, including Bias, on his computer screen. Sensing the students' interest, Lewis decided to show *Without Bias* to his health classes.

One class, of more than two dozen ninth graders, started at 8:40 a.m. When Lewis turned down the lights, I expected a few still-sleepy high-school freshmen to grab a quick nap. But the students sat riveted. Once the documentary ended, questions from the students filled the remaining 10 minutes of the class.

"Did he do it on purpose, buy pure cocaine?"

"How did his mom get through it?"

"Was it his first time doing drugs?"

"Did Tribble serve jail time?"

The last comment came from a girl in the front row. She says she learned that you never know what will happen to you if you abuse drugs, and abusing drugs even one time can kill you. "That's what we're looking for," says Lewis, sitting in his homeroom class during the next period. "They may use it one time. I want them to know what can happen if they do. That's the story."

KEITH GATLIN

In late October 1982, Keith Gatlin entered the Maryland basketball office just before lunchtime. A high-scoring guard from D.H. Conley High School in Greenville, North Carolina, who in 1983 would be named the state's high school player of the year, Gatlin had narrowed his college choices to Maryland, Wake Forest and N.C. State. As a North Carolina native, Gatlin had an affinity to the Carolina schools. But he liked how Lefty Driesell coached the Maryland team with an up-tempo style, and he did have relatives close by. Maryland was high on Gatlin's list when he entered the office, and his interest in the shool increased after Bias agreed to serve as his chaperone for the visit.

"He was just a regular guy," says Gatlin. "I hit it off with him when we first met. When you go to campus, to a visit, most of the coaches put you with somebody they know will be talkative, outgoing, show you a good time. He was the guy."

Bias and Gatlin went from the basketball office to lunch at the Student Union, where they met other Maryland players. After lunch, Gatlin attended a geology class with Bias before he watched practice later that afternoon. That day, Gatlin also witnessed Bias's strong personality for the first time. Bias kept things light, joking around and making sure everything was good and comfortable. A hard preseason practice was apparently not enough for Bias, who brought up the idea of an after-dinner basketball run.

Gatlin joined Bias and several other Maryland players, including sophomore forward Adrian Branch and senior forward Herman Veal, at the Leonardtown outdoor courts for an invigorating game of pickup basketball that lasted until about 10 p.m. After the game, Gatlin joined Bias and some of the other players back at the Student Union for a party, where Gatlin was impressed that Bias – only a freshman, but a regular on campus since attending high school nearby – seemed to know everyone.

Bias proved to be an effective recruiting tool: Gatlin says the pickup game and the general good time he enjoyed on his trip helped convince him to attend Maryland, where he enjoyed a strong freshman season, starting nine games, playing in 30 and averaging 8.6 points while leading the team in assists. Gatlin became a full-time starter during his sophomore season. He was the team's third-leading scorer, averaging 8.3 points per game, and became the floor leader who fed passes to Bias and Branch, the team's leading scorers. Gatlin handed out 221 assists that season, breaking John Lucas's Maryland season assists record of 178 set in 1973. Gatlin's record would stand until 2001, when junior Steve Blake recorded 248.

In Bias, Gatlin saw a great, raw talent adjusting to "how college coaches coach." He says, "You could tell basketball was something that came natural to him. Once the game slowed down for him and he got used to Lefty's coaching style, you could tell the sky was going to be the limit."

As the team's point guard, Gatlin learned to know where to feed Bias the ball. Against smaller defenders, Bias preferred receiving the ball near the basket, where he could convert turnaround jumpers. Against bigger defenders, Bias sought the ball on the wing so he could face them and take them one-on-one. "I had the toughest job in America," Gatlin says with a chuckle. "Len was complaining he didn't get the ball enough. Adrian wanted the ball. He felt like he was not getting enough shots. My friends were asking me why wasn't I scoring more."

Gatlin spent a lot of time with Bias off the court as well and even their families got together. The Biases, including parents Lonise and James, visited the Gatlin home in Grimesland, North Carolina, and Gatlin recalls Len embracing the horses and the spacious surroundings of the Gatlin property. "I remember Lenny saying, 'One day, we'll build a house down here in the country where it's peaceful,'" Gatlin said in the *Washington Post*. " 'Next year, you'll be a pro, and we both can make some big plans.' That's what we were both doing, making crazy plans that kids make."

They also found time to mingle with the Maryland student body in college, and unlike some others who say they never saw Bias drink alcohol, Gatlin recalls: "We had a little routine. We would go by the [Rendez] Vous for 10 minutes. We would go to Bentley's to get a bite to eat and then go across the street to the Cellar. He'd just stand around. He would drink a beer."

With senior Jeff Baxter sharing more of the point-guard duties with Gatlin during his junior year, Gatlin's assist numbers went down, but he ended the season as the team's second-leading scorer with a 10.2 per game average. Gatlin was also part of one of the biggest moments of the season, if not his and Bias's Maryland careers: the Terps' stunning overtime win on February 20 in Chapel Hill over North Carolina, ranked No. 1 in the country. With Maryland leading by three points with seven seconds remaining, the Terrapins were inbounding the ball under their own basket. Carolina needed to steal and convert a three-pointer quickly to tie the game again, or foul a Maryland player quickly and hope for missed free throws. They got the chance for neither when Gatlin deftly tossed the ball into the back of a Carolina defender who was facing the court – a play they had developed by complete accident during practice the night before. Gatlin calmly gathered the ball when it bounced off the defender's back and into his hand before turning and scoring an uncontested layup. It was the perfect punctuation to a marquee moment in Bias's basketball history at Maryland.

As he prepared for his senior season, Gatlin was poised to become the team leader in scoring and assists. And at 6 feet, 5 inches, he had the strong potential to become at least a role player in the NBA. Gatlin, who lived in the same four-room suite as Bias, had his last conversation with him before going to bed on June 18 so he could be ready to attend class the next day. "I said 'I'll see you in the morning,'" Gatlin recalled. "He said 'I'll see you in the morning.'"

For years, Gatlin couldn't shake from his mind the image of 6:57 on a clock. That's when he awoke the next morning to find Bias on the floor, unconscious, after snorting the cocaine that killed him. Gatlin remembers calling Lonise Bias, telling her incorrectly that her son would be taken to Prince George's Hospital when he was actually headed to Leland Memorial Hospital. On the way to Leland, Gatlin prayed that he would receive good news. "I knew it was serious," he says. "I was hoping for the best. But the doctor came out and he said, 'I'm sorry, we've lost him. There was nothing we could do.'"

"I was just loving life," he said in a *Washington Post* story in 1988. "I was playing pretty well, and I was surviving in class: not great, not bad, but surviving. Then, Lenny dies and everything just changed." Crying every day for weeks, Gatlin spent most of his time watching soap operas on television. He ordered pizza and ate it in bed. He was scared to leave his room, fearful of people whispering, "Hey, that's Gatlin. He was in the room when Bias died," which happened too often. Many days he sat and thought, "This is not fair. What hope is there for me? I didn't do drugs. I didn't die," he said in the *Post*.

Gatlin admits that he was in denial, struggling with the fact that his close friend had died from a drug he never saw or even heard of him using. He tried to escape by attending the graduation of a friend at Pepperdine University in California, but he quickly found that a change of venue even some 3,000 miles away did little good. "I get off the plane, and one of the first people I see says, 'Hey, ain't you Gatlin? Man, what happened to Lenny Bias?'" he said in the *Post*. "And I figured if I can't go to Malibu Beach to escape this stuff, then my mother is right. I can't run from it."

"I was getting ridiculed and I had nothing to do with it," he says in 2010. "I'm thinking this is crazy. I was guilty by association. Because we played at Maryland, everybody perceived us as being a pot smoker and bad kids. I felt like everybody on the team was being targeted. I was very bitter. We were young men having a great time in college."

After Driesell was removed and athletic director Dick Dull resigned, Gatlin felt he had lost any remaining support at the school. "You couldn't turn to no one and not think they won't stab you in the back," he says. Admittedly distracted, Gatlin failed to register for classes in the fall semester and was ruled ineligible for the 1986-87 season. (Media reports claimed that Gatlin couldn't register due to unpaid parking tickets, but he says the amount he owed would not have prevented him from signing up for classes.) Gatlin would likely have missed at least the early part of the season, regardless: He says he had knee surgery that summer to repair a damaged ligament. He admits that his thoughts were far from basketball and school. "I took the wrong approach," he says. "I was young, I felt like 'This is not fair.' Instead of handling it like an adult, I went into a shell and had the 'F the world' mentality. That lasted the whole year for me."

Gatlin thought about transferring out of Maryland, but his mother told him to "take it like a man" and he would come out smelling like a rose. "My mom told me 'This is not the way I'd like you to leave the university. If you're not part of the problem, stand up and make sure you have a stand-up year,'" he says.

Gatlin returned to classes at Maryland the following spring semester and continued with summer sessions. He maintained his basketball fitness by playing pickup games on campus with students and with Massenburg, who was also sitting out the year. Gatlin says he played every day, at times taking passes from his girlfriend, Jill, as he repeatedly shot three-pointers. Gatlin returned to practice in late December 1987 and was cleared to play on January 5, 1988, after Wade received Gatlin's grades from the fall semester. In his first game as a Terrapin since March 16, 1986, Gatlin scored 17 points as a reserve in an eight-point loss at Missouri, 10 games into Maryland's season. Gatlin played his first home game back at Cole Field House since the death of Bias on January 8. Most in the sellout crowd of 14,500 stood and cheered for him as he entered the game for the first time about midway through the first half. He scored 12 points and led Maryland in assists with six in a 15-point win over Clemson.

In early February, Gatlin scored 13 points in a five-point win over Old Dominion. Beginning the ACC tournament on March 11, Maryland – with only 16 wins – needed a win over 18th-ranked Georgia Tech to have a chance to advance to the NCAA tournament. Gatlin responded with a 25-point performance. He also was the roving defender in a diamond-and-one defense responsible for holding Georgia Tech's high-scoring freshman Dennis Scott to seven points. Scott had burned Maryland with 29 points earlier in the season. Gatlin also converted all six of his three-point shots, an ACC tournament record for Maryland players, and was named a second-team tournament all-star.

In Maryland's first-round game of the NCAA tournament, Gatlin had a hot night, scoring 23 points in a 10-point win over Santa Barbara. His Maryland career ended in a second-round game against Kentucky, who beat the Terrapins by nine points. Gatlin finished the season with a 12.1 points-per-game average, the best of his career, and shot over 50 percent from the field.

Gatlin was comfortable playing for Wade, who started his second year at Maryland the year Gatlin returned for his senior season. "I didn't have a problem with him at all," he says. "Bob was good to me. He was in a tough situation. He could never do the things he wanted to do. When we played for Coach Driesell, we always got the gym whenever we wanted it. Whatever he said, we got. When Coach Wade came in, the women's team had more pull than he did. It was unfortunate. I never thought the university gave him a fair shot. Coach Wade didn't have a chance in hell to survive at Maryland."

Gatlin hoped he had proved himself well enough at Maryland to build a strong NBA career. In late April, he was invited to try out for the U.S. team for the 1988 Seoul Olympics, but was cut after a few days. Later, Gatlin says, he felt stigmatized by teams in the NBA because of his association with a Maryland team that included Bias. "The best way I can put it, Derrick Lewis always said, 'When we came out as seniors, we couldn't be shit. We were guilty by association.' We didn't get a fresh start."

Gatlin wasn't drafted, but was given a tryout with the Milwaukee Bucks and lasted the entire summer before being cut. "Milwaukee told me 'We like you, but we just will go in another direction.' They told my agent 'We think there's a lot going on, and we don't want that publicity.' "

After an unsuccessful tryout later with the Indiana Pacers, Gatlin played for a few years with teams in Pensacola, Florida, and the Quad Cities in Iowa in the Continental Basketball Association, during which time he tore his ACL. "I didn't like it," he says of his CBA experience. "I was kind of bitter. I didn't like the bus rides. I stuck with it because I knew I could play. It's kind of tough when you have a great college career, and you see some of the guys you were playing with and they're playing pro. It was kind of tough to swallow."

During off-seasons, Gatlin worked at a law firm owned by a supporter of Maryland athletics and at a furniture store. He was finally able to focus on basketball full-time in 1993, when he began an eight-year pro career in Europe. He won the Germany Cup during his first year and later made all-star teams with clubs in France and Greece. He enjoyed his European experiences so much that he returns each year to France or Germany with his wife and son. Even when he played in Europe, however, Gatlin couldn't escape Bias's death. "Everybody in Europe wanted to know the story," he says. "It didn't bother me. I know that will follow me until the day I die."

Gatlin has settled into a comfortable life as a fitness trainer for college and pro basketball players and as the boys' high-school basketball coach at Wesleyan Christian Academy in High Point, North Carolina. He and his wife also started a trucking company, which they sold in 2006. They have one son, Kaleb. As a coach, Gatlin passes on the lessons he learned from Bias's death. "I tell the kids all the time you're lucky to get a free education but if you don't go to college for basketball it's also great," he says. "Don't put all your eggs in one basket. Sooner or later, you will stop playing a particular sport."

He also counsels them that it's OK to be who they are, to be true to their own nature. Had Bias heeded that kind of advice, Gatlin believes, he might still be alive. "I used to be teased a lot because I was a homebody during college," Gatlin says. "I was not trying to live fast. That's from my up-bringing. Lenny always fought with that off the court. On the court, he was a tenacious player. When he was with the crew [his local group of friends], he did what they did. But when he was his own person, people said he was too soft. I tell kids, it's OK to be different. Live to your own stan-dards."

BRYAN PALMER

Bryan Palmer, who grew up a Maryland fan in Glen Rock, Pennsylvania, about 75 miles north of College Park, readily admits that his basketball career there failed to match his lofty aspirations. In three years at Maryland, Palmer played in only 24 games and scored 15 points. In November of his fourth year at Maryland, at the start of the 1985-86 season, Palmer made a decision rare for a player at that level: He abandoned his basketball career, quitting the team after he realized practices conflicted with classes he needed to take to earn a degree in civil engineering, which he obtained after his fifth year of school.

Palmer entered Maryland the same year as Bias, and they were roommates their first and third years. Like his teammates, Palmer insists that he never saw Bias use cocaine, had no clue that Bias used it, and believed that Bias used the drug for the first time the night he died until he was told about Bias's recreational drug use during a phone conversation we had in 2011. Palmer remembers Bias as gregarious, silly and creative, drawing mocking caricatures of team members and hanging them in the locker room. Each Christmas season when Palmer hears "The Christmas Song," he thinks of Bias singing the smooth melody to perfection on a team bus late at night after a game. "I remember it so vividly," he says. "It was a perfect song for the night, everybody away from their families. 'Chestnuts roasting on an open fire'… still to this day that moves me when I hear that song. He had a great voice, a pitch like no other. And guys never gave him a hard time about it. They let him sing. That was awesome."

Palmer is constantly reminded of Bias as he travels throughout the United States in his job in construction management. Because of his 6-foot, 9-inch height, strangers often ask Palmer if he played basketball, and the conversation turns to Maryland. "His name is the first thing that comes up," he says.

When Palmer coached in youth sports, he often used the story about Bias as a lesson to teach his athletes to make the right choices. Fathers in his Washington, D.C.-area neighborhood tell him how they've told their kids that if a superbly fit athlete such as Bias can die from abusing drugs, so can they. "It's comforting in a way, taking that pain and turning it into something positive for the next generations," he says.

TONY MASSENBURG

Of all the players on the Maryland roster in 1985-86, Tony Massenburg was the one few predicted would be one of the more enduring pro players in Maryland history. But by the time he played his last NBA game in 2005, Massenburg had played in the league for 13 seasons for 12 different teams. The only former Maryland players who have forged longer NBA careers are Buck Williams (17 seasons), Joe Smith (16) and John Lucas (14).

At Sussex Central High School in Virginia, Massenburg was all-state in 1985. At Maryland, Massenburg twice earned post-season honors, making the ACC third team after his junior year and the second team the following year. His career there, however, was more noteworthy for other reasons. "I can honestly say there hasn't been anybody in the history of NCAA basketball – barring injury – that has had a rougher career at one school than I have," he said in early March, 1990, and his comment carries weight. As if the trauma of Bias's death weren't enough, he learned soon after that he would be suspended from the team his sophomore season for cheating on an exam. "I didn't think they had enough evidence," he said in 1990. "I felt I may have been made an example of during the time Maryland was supposedly cleaning up their program."

Like many of his teammates, Massenburg thought about transferring out of Maryland after Bias's death. "I thought that I'd seen the worst this program had to offer," he said, "so why should I leave for some place that may even be worse? I could've said, 'This is it. I'm not doing this anymore. Somebody is out to get me.' I kept striving. Besides, I really liked the area and the people I made friends with. I still thought I could make something of myself up here. I knew there would be a rainbow at the end of all of this."

During his time away from the team, Massenburg made sure to stay fit, working out after class. He stopped by the basketball office a few times a week to keep in touch with new coach Bob Wade. He played pickup games on campus with Gatlin, who also missed the 1986-87 season, and worked out often in the weight room, using memories of Bias as motivation. Academic problems forced Massenburg to miss the early part of the 1987-88 season as well. He played his first Maryland game since Bias died on December 28 and scored 25 points in a five-point win over South Carolina. Five games into his return, he was leading Maryland in points (15.8 per game) and rebounding (9.2 per game). He finished as the team's second-leading rebounder and fifth in scoring, helping Maryland advance to the second round of the NCAA tournament.

Tough times returned the following season. Maryland struggled through a 9-20 season, but Massenburg led Maryland in scoring (16.6 points per game) and rebounds (7.8). The next season started slowly. Massenburg was going to miss the first four games with an NCAA suspension for selling complimentary tickets to the 1988 ACC tournament, and there were signs in the preseason that he was disheartened. New head coach Gary Williams remembered him as lacking aggression in practices. "I wasn't sure he wanted to rebound or play defense, or any of the other things that require the work," he said in the *Washington Post* in 1990. "I think there was a tendency to think: 'Why me? Why did I have to go through this?' Funny thing about the suspension. All of a sudden, I think, he saw what it was like without basketball. And it bothered him. He came back from that ready to play."

Massenburg recorded career numbers in his first season under Williams, averaging 18 points and leading the team in rebounding at 10.1 per game. In early March of his last year at Maryland, he reflected on his five years there. "I've done a lot of growing up," he said in the *Washington Post*. "When you're younger, you just live for that moment. I now know how to make better decisions. I know who to trust, who not to trust. Everything has happened for a reason. As hard as it's been to deal with, I wouldn't change any of it. Sometimes it takes controversy to make you a better person, a little wiser."

The San Antonio Spurs made Massenburg the 43rd overall pick, in the second round of the 1990 NBA draft, and he played in 35 games for the Spurs during his rookie year. In 1991-92, he played for four NBA teams, including a 10-day contract with the Celtics to help the team when Larry Bird hurt his back. During the 1992-93 and 1993-94 seasons, he played for two teams in Spain.

After winning the NBA title with the San Antonio Spurs in 2005, Massenburg broke an ankle in a car crash and missed the next two seasons. At the age of 40, he attempted a comeback in 2007, but was cut by the Washington Wizards during the preseason.

Massenburg opened the Tony and James Restaurant in Kentlands, Maryland, north of Washington, in the spring of 2010. In the spring of 2011, I stopped by the restaurant to try and secure an interview. A manager contacted Massenburg, who agreed to talk and said he would call. Some two months later, he said in a text message that he had a "conflict of interest" and would not talk for the book. Massenburg, along with former Maryland star Walt Williams, was working on his own book about Bias.

JOHN JOHNSON

John Johnson returned to the familiar setting eager but wary. It had been more than two decades since he walked through the doors of RJ Bentley's Restaurant in College Park. As if propelled by a mystical force, Johnson moved to his right toward a corner of a back room in the restaurant, in the direction of the number 34 Len Bias jersey hanging in a glass-protected frame on the wall. "I didn't know it was there," he says of the jersey. "Seeing it was almost like confirmation that I was doing the right thing to talk. I could have never shown up, or I could have said 'I don't feel like doing this.' I was going back and forth in my mind whether or not I wanted to go through with it."

Johnson stood staring at the jersey for a few moments, calling it his own little private, spiritual moment with Bias. "I always feel him around me," he says. "Throughout my life I've had encounters where I know he's been around. I felt like at that moment he was there at the restaurant with me."

When Johnson had agreed to meet me at Bentley's to talk, he had asked if I could arrange for owner John Brown to be there. Brown was happy to oblige. As Johnson turned away from the jersey and walked to the bar, he recognized his old friend. Brown recognized him, too. "How you doin', big fella?" Brown said to Johnson as he stood to greet the former player. They shook hands and hugged, chatting briefly about the old days as if time had barely passed since they last saw each other. Brown told Johnson that he was proud of him. "I've always liked John," Brown explained later. "Len was a true hero and idol for a lot of these guys. John was young and looked up to him tremendously. He weathered the storm. He was tough."

As Johnson looked back across the room, he asked, "Do you mind if we sit next to Len's jersey?" Not waiting for an answer, he headed toward it. "Let's sit next to Lenny." Then he talked for three hours about the quarter century since the death of Bias, whom he calls a brother.

The two bonded within moments of meeting on Johnson's recruiting trip in the summer of 1984. As soon as Johnson opened the door to a dorm-room full of Maryland basketball players, he remembers Bias tackling him. They spontaneously started to wrestle, acting like two young teenagers testing their competitive edge: the out-of-place, impressionable country boy and the urban soon-to-be-legend starting to spread his influential wings.

John Johnson sits next to Len Bias's jersey at RJ Bentley's Restaurant. *(by Dave Ungrady)*

"One of the biggest reasons I came to Maryland was because he and I were down there wrestling on the floor, like he had known me all of his life," Johnson says.

Speedy Jones, a classmate and teammate of Bias's at Maryland, claims that no member of Maryland's 1985-86 team was as affected as Johnson was by the death of Bias, including Maryland teammates Terry Long and David Gregg, who were both with Bias when he died and later faced grand-jury indictments. Dave Dickerson calls Johnson "very loyal" and witnessed Bias and Johnson form a special friendship. "Throughout our first year," Dickerson says, "he had a natural bond with Lenny."

At Bearden High School in Knoxville, Tennessee, Johnson averaged about 25 points a game during his junior and senior seasons, with a career high of 46 points, and was named the top boys player in the state. He was also an All-America. He picked Maryland over such schools as Stanford, Georgia, Tennessee, Wake Forest and North Carolina because he liked what he called the culture shock of leaving a country setting for a strong urban environment of College Park and nearby Washington, D.C. But the biggest reason he says he chose Maryland was the connection he made with

Bias when he was being recruited.

"He welcomed me like I was a teammate or a brother," says Johnson.

Bias called Johnson about a dozen times during the recruiting process, which started during his junior year. He asked Johnson about his stats, his family, how he was doing. One time, Bias called Johnson from Alaska, where Maryland was playing in the Great Alaska Shootout.

"You think I care about what happened one night in a room, when you got a guy calling you from Alaska?" he asks, referring to the night Bias died. "I'm nobody. I'm just a kid that's trying to get into a university. But that's the type of guy he was."

During his freshman year, Johnson shared a dorm suite with Bias, Terry Long and Speedy Jones. He relished his first year at a major university far from his home in Knoxville. Sue Tyler, an associate athletic director at Maryland while Johnson attended the school, remembers Johnson during his freshman year as a person with a promising future. "The first time I met him, he was like a little kid, always upbeat and positive, a fun guy with a smile and a nice word for everybody," she says. "There are kids you just kind of think, 'This guy's gonna make something of himself.' "

Johnson, at 6 feet, 4 inches and 170 pounds, made in impact early in his Maryland career. On December 28, 1985, he hit an 18-foot shot with four seconds remaining in the second overtime as Maryland beat Stanford, 67-65, at a tournament in Hawaii. A few weeks later, Johnson, along with Bias and Baxter, attended the "Freak Momma" party after a game against N.C. State, resulting in the one-game suspension for all three players. Johnson remembers Bias asking, "Are you coming with me?" Johnson quickly obliged. "I don't regret it at all," he says with a smile. "We had a great time. Oh, man, I'll never forget that."

While Johnson wondered if his Maryland career was over, Bias talked about the suspension on the phone with his mother, Lonise. After the call, Johnson noticed that Bias was ready to move on. "I'm sitting there thinking that I'm going to be kicked off the team, but he got off the phone and he was good," says Johnson. "You could tell he had his mom's God spirit in him. He had such a strong will and mindset, like his mom."

Johnson, who averaged 15.9 minutes of playing time per game, finished the year with the best numbers of any of the five Maryland freshmen. He tied Massenburg for the most starts by a freshman with eight but led the class in overall appearances with 30 and points with 5.8 per game. Johnson also ended the season enjoying his bond with Bias, feeling it was unique for a freshman to be spending so much time with a senior – especially one of Bias's stature. He remembers Bias embracing his Tennessee country leanings and Johnson's fondness for pop bands such as New Edition, despite Bias's taste in go-go music. "I guess he never thought he'd be listening to New Edition and Bobby Brown," says Johnson. "But he started listening to my music, and we started joking about it, how the catchy songs were starting to grow on him."

When Bias left College Park to play in the ACC Barnstorming Tour in April 1986, he gave Johnson the keys to his new Nissan for a long weekend. "He could have given those keys to anybody," Johnson says wistfully. Johnson remembers their last conversation. It was on June 18 while Bias was in Boston visiting with representatives of Reebok and meeting members of the media. Bias called Johnson a little after noon to tell him that he had his phone card, which he'd been using. "It was no big deal to me," Johnson says. "We would always loan each other money. He would say, 'You got this? I'll pay you back on the next road trip.' "

Around midnight, Johnson remembers being surprised when he and teammate Greg Nared walked past Bias's suite in Washington Hall and noticed the light was on. They didn't stop by, however, because they didn't think Bias was on campus. The next morning, Johnson was abruptly awakened when someone – he doesn't remember whom – stormed into his room and roused him from a deep sleep, yelling that Bias had had a seizure. "I laid back down because I figured someone's got to be joking," recalls Johnson.

When other teammates began to gather in his dorm suite, he knew it was serious, and when he finally arrived at the hospital, he remembers Lonise Bias asking if anyone knew why her son might have had a seizure, so she could inform the doctors. Even after Bias's mother announced that he had died, Johnson still thought Bias was going to be all right. He didn't admit to himself that his friend and teammate was gone until he witnessed a group of frenzied reporters outside his room.

Johnson says he and most of his Maryland teammates went back to their rooms and stayed there, relying on friends to provide food for up to a week until the media throng finally left the area. They turned away a grief counselor. "I remember Speedy [Jones] [telling them] we didn't need any help," he says.

It wasn't until a woman who Johnson says was close to Bias stopped by the apartment and was consoled that he realized the full impact of what had happened. Before that, he says, "Everyone was locked in their own little mourning," he says. Johnson remembers finding comfort in a darkened, somber room, with curtains drawn, repeatedly listening to Prince sing "Sometimes it Snows in April." The song tells of the death of a friend. "The irony of that song, snowing in April, some people think it's unheard of," he says. "There it was for me, a situation I would have never believed in a million years. It took a lot of fortitude and prayer to come out of that situation and not be a basket case."

Johnson's Maryland mojo faded the night Bias died. The game became – and remains – a chore. Upset about the negative reports about Maryland players using drugs and failing classes, he shut down, mostly giving up on summer school. He recalled the first class he attended after Bias died, which took place in a huge lecture hall. He and a friend walked through a door at the front of the hall, visible to all who had already taken their seats. The buzz of idle chatter suddenly stopped. He walked through row after row of students, all silent, taking a seat at the back. "You could hear crickets," he says. "I don't know what they said about me. Did they associate me with being a drug head? I started feeling bad. 'What are these people thinking?' I wasn't ready for that."

He lasted 15 minutes, then left.

Johnson spent time after Bias's death at a friend's house in Columbia, Maryland. When he returned to classes later that summer and through the fall, he stuck with a routine of going from class, to the gym, to the training table and to his room. He often read scripture for comfort and considered transferring – to anywhere. He struggled with what people were saying about Bias, the team and

Driesell.

"I thought he was one of the kids mostly affected," says Tyler. "He changed. He turned into somebody who didn't give eye contact. He had more rounded shoulders. You could tell in his body language. I think it shattered his world."

Johnson agrees that he became more introverted. He chose to stay at Maryland out of loyalty to his fellow classmates on the team, and a strong bond helped keep the team together. Johnson credited the support of his mother and the mother of teammate Derrick Lewis; they were both strong Christians, he says. He also credits the comforting words of Lonise Bias. "She had so much to say," he says, recalling the time a few months after Len's death that he ran into her at a shopping mall near campus. " 'Lenny loved you' and 'You keep doing what you're doing because God wants you to be at Maryland.' She had so much conviction in her spirit. I was shaking. She said 'Lenny used to talk about you all the time.' She gave me the will to fight. Up to that point, I was wandering a bit."

Johnson found more inspiration from Brian Tribble during a chance meeting in the fall of 1986. As Johnson approached a barbershop in Takoma Park frequented by Maryland players, he saw Tribble sitting in a chair. Stunned, he turned away and went back to his car, where he sat sorting through his confused feelings. He had heard from news reports and friends that Tribble may have provided the drugs that killed Bias. Johnson described his relationship with Tribble as "really, really cool." But sitting in the car, he wondered if he should be angry with him.

Still unsure of his feelings, Johnson returned to the barbershop and sat next to Tribble. Soon the two starting talking. "Tribble said, 'You know, Johnny, Lenny used to always say that the next person that is going to come out of here is going to be you,' " says Johnson. " 'I used to ask Lenny, who is going to take over after you leave? Lenny would always say Johnny Johnson.' Hearing Brian say that is almost like Lenny talking to me. It kind of shocked me because Lenny and I never talked who was going to be this in basketball and who was going to be that."

Still, the fight continued for Johnson, who continued playing basketball primarily as a way to keep his scholarship and earn a free education but described his next three years at Maryland as a chore.

Johnson recorded strong numbers during his sophomore year, starting every game and averaging 10.8 points and 3.2 assists, but Maryland lost all 14 ACC games and finished 9-17. His junior year, Maryland qualified for the NCAA tournament but Johnson had little impact on the team's success. The year before, he had shared starting guard duties with Teyon McCoy, but now the addition of junior college transfer Rudy Archer, a guard from Baltimore's Southwestern High School, and the return of Keith Gatlin limited his playing time. Johnson played in 23 games but never started, averaging just 2.2 points a game. Archer started all of Maryland's 31 games. Furthermore, Massenburg returned after missing the previous season due to academic problems and Wade recruited freshman Brian Williams, who would be one of the top centers in college basketball that season. Both additions further affected Johnson's playing time.

Johnson says he used the memories of Bias as inspiration to make the best of a trying situation. In practice, he channeled the joys of playing loose and free pickup games with Bias and others during the offseason, hopping in a car and heading off to courts at local colleges. "I played like Lenny and I were playing," he says.

With Gatlin's eligibility expired, Archer ruled academically ineligible and Williams gone after transferring, Maryland faced another transitional year during Johnson's senior season. He ended the year as one of the team's top players, starting all 29 games and posting career-best numbers, averaging 15.5 points, 3.3 assists and 3.2 rebounds per game. Still, Maryland struggled and finished 9-20, and the effects of Bias's death still lingered. Once, while Johnson sat in Massenburg's dorm room, they suddenly both grew silent. Moments later, Massenburg erupted in a spasm of crying. "What do I do? What do you say?" says Johnson. "You can't say anything because we've already been through so much. I just remember the big fella broke down and I'm pretty sure I teared up, too."

Johnson admits that, during his senior year, he and a couple of other players threatened to quit the team after a loss to eighth-ranked North Carolina in late January dropped Maryland to 6-8. "It wasn't working out," Johnson says. "The experiment [with Wade] was over. What are they going to do to me, take away my scholarship? I had nothing to play for anymore." Johnson remembers staying on the team after meeting with athletic director Lew Perkins, who told him that quitting would set Maryland back for years. "Nobody wanted to make Lew look bad," says Johnson. "Everybody respected Lew."

Remaining on the team allowed Johnson to share a tribute to Bias with Massenburg during their last play in a Maryland uniform. It took place in the first round of the ACC tournament on March 10 when Maryland, the lowest seed, defeated top-seeded N.C. State 71-49. It was Maryland's biggest win of the season, and on the last play of the game Johnson took an outlet pass off a rebound and looked up court as Maryland began a breakaway. He threw a lob pass to Massenburg, who responded with a resounding, Bias-like dunk. Massenburg then ran to greet Johnson, who met him with open arms by the Maryland bench for an emotional embrace before being subbed out of the game.

"It was like an exclamation point to my career," Johnson said then. "Me saying to Tony, 'Hey, big fella. This is my last pass to you. Tear that rim down, and let's have a little Lenny Bias celebration.'"

Johnson earned his degree in criminal justice in four years, but his dream of playing pro basketball ended when he broke a toe two days before a scheduled tryout with the Celtics. For about a year, he sold copiers. Then a Maryland alumnus connected him with Coca Cola, where he worked for 13 years and reached a position as distribution district manager. Because his coworkers knew his background, however, it was difficult for Johnson to avoid questions about Bias and his days at Maryland. He enjoyed the anonymity at his subsequent jobs. He even avoids the topic of Bias with his wife, Yolanda Robinson, whom he married in 2008. As Johnson's life evolved further away from the death of Bias, his passion for the game continued to fade. He would not even play in a recreational pickup game.

For a brief time Johnson discovered the fun again in basketball, back at his home in Tennessee from 2005-2007. The mother of a player chasing Johnson's records at Bearden High School called him to ask if he would train her son. At first he said no, but the boy's connection to his high school was too much to resist. Johnson found the sessions with Tony White, Jr., a 6-foot, 150-pound guard who later played at the College of Charleston, a good form of therapy. "By working out with him, it actually made me grieve again," he says. "I was transferring something that Lenny and I shared together, that fire, and I'm getting it back on the court. Man, it freed me from that proverbial monkey on my back saying that basketball was no fun anymore."

Johnson also coached a boys' freshman team at The Webb School, a private school in Knoxville. His coaching career, which functioned as the therapy he avoided soon after Bias died, lasted one rewarding year, bringing back the joy of playing the game. But the ending brought disappointment. Johnson expressed interest in the head coach's position that opened up for the boys' varsity team. Not only was someone else chosen, but the school decided not to bring back the freshman team. Johnson felt as if he had been elbowed in the gut.

"Man, it crushed me because of the freshmen that I had cultivated during that time," he says. "I'm working out with them doing personal sessions. I got that feeling again. I'm looking at little 'Bobby' develop his jump shot every day. I want to see the little kid that's 5 years old dribble behind his back and you say, 'Go, buddy!' I want the fun part again."

Johnson returned to Maryland in 2008 to get married. He lives and works in Laurel for the Maryland State Highway Administration as a field maintenance technician; before that, he was a mobile unit driver for the American Red Cross. He rarely, if ever, watches basketball on TV and has not seen a Maryland game since the early 1990s, despite the efforts of former Maryland coach Gary Williams, whom Johnson says has invited former Maryland players to games at Comcast Center, their home arena.

"He's always made it known that we are part of the family," says Johnson. But he says he's just not interested. Even the NCAA Final Four in Atlanta in 2002, when Maryland won its last national title, was not enough to persuade Johnson to attend a Terrapins game. Dickerson, a Maryland assistant coach at the time, offered him tickets and he traveled to Atlanta, but Johnson chose to watch the game from his hotel room, preferring to support the team in quiet anonymity rather than join some of his former teammates at the Georgia Dome.

It was not an easy decision for Johnson to discuss Bias; he had not talked with the media about him since 1990, in a *Washington Post* feature about Massenburg. Johnson first approached his mother for counsel on whether he should talk about Bias for this book. Just as she did when he sought her comfort after Bias died, his mother suggested he turn to the Bible for guidance.

"There's a scripture that says you've got to watch the way you treat people because we don't know when we have entertained angels," he says. "And I look at that and I think to myself, 'Could he have been an angel?' This guy was 22 years of age, he made a huge impact on a lot of different lives. Who's to say he wasn't an angel, because of the fact of how many people he saved? How many people actually went to Christ because of the fact that they threw away a lot of drugs that same night they found out [about Bias's death] and decided they were going to change their lives for the better?"

With all the setbacks and challenges he endured during his years at Maryland, Johnson expressed pride for not falling into a deep, prolonged despair. "There are two ways I could have gone," he says. "I could have crashed and burned, or I could just pick myself up and use Len as a motivator to go forward. I've never been arrested, never been locked up. My record is clean as a whistle. It's important for me to tell my story, as far as how he impacted my life. I carry him with me every day. That fire in his eyes, his personality, his spirit, his attitude about the game and his love for the game. Let me keep it right there and everybody else can have the rest. They can have the negatives. They can have the positives. What he gave to me is eternal. I'll always remember that."

Johnson paused, as if drawing peace from Bias's jersey hanging almost within reach. "He was an angel," he says. "But how many other people look at him and thank him because he saved their lives? Without Len Bias, where would those people be?"

JEFF BAXTER

Jeff Baxter sat restlessly in a booth at J. Paul's Restaurant on M Street in the heart of Georgetown, not far from where he and Len Bias walked the streets, enjoying the shops, restaurants and clubs that occupy a couple of square miles of the upscale Washington, D.C., neighborhood. Lean and fit, his 6-foot, 1-inch frame carried what appeared to be not much more than his 165-pound playing weight from his days as a Maryland point guard. If his lightning-quick responses to repeated text messages during a three-hour conversation are any indication, he still possesses the dexterity that helped make him a frisky floor leader on the basketball court.

And it was not surprising to hear that Baxter still plays basketball about three days a week. His reputation as a former Maryland player and highly recruited point guard out of Archbishop Carroll High School in Washington, D.C., combined with his work with the federal government, prompted the Obama administration to invite him to participate in pickup games with the president at Camp David a couple of times in 2010.

Once burdened by the death of Bias, his close friend and roommate of four years, Baxter now talks comfortably about the trying times he endured in the few years that followed. He agreed to be interviewed for *Without Bias* but says that in the past he has mostly been very guarded about what he has discussed. Baxter agreed to talk at length because he says he has nothing to hide. "It took a while for me to come to grips with it," he says. "I avoided countless interviews with numerous people over the years, and only because I thought at the time that it may be a target session for Coach Driesell and Lenny's family. I can see why it haunts a lot of people."

Baxter sat with his back to a window through which a vibrant, early evening in late fall unfolded behind him on the crowded streets of Georgetown. Over his right shoulder, across the street, were the words "Saloun" above a door that led to a small nightclub known for showcasing top local jazz talent. It was one of Baxter and Bias's favorite places to chill out in Georgetown, about a 45-minute drive from College Park. It was also where Baxter sought solitary refuge the night of Bias's death. After the chaotic day, he sat by himself at the bar, from 9 p.m. to 3 a.m., drinking Sprite and apple juice. He said other patrons, respecting the moment, left him alone.

"It was reality, but it felt like a dream," he says. "It was just a time away from it all."

Baxter and Bias were two of the top players in the D.C. area during their senior years of high school in 1982, but, perhaps surprisingly, Baxter doesn't think they ever played against each other: Baxter's high school competed in a private-school league while Bias went to a public school in Maryland. And while Bias learned basketball playing at The Rec in Columbia Park and other recreation centers in the D.C. area, Baxter played his pickup games at either boys clubs or hoop hot spots such as Turkey Thicket Park and Candy Cane Park in northern D.C.

Jeff Baxter stands across the street from the Saloun, a bar in Georgetown he and Bias used to frequent. (*by Dave Ungrady*)

Both were all-area first team selections in high school but Baxter was a third-team high school All-America while Bias did not earn All-America honors. Both were highly recruited by colleges. Like Bias, Baxter says he received interest from about 100 colleges, and that the only top programs that did not recruit him were Kentucky and Indiana. Like Bias, Baxter put N.C. State high on his list and also like Bias, Baxter, the youngest of six siblings, chose Maryland in part because his family wanted him to stay close to home.

The two first met during a high school senior-class trip to Kings Dominion, an amusement park about 75 miles south of D.C. Baxter remembers Bias approaching him with a "what's up, man?" before they exchanged high fives. True to their competitive spirits, Bias and Baxter agreed to see who was better at a basketball-shooting game in front of a large, curious crowd. Baxter doesn't remember who won. "They're set up for you to lose," Baxter says. "I think we both lost a lot of money because you had to be perfect to make it."

Even though Baxter didn't need to attend summer school before starting fall classes at Maryland, he felt compelled to join Bias early, and by late June 1982, he was living on campus and beginning preseason workouts. The two were roommates and developed a comfortable bond from the beginning.

"He was kinda like myself," says Baxter. "We could both be serious and really silly."

On some nights before games during their freshman year, Bias and Baxter fought off the boredom of curfew by holding their own little dance parties in their campus apartment, two energetic freshmen dancing alone but to the same songs. Baxter would tell Bias to dance, then Bias would urge Baxter to perform his solo routine. The music, loud and lively, laid the beat for hilarity. "For a guy who was a 6-8 basketball player, he was an amazing dancer," says Baxter.

Baxter and Bias started spreading their social wings in their junior season, venturing more often into Georgetown to shop or hang out at clubs and bars. Bias was fond of its upscale clothing shops, and Baxter says that a Georgetown store gave Bias the white pin-striped suit he wore at the NBA draft. One of their favorite places was the Saloun, where they would stay for a couple of hours and listen to jazz music before moving on to dance clubs. Baxter claims that he never saw Bias drink alcohol. As for himself, Baxter says he drank only wine or champagne during celebrations.

"Lenny would never drink in front of me," says Baxter. "When we went out, we partied, we danced, we chased the girls, that's it. We didn't go out and were like 'We got to get something to drink first or we've got to get high.'"

Both Bias and Baxter played in every game for Maryland during their freshman season, but Bias started 13 while Baxter was a reserve who averaged 3.4 points per game. Both players worked on their games the following summer during what Baxter described as successful campaigns in the Urban Coalition summer league, at the time considered one of the best such leagues in the country. Baxter remembers Bias learning a move from D.C. native Adrian Dantley, at that time a seven-year NBA veteran with the Utah Jazz, that Bias used to his advantage later at Maryland.

Positioning himself in the low post, Dantley would lock up Bias with an elbow as he moved past him, preventing Bias from recovering defensively. Baxter remembers Bias using the move against Dwayne Ferrell in 1984 to help close a large deficit in a game against Georgia Tech. "We were down by 20, and we came back," Baxter says. "[Bias] said, 'Shorty, I got him on the move,'" Maryland still lost by one point in overtime.

Baxter didn't start his first game until his senior season, during which he started 30 and averaged 9.5 points per game. After the season was over, Baxter joined Bias on the Barnstorming Tour that featured ACC seniors playing games at high-school gyms in the Raleigh/Durham/Chapel Hill area. Baxter reacted with surprise when told about Chris Washburn's account of Bias introducing Washburn to cocaine during the tour. Although he acknowledges that he and Bias did not share a hotel room and that he returned to Maryland twice to take tests, he insists Bias did not use drugs before the night he died. "I had heard things but had not heard anything validated," he says. "Len doing cocaine prior [to his death] is crazy. I would go on trial and deny that."

As their college careers neared an end, Baxter and Bias pursued different paths. With a lucrative pro contract looming, Bias let his studies falter. With a pro career more dubious, Baxter stayed focused on earning his degree, needing to earn six credits to graduate. Had it not been for a summer school exam he needed to take on June 19, Baxter would likely have stayed at his girlfriend's house, where he had fallen asleep the night before. But he returned to the dorm suite shortly after midnight expecting to study a bit more before grabbing a few hours' sleep. It was common for Baxter to study through the night.

When Baxter returned, he heard sounds of elation emanating from the room shared by Terry Long and David Gregg where they, Brian Tribble and Bias had gathered to celebrate Bias's draft success. He knocked on the door and remembers a couple of minutes elapsing before the door to the room opened. He says it didn't cross his mind that it might be because the group was using drugs.

"I saw a couple of eyes that were blood-shot red, but my mind thought it was liquor," says Baxter. He stayed with the group for about 10 minutes. At one point, Bias gave Baxter some too-small Reebok gear he had been given during the trip to Boston after the draft. Then Bias told Baxter that Larry Bird was so excited about him joining the team that Bird was planning to join him at rookie camp.

Baxter left the revelers at about 2 a.m. to sleep. A few hours later, Gregg woke him up, saying, "Come on, come on, Lenny fell down." Baxter tried to shake off the fog of sleep and figure out what was happening as he walked into the living area of the dorm suite and saw Bias sprawled out on the floor. Baxter knelt down and stared at the inert Bias, whose eyes were closed and who was not breathing, afraid to touch him.

"When things happen like that, you can think of the craziest things," Baxter says. "The whole time, when he was unconscious, I was thinking that the gold necklace he had on his neck was the cause of it. So I reached down and tried to remove the necklace as the paramedics came in. It was the weirdest thing. You think a guy who was perfectly sculpted, who didn't need to get any bigger and stronger, how could he be lying on the floor dead?"

Amid the blur of the moment, Baxter remembers not being able to find his car keys, so he grabbed the keys to Bias's car. He remembers driving by himself to the hospital, not realizing until he arrived that he had driven through every stop light along the way, about eight total. At the hospital, Baxter had difficulty figuring out what was happening. Keith Gatlin was crying in a corner. After he heard people mention the word "drugs," he grabbed the 6-foot, 8-inch Gregg by the jacket and pulled him aside to ask what happened. "He fell out, he fell out, he fell out," Gregg responded. The answer did not satisfy Baxter, who persisted with more questions. "Was it drugs?" he asked. When Gregg responded by screaming and wailing, Baxter knew: It was drugs. He dropped to the floor, crying.

Amid the chaos, Baxter remembers a calm Lonise Bias hugging and consoling anyone who needed it, soothing the forlorn by rubbing their backs and assuring them everything was going to be all right. Baxter wondered how she could be so calm in such a stormy emotional scene. For Baxter, serenity was hard to find in the coming months. After his solo reflection at the Saloun the night Bias died, he drove to his parents' house in D.C., where he stayed through most of the summer. Unlike other Bias teammates, who hunkered down and tried to avoid the public, Baxter did not. "I was weary of conversations with people who would talk about the event," he acknowledges. "Everybody had an angle. Everybody was talking about you. [But] I was trying to get back in the groove to play basketball, was trying to move on as quickly as I could."

Baxter again played in the Urban Coalition league, this time trying to improve his chances of playing in the NBA. He returned to classes during the second summer session, but soon realized it was not a good move. "Being there was not the thing to do," he says. "Everybody was talking about you."

Soon after Bias died, Baxter was surprised when his oldest brother asked him if he was using drugs. "The second-guessing was coming from everywhere," Baxter says.

His goal of graduating from Maryland that summer ended after he dropped out of summer school, but he had not given up his dream of playing professional basketball and tried out for two NBA teams. He felt slighted when he was asked by one team, which he did not want to identify, to perform three drug tests a day for five days while other players faced just one test during their tryouts. Baxter feels the excessive testing was due to his connection to the Bias death: "I found out afterward I was an unapproachable commodity," he says.

With his basketball career going nowhere and his academic goals stalled, Baxter started working for Federal Express in the fall of 1987 as a courier delivering packages and returned to Maryland two years after Bias died to complete the six credits he needed to earn his public-relations degree. He worked for Federal Express for 13 years, advancing to a senior position, and made money through real-estate investments before taking a job as a superintendent with the U.S. Department of Transportation about six years ago.

Baxter says that, until a few years ago, something would happen every day that would make him think about Bias. Now, he mostly reflects on his friend and teammate only when asked. At the D.C.-area premiere of *Without Bias* in 2010, Baxter abruptly walked away from the entrance before the showing when he saw cameras. He says he waited across the street until the excitement faded. "That wasn't a celebratory moment to me," he says."That wasn't a moment to gain or regain fame."

During a bathroom break that night, Baxter spotted Steve Francis, a Maryland star for just one year in 1998 before joining the NBA. Francis was crying so hysterically that Baxter remembers him barely able to stand up. "He said 'You guys were the reason I went [to Maryland],' " says Baxter. "But I'm sure he meant Lenny, because he was the star."

To Baxter, Bias's legacy is simple: He was a great basketball player who made a bad choice. As he sat alone at the Saloun the evening of June 19, 1986, Baxter realized that life was too short and that one never knows what will happen next. He says Bias's death solidified lessons his parents had taught him. "You've just got to be careful about the choices you make, because not all of them are going to be right," he says.

SPEEDY JONES

Within a few minutes of beginning a phone conversation in May 2011, Tom "Speedy" Jones says that Bias's death renewed his faith in God. Jones, a classmate and teammate, admits that by the time he began his Maryland career in 1984 as a junior college transfer, he had stopped going to church. "The sad thing is, it's a hard thing to say, but it was a positive thing for me," he says. "It made me take a look at how I was living my life. During that year, I was the worst. I had no respect [for anyone], period. Anyone would tell you, if I went into a restaurant, I treated everyone with dis-respect. When [Len] died, I knew I had to get my life straight. I'm here by the grace of God."

John Johnson backs him up. "Speedy was always that guy that it was all so about him," he says. "He was a jerk sometimes. But one of the times that I talked to him afterwards, I could tell he had changed. He was more considerate of other people and other people's feelings. It was like he was a different person."

Jones earned All-America honors at Oak Hill High School in Mouth of Wilson, Virginia, where he graduated in 1982. A 6-foot, 6-inch forward known for a strong inside game and rebounding, Jones picked Maryland over West Virginia after he played two years for Allegany Community College. At Allegany, Jones was an All-America and the team's leading scorer. He averaged 23 points and nine rebounds a game on an Allegany team that finished 34-4.

At Maryland, Jones started 20 games as a junior and averaged 7.1 points and 4.2 rebounds per game. He started only nine games during his senior year, but his per-game averages improved, to 8.1 points and 4.7 rebounds. One newspaper report described him as a "Bias-like leaper."

Jones said in the *Calgary Herald* in 1992 that he had planned to earn a computer-science degree at Maryland but instead finished with a general-studies diploma because of the realities of playing basketball at a prominent Division I program. "At Maryland, basketball and computers didn't mix," he said. "I had to make my choice."

To avoid the unwanted attention that was engulfing Maryland's players after the tragedy, Jones said in the *Herald*, "I took the first flight out to Europe. I couldn't come out of the apartment without a camera getting into my face." He played one year in Europe, when he found out he couldn't avoid the topic of Bias's death. "I thought I could get away from it over there. But over there were the same questions."

Jones then completed his general-studies degree at Maryland in one semester before working various jobs for a few years. He played for minor league teams in Greensboro, North Carolina; Erie, Pennsylvania; and Calgary, Alberta, before returning to Europe to play for three more years. At the time of our conversation in the spring of 2011, Jones was operating a construction business and working as a special-education teacher at West Potomac High School in Alexandria, Virginia, where he helped secure Lonise Bias as a graduation speaker in 2008. Jones mentioned that he has written a book about his own life, including his time at Maryland, but says it was "too controversial" and he had not found a publisher. He says the book addresses the powers of the National Collegiate Athletic Association and the influence coaches have over players.

"I'm hopeful parents and players would read it and look out for some things to tell their son, so they don't end up like [Bias] ended up."

DAVID GREGG

More than any other member of the 1985-86 team, David Gregg – coming from the same high school, playing for the same coach – lives in the large and looming shadow of Len Bias. During his freshman year at Maryland, Gregg developed a strong friendship with Bias. At 6 feet, 9 inches and just under 200 pounds, Gregg could have passed as Bias's brother; in fact, they jokingly referred to each other as cousins.

Charles Payne, now an assistant basketball coach at Stanford University, met Gregg when they were 11 years old and played basketball with him at Northwestern High School, where he was known to be quiet and shy. "Once he got to Maryland, he came out of a shell," says Payne, who still talks to Gregg every few weeks. "I'm sure it's because of the friendship he struck up with Len. Once they became friendly, Len showed him a different side of a social life."

Gregg's transformation brought temptations that ultimately changed him, and not always for the better. He admitted in the *Miami Herald* in 1988 that he stopped going to classes during the second semester of his freshman year, choosing instead to "date girls, talk to friends, just hang out," Gregg said. Maryland teammate Terry Long admitted during testimony at Brian Tribble's trial that he snorted cocaine with Gregg and Bias at Tribble's apartment after a game against N.C. State in College Park. It took place on January 23, 1986. Phil Nevin, a classmate and teammate of Gregg's at Maryland who shared a suite with him, says he didn't get along with Gregg. "He was a pothead and he was kind of arrogant to me," says Nevin.

Deeply entrenched in a seemingly fun and life-altering friendship with Bias, Gregg found himself in a precarious position during the early-morning hours of June 19, 1986. As he states in *Without Bias*, Gregg was in his dorm room talking on the phone, "chillin'," when Bias knocked on his door wanting to party. As Gregg remembers, he walked into Long's room, where Long, Bias and Tribble were drinking cognac.

Bias wanted Gregg to help celebrate the start of his new career with the Celtics. After they started doing cocaine, Gregg became concerned that Bias was snorting too much of it. In the documentary, Gregg called the cocaine they were snorting "fishscale" and described it as 98 percent pure. "That means it's real potent," he said. "Nobody can do that much of that stuff at one time, I don't care who you are."

But how could Gregg convince his friend and mentor, especially one as strong-willed and confident as Bias, that he was about to do something foolish and possibly even fatal? He couldn't. Mike Morrison, a friend of Gregg's since the third grade and a high-school teammate, remembers talking with Gregg by phone in the evening after Bias died.

"He said, 'I can't believe he's dead. I can't believe this happened. I told him to stop and he wouldn't listen,' " says Morrison. When Bias died, Gregg's life changed from one of basketball promise to one of displacement and despair. A McDonald's High School All-America who was still growing into his body, Gregg started only one game as a freshman and played in 15, but with forwards Bias and Speedy Jones using up their eligibility, his minutes were likely to increase the next year.

But Gregg never got the chance to prove his worth at Maryland. Instead, he spent the summer of 1986 as a recluse, a reluctant participant in a great tragedy. His testimony before a grand jury investigating Bias's death resulted in an indictment against him for possession of cocaine and obstruction of justice. The charges were dropped in exchange for testifying against Tribble at Tribble's trial.

In May, 1987, Long testified at Tribble's trial that after Bias went into seizures the morning of June 19, he tried to resuscitate him with CPR while a shaking Gregg held the unconscious player. Long said Gregg then took the cocaine and a mirror used to snort the cocaine out of the room. During his testimony at Tribble's trial, Gregg said that he placed the cocaine in a container, then placed the mirror and the container in a dirty bag in Long's closet. According to a paramedic who attended to Bias at the room, Gregg and Long never told him that Bias had been using cocaine, a fact that could have saved his life.

Once at the hospital, Gregg said in *Without Bias*, that he felt so numb he could barely stand up. "I felt nervous, scared; I had to hold on to the walls, feel the walls, to walk through the halls of the hospital, to keep my balance," he said. At the hospital, Gregg called his high-school coach, Bob Wagner, who says that Gregg suffers from asthma that sometimes makes it difficult for him to speak. "David was having a hard time," Wagner says. "He says 'Mr. Wagner, Leonard's gonna die, he's dying.'"

Shortly after Gregg returned to campus later that morning, he called Payne and asked to be picked up in front of Cole Field House. Payne drove a devastated Gregg to coach Lefty Driesell's house, where the Maryland team gathered to sort out the tragedy. In mid-afternoon, Payne drove Gregg to his mother's house a few miles from campus, where they ate some lunch and talked. Gregg and Long later went to Wagner's house for a few hours while they waited to secure an attorney. Gregg spent the next two weeks at his mother's house, keeping mostly to himself. "He was no longer David Gregg," says Payne, who talked to him daily. "He was David Gregg Who Was in the Room with Len Bias."

"I had never known David to cry, but he did then," says Morrison, who calls Gregg one of his closest friends and talks to him at least once a month. "David's not a real talker. He got real reclusive. A lot of people blamed him for Len's death. A lot of people assumed because of his easygoing lifestyle that he had something to do with Len's choices."

Payne recalls Gregg telling him that death threats against him and Long were sent to their attorney, Alan Goldstein. "We took those seriously," Payne says. "Whenever we went places, we made sure we went with a group of people to make sure people knew he had friends and support."

After he was indicted, Gregg was suspended from the basketball team for the next season, but he continued to attend classes and played in occasional pickup games. In early July 1987, Gregg announced that he would transfer from Maryland. "It's been very tough," Gregg said at the time. "Wherever I go, people point and say, 'Oh, there goes David Gregg.' I've been getting more attention for this than I did for my basketball."

At the urging of Payne, who was about to begin his junior season there, Gregg chose to attend Florida International University in Miami. Because he was academically ineligible to play there, however, Gregg took classes at Miami Dade Junior College as well as FIU throughout the 1987-88 academic year. To attend classes at Miami Dade, Gregg rode a bus 45 minutes each way from where he lived with Payne on the FIU campus. He even made arrangements to take two classes that overlapped by an hour during his last session of summer school at Miami Dade in 1988 to earn enough credits to play at FIU for the 1988-89 season. Payne closely monitored Gregg's progress at Miami Dade, even spending that summer in Florida to help Gregg get through his courses.

"He never got less than a C+ in any class," Payne says. "This was his chance at redemption. All we did was go to class, come home, study together, make sure he did everything he needed to do because I knew how important it was for him not just getting the basketball going again but to get his college degree."

In June 1988, a *Miami Herald* story touted Gregg's pending arrival at FIU. "If all goes well," it read, "he could be the player who lifts the program to respectability." A couple of years earlier, FIU had applied to become a Division I athletic program. Rick Walker, then the school's head basketball coach, hoped the addition of Gregg to the team would help FIU earn its new status. "He was a sense of hope for a growing program," Walker, an assistant athletic director at the University of Iowa, told me.

In late December 1988, in his third game for FIU, Gregg scored 18 points and grabbed 11 rebounds in a home loss to Radford in front of only 476 spectators, hardly the energy and intensity of Cole Field House. Oddly enough, he appeared to enjoy playing the game more than he ever had in his life.

Morrison and Payne both say that Gregg had never really loved the game; Morrison says he felt Gregg played college basketball only because people expected him to. Walker hadn't known him very long but says that by the time Gregg arrived there he was "so beat up" that he showed little passion for the game, doing what he was asked but no more. But once he started playing at FIU, all that appeared to change. Payne remembers Gregg being happy again, with both life and basketball. "He was having a great time." he says. "We were teammates again. It was away from home. He met a lot of people who didn't identify him with Len Bias." Gregg even talked about trying to play professional basketball in Europe.

Through early February, Gregg played 12 games for FIU, averaging 16.7 points and 7.8 rebounds. Then, on February 7, 1989, according to a report in the *Miami Herald* at the time, FIU placed Gregg on indefinite academic suspension after Terry Kelly, the Miami Dade vice president, claimed Gregg did not earn credits "appropriately" in three classes at the school. Kelly did not offer specifics in the report. Payne says Gregg needed to sit out the rest of the year at FIU and take the classes in question again at Miami Dade before he could return. Gregg left for home two days later, disgruntled and disheartened. His family could not afford to pay for him to take the classes over.

"No one wants to take responsibility," Payne says angrily of Gregg's exit. "He was treated unfairly, and that's the bottom line. The way adults acted in that situation was shameful. That was the last straw in terms of killing his spirit for continuing on in college athletics and college, period."

Gregg settled in back home in Hyattsville and started working at the National Institutes of Health, where he has been ever since, according to both Morrison and Payne. Still, Gregg's life has not been without challenge and further heartbreak. Court records show that he was charged with driving under the influence of alcohol in September 2010; Morrison says he was involved in an automobile accident after drinking and ordered to perform community service. And in 2008, he lost his 9-year-old son to brain cancer.

Payne says Gregg has attended Maryland basketball games, but he appears to have kept a low profile among his Maryland teammates over the last quarter century. Neither Jeff Baxter nor Derrick Lewis, who both live in the Washington, D.C., area, knew how to contact Gregg or where he was living. Lewis and Baxter attended the D.C.-area premiere of *Without Bias*, and Lewis claims he did not see Gregg at the event. Speedy Jones has tried to counsel Gregg. "He's dealing with some personal issues as a result [of Bias's death]," says Jones, without elaborating. "I don't know that he's ever sought help to deal with it. I think he needs to. I told him he needs to."

Payne says Gregg maintains contact with a small group of former players from high school. Each year the group, which includes Wagner, Payne, Morrison, and Clint Venable – all of whom knew Bias well – meet to eat pizza and talk about the good old basketball days of the 1980s at Northwestern, which won a state title during that time and has sent dozens of players to college basketball programs. They see in Gregg someone who enjoys life despite his setbacks. "When we're around and everybody is together, he manages to laugh and have fun even though you have to know in the back of his mind, [the death of Len and his son] kind of weigh heavy on him," says Payne.

Gregg chose not to talk for this book, because, Payne says, he fears a negative reaction. He applauds Gregg for figuring out how to maintain a job, raise a family, sustain relationships and be a productive member of society despite everything he has faced. "Any one of those events alone could negatively impact people," he says. "Dave's figured out a way to move on with his life."

TERRY LONG

In early November 1982, just before his senior season at Heritage High School near Richmond, Virginia, Terry Long announced that he would attend the University of Maryland on a basketball scholarship beginning in the fall of 1983. His comments on the announcement in a news report about his signing appeared to reflect more relief than jubilation. "I just wanted to get it all over with," said Long, who, according to the report, picked Maryland from among some 400 schools. "The last few months have been [a] disaster. The phone would start ringing about 8 o'clock at night, and I'd be talking to coaches until 11 or so. It just got to be too much."

As one of three people with Bias when he passed out while snorting cocaine, Long achieved more notoriety for his connection to the death of the Maryland star than for his accomplishments on a basketball court. Long, a 6-foot, 8-inch forward, posted supportive-role statistics at Maryland. He played in 27 games during his freshman year, averaging 2 points and 1.9 rebounds per game. As a sophomore, those numbers were 2.3 points and 1.9 rebounds per game in 37 games, including eight starts. As a junior, he played in 28 games and started in 21 of them, averaging 3.3 points and 3.1 rebounds a game. With the death of Bias, that would be the end of his Maryland career.

Long was described in a *Washington Post* story as "a polite, soft-spoken sort with an easy smile, but an anxious demeanor." The report claimed he was frustrated with his lack of progress as a player at Maryland and considered transferring to another school during his sophomore season. Long sprained a knee in the season opener during his junior year and later that season was declared academically ineligible for a couple of games for not completing a course. The birth of daughter Jovan, about 18 months before Bias's death, was an additional challenge. He visited Jovan about once a week. "It was something for me to get adjusted to [having a daughter]," Long said in March, 1986. "Overall, I think it's the best thing that's happened to me. It's made me mature faster."

By that time, Long occasionally used cocaine. He was charged with possessing cocaine and obstructing justice related to Bias's death, but the charges were dismissed in exchange for his testimony against Brian Tribble. He said in testimony during the Tribble trial that Bias introduced him to cocaine in 1984 at the beginning of his sophomore season, when Bias gave him the drug in a folded dollar bill. Long said during his testimony that Bias knew Long had used marijuana. Long also said during his testimony that he used cocaine only in his dorm room except for one time at Tribble's apartment after an N.C. State game in College Park. "Lenny drove us in Brian's car," he said during his testimony, according to the book *Lenny, Lefty and the Chancellor*. "We sat down and [Tribble] offered us a beer and we started using coke." During Long's testimony, Tribble's attorney, Thomas Morrow, tried to discredit him as a prosecution witness by pointing out that Long did not tell members of the responding emergency squad that Bias had been using drugs. "I don't recall what I said," Long said to Morrow.

"When the emergency medical team came you lied to them," Morrow said. "You lied to them because you didn't want to get into trouble, didn't you?"

Len Bias, left and Terry Long relax at Cole Field House during a workout. *(provided by Tina Maynard)*

"No," said Long. "I lied because I didn't really believe Lenny would pass away, and I didn't want to ruin his reputation."

Long's cocaine connection to Bias was not a surprise to Jones, who lived in the same suite with Bias and Long. He says that at the time of Bias's death, "Terry Long was hooked on cocaine." Jones says that if Bias hadn't died, cocaine might have eventually claimed Long.

Instead, Long's life took several dramatic turns. He returned to the Maryland campus two days after Bias died along with a police escort, Long said at the time, "for his safety" following death threats. He had been dismissed from Maryland at the end of the spring 1986 academic semester and needed to pass two classes at the end of the second summer session to retain eligibility for the following season, and his future at Maryland was made more precarious after he was suspended indefinitely from the team following his indictment. In October 1986, Prince George's County prosecutors dropped the charges against Long because they said he had testified "honestly" to the grand jury. He withdrew from Maryland in late December 1986.

Long appears to be the only member of the 1985-86 Maryland team who has not talked publicly about the Bias death aside from his statements made under oath during the Tribble trial. During a brief phone call in the spring of 2011, he was asked to talk about how Bias's death has affected his life. He responded twice, politely and calmly, saying, "I'm not interested." In subsequent calls he provided only brief background information.

Baxter says Long returned to the Maryland campus for the first time when the school's athletic department honored Driesell at a Maryland basketball game against North Carolina State in 2003. "I think Terry's been deeply hurt about this whole event," says Baxter. "He's very standoffish. I think Terry thinks this is his fault. I think he would put that type of pressure on himself."

Jones says Long broke down and "told him everything" about how Bias died, but he did not provide details. He says that every time he talks to Long about Bias, he can still see the pain in Long's eyes. Keith Gatlin, who entered Maryland the same year as Long, talks with him occasionally and visits him in Baltimore. He wishes Long would talk. "It would be therapeutic for Terry," he says. "And the perception of Terry that he was a bad guy or not a good kid is something that is really not true."

As of July 2011, Long was living in the Baltimore area with his wife – the mother of Jovan – and three other children. He worked at the W.R. Grace Company and as a part-time high-school basketball referee.

PHIL NEVIN

Phil Nevin rarely thinks about the two years he spent at Maryland as an infrequently used big man. After getting only 4 points and 17 rebounds in 13 games as a redshirt freshman during his second year, he was removed from the roster.

"It was an interesting time in my life," he says with little emotion during a phone call in July 2011.

Nevin, a 6-foot, 11-inch center out of Kiski Area High School just northeast of Pittsburgh, was a Street & Smith All-America. He chose Maryland over Virginia, Duquesne and Pitt because "it was not too close but not too far away," he says. Unlike many of his teammates, Nevin did not consider transferring out of Maryland after Bias died, but he did transfer later. He said in May 1987 that coach Bob Wade was trying to take away his scholarship. In August 1987, Maryland announced that he would not play for the team but that he would retain his full scholarship. Wade claimed that he and Nevin had a misunderstanding, and that it was Nevin's decision not to play for Maryland.

Nevin did not embrace Wade's stricter approach to coaching a team, on and off the court. "Lefty treated us like adults," he says. "After [the death of Bias], they treated us like children. They checked your schoolwork. They had people checking on us every other day. Wade tried to run your life 24 hours a day, with a military attitude. I didn't enjoy playing for Wade at all."

Nevin, a biology and chemistry major, focused on his studies for one more semester before announcing in January 1988 that he would transfer to Millersville University in Pennsylvania. John Kochan, an assistant coach at Maryland under Driesell before Nevin arrived, was the head coach at Millersville. Nevin now wishes he had stayed at Maryland to get his degree, in part because Millersville didn't accept all of his credits.

Nevin played only one year at Millersville, starting 24 games and averaging 8.7 points and 6.3 rebounds a game on a team that finished 26-7, won the Pennsylvania State Athletic Conference regular season and tournament titles and reached the Elite Eight at the NCAA Division II tournament. Nevin left Millersville in 1989 before earning a degree, in part because Kochan, he says, was "too easily excitable," and took a job as a health-physics technician for a nuclear support service company.

In July 2011, Nevin was working as a technician focusing on fuel repair and modifications for Master-Lee Energy Services, based in Latrobe, Pennsylvania, and living in the home where he grew up in nearby Markle. "I'm pretty happy," he says. "I've got a job that I work when I want to. I have a family and I'm close to the families I grew up with. I could be doing a lot worse." Nevin has a son but is not married.

Nevin says that he dealt with the death of Bias years ago. Asked if he harbors bitterness about his time at Maryland, he says, "I did when all this first happened. But it's 25 years ago. If I was still bitter about this now, I'd be a hateful person. I've put it in the past. "

He says the last time he thought about Bias was when he wondered how much money he could make from selling his door-sized poster of Bias on eBay.

Chapter 5
Family and Friends

BOB WAGNER

For a year and a half after Len Bias died, Bob Wagner fought a deep depression. He stopped coaching and teaching and returned to school, taking computer-technician classes. In the evenings, he worked as a night manager at College Park Towers, an apartment complex that catered to students who attended his alma mater, the University of Maryland.

"That's where I disappeared," says Wagner, Bias's head coach at Northwestern High School.

When not at work or in school, Wagner retreated to his house in Hyattsville as much as possible. "I wanted to get away from [high-school] kids," he says. "I didn't want anything to do with basketball. I didn't answer the phone. I didn't have much of a life at all. I was sleeping, studying and working. … There wasn't anything I could do."

As Wagner sat on the hallway floor of a suburban Maryland high school, or behind the closed door of a classroom between sessions of a basketball camp he helps run, his voice was somber. The compact build from his high-school coaching days has softened, but time hasn't changed everything. Even in the summer of 2010, Wagner was still visibly pained at losing someone he called a son. At first, Wagner was reluctant to reminisce. Time has passed, and he wondered if it was worth reliving that unsettling period of his life. But he agreed to talk after I appeared, unannounced, at the high school during a camp session.

Wagner says he still thinks about Bias every day. Sometimes, he cries. After Bias died, he endured typical stages that accompany a loss. "Depression. I questioned myself, what did I not see, what really transpired," he says. "Not knowing any of that side of him partying. In those days, I was the big brother to all the kids. We had a unifying spirit around basketball. It gave us a positive identity within the community. That's what hurt a lot of people with the tragedy. Here was a P.G. County public-school kid who did just as much if not more than a kid that might have gone to DeMatha or St. John's or some other top D.C.-area program. He wasn't given anything along the way. He had to work for what he got. It hurt the whole community. He was part of us. Most of us were part of him. So when he died, part of us died with him. The pain of his loss and the death of hope. He represented hope for a lot of kids."

Wagner had been tied into the D.C.-area basketball community since he was young, learning the game while playing against some of the top players in the area in his North Brentwood neighborhood in the 1950s and 1960s when Chuck Taylor canvas basketball shoes were in high demand and kids, as today, hoped their basketball talents would help them escape the ghettos and secure invitations to the top basketball schools in the area.

Wagner played basketball for Northwestern and later attended the University of Maryland, graduating in the late 1960s. By the time Bias had entered Northwestern, Wagner was beginning his second year as its head basketball coach and still developing his philosophy, still learning how to coach players. "I told [Bias] 'We're going to share this together. I need to learn,' " he says.

Wagner, a science and math teacher, had developed one of the top teams in the area with a militaristic approach to practice. "My goals as a coach and a teacher are that there was never a situation in a game that we did not go over in practice," he says. "We respected everybody and feared no one. Never had a player who played for me and went to college and had a harder practice. Ask Clint Venable."

Venable, five years younger than Len Bias, was a teammate of Len's younger brother, Jay, at Northwestern, as well as his best friend. He learned the game watching Len and developed his skills with Jay and under the guidance of Wagner and Len Bias's basketball mentor, Johnnie Walker.

"He kept me on a straight path," Venable says of Wagner. "If there was anything wrong, he would get on us. He said the same things my dad told me. 'You watch what you say and do; you never know who's watching you.' We went to school to learn, get our lesson and play basketball. Stuff that schools were doing five or six years later, Mr. Wagner was already doing. Mr. Wagner was disciplined. We had study hall, studied before the game, watched film. A lot of kids when we were in school didn't watch film. We wore a shirt and tie to games. He said 'If you don't have it, I'll get it for you.' Mr. Wagner was one of those cool coaches, someone you could get along with and talk with, and he understood what was going on."

Most of Wagner's top players from Northwestern, including about a half dozen who played in the NBA or professionally overseas, such as Boyce Cherry and Mike Morrison, left the area after high school to pursue their basketball dreams. Not Bias. Aided by that proximity, he kept in touch with Wagner during most of his time at Maryland, and the two developed a relationship that Wagner never had with any of his other players. Wagner often took the mile and a half trip from Northwestern to Maryland's gym, Cole Field House, to watch Bias practice with the Terrapins.

The road went both ways. After his freshman year at Maryland, Bias would stop by Northwestern, where the two would walk the halls. As Bias mostly talked, Wagner mostly listened, letting Bias express his frustration about his growing stardom. "He'd come by school and say, 'Mr. Wagner, I'm having fun, but I get tired of this, girls coming by constantly. I'm trying to study. If I say 'No,' then they'll go, 'Well you were with *her* ...' "

Wagner noticed that after his sophomore year Bias was growing into a more emotionally mature player, that he started hearing what Driesell was saying rather than how loudly he expressed it. "I asked Leonard, 'What happened? All of a sudden you're playing, and you're not whining anymore,' " says Wagner. "A lot of kids don't get through that phase with college coaches because their high-school and club coaches are patting them on the back. After his sophomore year, I don't think he ever came in second in anything, sprints, lifting, whatever it was."

Wagner also watched Bias grow into a dominant presence and saw how he handled the brutal physical demands of playing college sports at the highest level. He taught Bias the realities of basketball at that level, telling Bias that he's a player for hire and that Maryland will use his body to make money. "He could either get screwed and not get paid, or he could get paid," says Wagner. "If you want to get paid, you have to go to class and get your degree. Otherwise you're a prostitute not getting paid. They're using your body, wearing you down. What else are you going to get out of it? How are you going to get something out of it besides smiles and interviews and all of that?"

Wagner liked to assess his success as a coach by how his former players have adjusted to their adult lives. He asked them to come back in 10 years and tell him how they were doing. "Do you get up and go to work when you don't feel like it? Does your wife complain you're not making enough money? Are your kids complaining that they don't get this or that? Are you getting up on a Saturday or Sunday morning and working out? Are you willing to work hard to make it easy later? Leonard never got there, but he was close."

Wagner found out about Bias's death in a phone call from David Gregg, who played for Wagner at Northwestern. At the hospital, Wagner remembers standing in the room where James Bias held his dead son in his arms. Wagner fell quickly into a deep personal abyss. Not only had his most accomplished player died, a young man he loved like a son, but another of his former players, Gregg, was in trouble. Gregg had partied with Bias and ingested the same cocaine that killed his friend and teammate. On top of it all, Wagner's close friend, Lefty Driesell, was also confronting the traumatic loss and its ramifications.

Wagner remembers telling Gregg and others something about making sure they cleaned up the room where they had partied with Bias earlier that morning because "people would come into the room." A few months later, Wagner testified before a grand jury. Prosecutors were trying to determine if he had obstructed justice by telling the players to clean the room where Bias died, but Wagner was never charged with any crime related to Bias's death.

Wagner resigned as Northwestern's head coach a week before the regular season began in the fall of 1986, citing personal reasons. He left behind a 119-78 record from nine years as Northwestern's head coach. Wagner was not ready to return to coaching when, just over a year after Bias died, Jay Bias approached him in the bleachers during a basketball game at Prince George's Community College. "Jay said, 'My mom's on the road, my dad's a mess. I don't have anybody to talk to.' It was the hardest on Jay. I said, 'You gonna play again?' I always remember him saying, 'I thought about it, and my brother would have wanted me to continue playing.' I stewed on that for a long time. I thought Len probably would have wanted me to continue coaching."

Wagner returned to coaching in 1988 at St. John's College, a private high school in northwest D.C., as an assistant varsity coach. After three years, he took over the program and was its head coach for six years while he worked with special-needs students and taught science and math in middle school. When we talked at the Buzz Braman's Sure Shot Basketball Camp in July 2010, Wagner repeatedly expressed regret about what he could have and should have done to save Bias before that fatal night. "I allowed him to get a little disconnected from me because I felt like the principles and the things we stood for and he knew, they were ingrained, that they would continue," he says.

But they clearly did not. Bias had somehow learned to hide the biggest secret of his life: his drug use. Wagner can even justify why Bias chose to hide the truth from him and others. "We lie to the people we love," he says. "Leonard loved me, and his parents and other people. Whatever he was doing, he kept it from us. He knew we'd be disappointed in him."

Wagner realized that toward the end, Bias lacked a commanding and perhaps controlling presence in his life, someone who could keep him balanced and humble and focused. "One of the things I've learned, and what I tell kids today, is if you become popular or notorious, you have one person, it could be your wife, who says 'It's time to go,'" he says. "They have absolute veto power over whatever you're doing. You cannot object to it. Celebrities need something like that. Usually when they fall down, there was nobody around who would say 'No.' He had nobody like that."

Wagner spoke of a dream he often has. In it, Bias has spent his free time since dying practicing and practicing, getting ready to face Michael Jordan. Finally, they go one-on-one in the afterlife. No one wins, but Wagner says the play is fierce. When he's asked who was the better player in life, Wagner offers a multilayered answer. "Leonard had the bigger heart, and the better body," he says. "But I always answer Jordan because Jordan lived and Leonard died. When your warrior image gets old, you can now be the leader. And he can give back the wisdom. Leonard never got to do that. He never got to give back. Jordan had an opportunity to do this. Today, you do drugs and get busted and come back and they write a story about you because you survived it and you can pass along that message. Leonard didn't get a second chance."

To Wagner, the legacy of Len Bias is laced with mixed messages. He commends Len's mother, Lonise, for doing "a great job" teaching the perils of drug abuse and encouraging people to work through personal struggles. "She has had more of an impact than Leonard did to stop [kids from] using drugs," he says.

But he does not agree with Lonise Bias that God had some plan for Len's death to have an impact on drug use. "What a waste. One life? I'm not trading one life for one life. I don't agree on the concept that God had some purpose. If he did, I don't see it. I think he could have been a successful basketball player and gotten that message across without having died. The lesson is that the 99 percent things you do right, and the 1 percent thing you do wrong is what they remember you for."

For Wagner, the memory of Bias has taken on a new form as he coaches a young player who reminds him of Bias: the smile, the innocent glow, the gleam in the eye. He's got not only the leaps that made Bias famous, but also the style that helps him hold the ball high on his jump shot, making the defending task that much more difficult. "I told his dad that if we can get that going, he's gonna have Leonard's jump shot," he says, ever wistful.

BRIAN WALLER AND JOHNNIE WALKER

On the evening of June 18, Brian Waller and Johnnie Walker joined some of the other regulars for their weekly pickup game on adult night at The Rec, the perfect place for the three to celebrate the choice of Bias as the No. 2 overall pick by the Boston Celtics in the 1986 NBA draft the day before.

Waller had talked with Bias on Sunday and again on Monday, the day before the draft. Bias hadn't said he would stop by that night, but Waller and Walker still held out hope that he would surprise them. They were so excited about Bias being selected by the Celtics that they cut their game short and talked most of the night about his good fortune. "We were just hanging out talking and waiting for him to walk through the door," says Waller. "Every time the door opened, we looked to see who was gonna walk through, thinking and hoping it was him."

Bias's buoyant presence never materialized. Waller was left to wonder: Could he have saved his best friend's life if only Bias had walked through those doors at The Rec that night? "I can remember, long after he passed away, I would come home from work, I would sit in the basement in the dark, for a couple of months," he says. "No TV, no radio. If I was there, he'd still be here." Waller says Bias never used cocaine around him.

Waller and Walker shared their thoughts about Bias at Waller's sprawling house in an upper-middle-class section of southern Prince George's County some 12 miles from the simpler middle-class surroundings of the Columbia Park neighborhood that shaped their youth.

Waller's eyes widened and filled with tears. "It was probably more sadness, not really guilt," he says, staring into space. "Man, if I was there, I could have done something. I don't think he would have been comfortable …" Waller pauses and takes a deep breath, "doing any kind of drugs around me. I would have been, 'What are you doing?' I would have been totally against it. He probably wouldn't have brought that foolishness around me."

Waller accepted a basketball scholarship to Providence College, where he played for four years and graduated with a degree in business management in the winter of 1985. After college, Waller returned to Maryland and worked as an insurance salesman, often not finishing until 9 p.m. Waller's schedule prevented him from visiting Bias more than a couple of times a month during the spring

1986 semester. He attended games with tickets that Bias left for him but rarely saw him afterward, choosing instead to get a good night's sleep for work the next day.

"He knew I'd be at the game, but we didn't hang out a whole lot his senior year," says Waller.

Waller insists he never saw Bias use drugs. "I've said this before, and I'll say it again," he says. "All the time we spent together, I've never seen him do drugs or bring drugs around me. If he was doing it, he hid it well. We used to drink a beer, and two or three hours later, late at night, he would go out and run because he drank a beer."

Waller was driving to work on the morning of June 19, on a street a couple miles from their homes in Columbia Park, when he heard the end of a radio report that mentioned someone died from a drug overdose two days after achieving his or her dream. Waller quickly found another radio station and heard the whole story of Bias's death. "I immediately pulled over to the side of the road because I'm shaking," he says, talking quietly. "I get myself together, drive to a shopping center and call his parents' house. I could tell by the way [Len's sister] Michelle answered the phone that it was true."

For a while after Bias died, Waller floated through life. He didn't touch a basketball for at least six months and struggled to interact with the youngsters at The Rec, where he volunteered three days a week to teach them basketball.

"I would sit in a chair in the gym and I wouldn't play with the kids," he says. "I shut it down for a long time. I just sat there and looked at the kids. Before that, I'd play with them, pass them the ball. I couldn't even get up there. I was thinking, when's he gonna walk through this door? You look at the kids and have all these flashbacks and not have enough energy to play with the kids. For years, it always seemed like a bad dream. One day you're going to come out of the dream, and he'll be there. He will walk through my front door or the gym door. For years, it felt like a nightmare. One day I'm gonna wake up from this dream."

While Waller was away pursuing his own basketball career at Providence, Walker had moved back to the area after finishing college. After playing two years on the varsity team at Northwestern High School – with Wagner as his head coach his senior year – Walker says he played basketball at Prince George's Community College for a year and later for Iowa Western Community College and Tarkio College in Missouri.

When Walker was home from school, Bias and Waller took full advantage of his return to play basketball what seemed like every waking hour. It mattered little that Walker, who was four years older than Bias, may have partied late on a Friday night. The two teenagers often knocked on his door around dawn on Saturday mornings, knowing that Walker, who worked at The Rec and had a key to the center, was their ticket to basketball nirvana and would let them play all day.

Upon arrival, Bias and Waller eagerly mopped the gym's floor, cleaning away the residue from Friday night go-go concerts that Walker organized and monitored at the center. They were then ready to play ball all day with dozens of other hoop addicts including, Walker insists, the acrobatic and over-40-inch leaper World B. Free, an NBA player at the time. The only people who seemed to mind the gatherings were residents who lived nearby, who complained about the noisy kids with their noisy cars.

At other times, Waller and Bias would pack into Walker's cramped, 4-cylinder Ford EXP two-seater that barely had enough juice to run the air conditioner when the car sat in idle. In it, the well-over-6-foot-tall sardines happily traveled the local recreation-center circuit, playing games against teams from Glenarden, Palmer Park and Fairmont Heights. What was a little discomfort if there was a basketball game out there somewhere? Waller remembers playing against a guy they called "Space," who was maybe 6 feet, 2 inches tall but jumped so high that he touched the top of the square on the backboard. Space, he says, once broke Bias's finger when he pinned his shot against the glass.

It was not rare for Walker to come home and find Waller and Bias working out on the plywood weight bench in his back yard. Waller repeatedly credits Walker with keeping him and Bias on the busy basketball path, away from the temptations of drugs and alcohol that consumed many other teenage boys.

By the time Bias entered the University of Maryland, Walker had returned to the D.C.-area full-time after college. He joined the D.C. police force in March 1985, and worked for the department for 16 years. For four years, he walked the D.C. streets as a patrol officer, at times working on drug details. He claims he heard nothing about Bias being involved in any way with drugs, although he says he heard that Bias's friend Brian Tribble, who was with Bias when he died, was selling them.

"The furthest thing from my mind was that Leonard was using any type of drugs like that," says Walker. "We had that conversation over and over about drugs, how people's careers ended on drugs. I always used to talk to him about when you watch movies about musicians and how they end up shooting drugs. We used to say 'How does he end up shooting drugs when he sees all the things that drugs do to other people? What leads him to believe that he's so invincible against drugs?' "

At Bias's urging, Walker took a week off from work in the spring of 1986 and joined him on the ACC Barnstorming Tour, serving as a traveling partner as well as the proprietor of the Len Bias "Everything Must Go" vending stand set up at the games. Walker says Bias gathered a range of Maryland basketball gear that included practice and game shorts and jerseys as well as a life-sized poster used as a Maryland promotion during the previous season to sell the gear at the game venues. Bias was so elated at his earnings for playing in the games – up to $1,500 each for about a half dozen games – that he let Walker keep all revenue generated from the gear sales.

"He said 'Whatever it is, just keep it,' " says Walker.

Later that spring, Walker joined Bias on a couple of getaway trips to Virginia Beach, including one the weekend before the NBA draft. He shared his last words with Bias during a phone call the night of the draft. During the call, Bias promised Walker they would have everything they ever wanted. "I was sleeping," says Walker. "I had to go to work the next day. I said 'Just call me tomorrow.' He said 'Man, you won't have to work no more after this. We're gonna do everything and anything we ever wanted to do.' I said 'OK, Leonard, OK.' "

After Bias died, Walker could not bring himself to return to The Rec, where he was still volunteering, and work with the players. "It kept me away from a lot of things," he says. "I didn't go to The Rec for a long time after that."

The death of Bias affected how Walker's coworkers perceived him as a police officer. Many of his fellow officers knew Bias, having seen him play basketball with Walker at the police-academy courts, and wondered how Walker could be unaware that Bias used drugs since Bias was spending a lot of time with Tribble, whose activities were already suspicious. "It seemed like maybe people looked at me as if I should have known more than what I knew," says Walker. "People who knew me said 'How didn't you know, because you usually don't miss anything?' People were like 'How do you know he wasn't using drugs? He was with a drug dealer. You didn't know [Tribble] was a drug dealer? You didn't know he was using drugs?' It created a problem for me. People perceived me different after that for a very long time."

Prosecutors in Prince George's County investigating the death of Bias wanted to know why Walker had removed items from Bias's dorm room the day Bias died. Walker testified before a grand jury, but no charges were brought against him. He says he took Bias's personal belongings from the room only after receiving permission from police to do so and because the Bias family had asked him to remove the items. He placed the items in Bob Wagner's van.

"Once the police said everything could be taken out, I cleaned the whole room out," he says.

Most often Walker has been left to wonder why Bias would fall prey to the temptations of drug abuse. "I think the drug thing with Leonard to this day was his perception that no matter what he did, he was just better and stronger, and it wouldn't have that effect on him," Walker says.

Walker became the girls' varsity head coach at Dunbar High School in Washington, D.C. in 1996. In 2001, he left the D.C. police force and took a job as a registrar for the city's public schools. He moved to Dunbar High School in D.C. as its attendance counselor in 2006, the same year he became the head coach for the boys' basketball team at the school. In the summer of 2010, Walker was named the athletic director at Dunbar.

He still wonders what more he could have done to prevent his friend's death. "It may not be true, but I felt like even when I was around his mom and dad, that they blamed me, that I should have protected him better," he says, his voice quiet and his tear-filled eyes staring at a television showing sports. "I felt for a long time like it was my fault. Still feel that way."

CLINT VENABLE AND JAY BIAS

Windowless and bleacher-less, the drab beige box with the synthetic floor isn't much to look at. But typical of basketball courts in the rec centers of middle-class black communities for more than a quarter century, it's not the floors and walls that count. It's what happens on the former and what decorates the latter. On the far wall of the court at Columbia Park Recreation Center – The Rec – in Landover is a poster announcing the dedication of the Wharton "Mack" Lee Madkins Gymnasium on November 25, 2002. For decades, Madkins was the director of the center and helped coach Bias and others in both football and basketball.

The poster contains a collage of photos that reflect Madkins's influence on the thousands of children he guided during his reign at The Rec. Madkins poses by a mantle of trophies. Madkins comforts a young boy. Madkins stands with his assistant coaches in a football team picture. Madkins tucks a football under one arm as he gently places the other around the shoulder of a young, smiling player, above words attributed to Madkins that read: "They may leave, but they always find a way back."

Many of those who Madkins coached or mentored through the years have indeed returned to the Columbia Park area. Some, such as Waller and Walker, not only returned but took on roles similar to that of Madkins, teaching younger boys about sports and life. But some were not so lucky. One, Jay Bias, is part of the picture on the bottom right of the poster. He flashes an easy smile and wears a green T-shirt emblazoned with the words "Boston Celtics" in bright, white letters. Jay's legend at The Rec is as profound as Len's, for different yet sadly parallel reasons. Neither made it back.

In the picture, Jay Bias leans forward slightly, his arms extended to his knees. Next to Jay is best friend Clint Venable, his left arm flexed at a 90-degree angle. His bulging biceps take the shape of a tennis ball; his triceps seemingly tear through the skin. Waller is crouched down in front of Venable. The picture was taken the winter after Len died, when a Columbia Park team won a club tournament in North Carolina.

In his early 40s now, Venable isn't as lean as he used to be and carries himself slowly, due in part to a problematic back that has kept him out of work for about three years. In the summer of 2010, Venable took me on a tour of The Rec, just a few blocks from the house where he grew up and still lives. We walked past the two outdoor courts he and his boys used when the weather allowed. Inside, moments after we entered the gymnasium, Venable fondly pointed out the poster and savored the image of his long-lost friend Jay.

Earlier in the day, over lunch at a restaurant in Landover near his home, Venable had talked more emotionally, often near tears, about the fond times spent with Jay. The two had met in Columbia Park. Their friendship took time to grow, basketball playing a large part in their developing bond. "We hung out and played ball at the gym 90 percent of the time," he says. "We hung out at each other's house and had each other's backs. All the guys came to The Rec to play ball. We'd play all day. If our parents wanted to find us, they knew where to get us. That's all we knew, basketball. If the gym wasn't open yet, we'd play outside."

Jay Bias was a year younger and became like a brother to Venable, who has two sisters. Venable talks reverently of the mentors such as Len Bias, Waller and Walker, who taught them about basketball and life at The Rec. The boys at The Rec were Venable's extended family. "They were like big brothers to us," he says. "We couldn't go to our parents to talk to them. Being around those guys was real good."

When not playing, Jay and Venable sat and admired how hard their idols worked on the courts. The older guys at times kicked Venable and the other middle schoolers off the court so they could get their own games in, but that was OK. The younger kids would marvel at their work ethic, watching Walker put Bias, Waller and others through the same technical and conditioning drills that Coach Wagner would later put them through when they played at Northwestern. If they were lucky, the older guys would ask Clint and his buddies to join in a game. "We wanted to be like those guys, wanted to do what they were doing," says Venable.

Waller knew early on that the young group admiring him and Len Bias had potential. At times Waller would pick Jay, Venable or Henry Hall – who Waller claims was better than any of them before a drug addiction curtailed his promising future – as a fifth player on a team that would travel to the courts at the National Institutes of Health in Bethesda, Maryland, for some of the best pickup games in the area. "They were middle-school kids playing with college players," says Waller. "People were like, 'Man, where you all go to school?' They couldn't believe they were in middle school."

Jay and Clint were still in middle school when Len began his career at Maryland and the two enjoyed Len's adventures as spectators and close admirers. Still, they looked at Len as just another guy from the neighborhood. They often hung out together at the Bias family home just a couple of blocks away from The Rec, gathering around the television set in the Bias basement, watching the video highlights of Len and Maryland that only Maryland players and coaches had access to as Lonise Bias made sure everyone had enough food to eat.

Clint Venable stands near a basket at the Columbia Park Recreation Center, "The Rec." (photo by Dave Ungrady)

"We'd watch some of the dunks you couldn't see on TV," he says. "We'd watch them and say, 'Did you see the pass Gatlin threw?' "

Playing pickup games with Len and other Maryland basketball and football players under the lights on the outdoor courts on the Maryland campus, Jay and Venable were living a dream. Guys like Gatlin, Baxter, Derrick Lewis and Cedric Lewis would be there, and Venable took advantage of the opportunity of being around such basketball greatness by trying to learn as much as he could, especially from Bias. Watching Len play convinced Venable that he wanted to go to college, ideally at Maryland. "I watched how he worked on the court, without the ball," he says. "How he cut off a guy, how he squared up to the basket, how he boxed out. A lot of it was straight basic basketball."

During the rare times Clint played on the same team as Bias, he understood his role. "When you play with someone like that, you're thinking, 'Man, I've got to get him the ball.' " And when Jay played against Len, the elder Bias did not play favorites. "He didn't take it easy on him," says Venable. "He would knock him down, play him the same way as anybody else."

When it came time for Jay Bias and Venable to pick their high schools, how could they not pick Northwestern? It was the only place they would be comfortable playing basketball. Len's and Waller's success at the school was enough to convince Jay to play for the same coach who had guided them to the state finals in Len's junior year. Venable had received an offer for a partial scholarship to attend DeMatha High School, at the time the top program in the D.C. area and one of the best in the country, but begged his parents to allow him to go to Northwestern because of Coach Wagner's reputation for developing players. "You watch the older guys play and you want to be in their shoes," he says. "I got lucky. We had the best cheerleaders, the best school, the best school spirit."

Wagner picked Jay to play half the year for Northwestern's varsity team as a sophomore, feeling it was best to keep Jay close to him rather than have him remain on the junior varsity. "He would be a challenge for other coaches," he says.

Wagner remembers Jay as possessing more balls skill than Len and hoped to use him more as a point guard or shooting guard on the court. Baxter thought Jay's abilities in high school were far superior to Len's. "Jay could handle the basketball better, he had more court awareness at the time and he could get off the floor," says Baxter. "But he couldn't get up as high as his brother."

Wagner thought that if Jay could settle down, he could be as good as Len. But Jay's vocal tendencies proved a hindrance. "He had more mouth, and that held him back in his development," he says. "He was like that even before Len passed away." On the day Len died, Jay scored 20 points in a summer-league basketball game, leading Northwestern's team to a 21-point victory. But Jay soon showed signs of trouble dealing with his brother's death. When he returned to school in the fall, he lost focus on academics.

"When my brother died, I got a chip on my shoulder," Jay said in a *Baltimore Sun* story in March 1989, while he was in junior college. "Nothing worse could happen. Since he was gone, I saw no reason to do what I was supposed to do. My attitude was, 'forget the world.' I found myself doing things I shouldn't have. I wouldn't do my schoolwork. Instead, I'd hang out at clubs, with friends. My mother and friends counseled me. I straightened up."

"His parents worked hard to help him with a lot of issues, but it was a lot for him to handle," says Wagner. "Jay was full of excuses. He'd say 'They're picking on me because of my brother.'"

Venable remembers players acting cruelly toward Jay about Len's death, and the younger brother at times struggled to control his emotions on the court. "They said a lot of bad things to Jay on and off the court," Venable says. "I don't care who you are, you can only take so much. It was rough on him. Kids on the other team kept nagging him. That was probably part of their game plan to get in his head to beat us."

During his junior year, Jay was ejected from one game for throwing an elbow and was involved in a shoving incident in another. The most dramatic incident happened in a game with county rival Eleanor Roosevelt, when Jay's fiery rhetoric and aggressive play rubbed someone the wrong way. Roosevelt players were trying their best to prevent Jay from dunking the ball on fast breaks, and after Jay completed an alley-oop play on a pass from Venable, he ended up on the floor.

"Jay said a few guys on the team were saying things, harassing him," says Venable. "He got the ball and threw it down. I turned around and then Jay was lying on the ground. There was a full brawl. People came out of the stands. It was terrible. A lot of people got hurt in that fight. Mr. Wagner used to say we're not gonna start fights, but if one of us fights, we all fight. We were out there swinging."

Jay admitted he had trouble controlling his temper. "I felt a lot of pressure after Len died," he said in a *Washington Post* story in March 1987. "I think people expected me to do what Len did when he was here. It bothered me a lot and I didn't have the patience to deal with it. I'm better now. I can control myself much better. I was also getting sick and tired of always being referred to as Len Bias's brother. I am not Len and I cannot be another Len. For the rest of my life, I will be Jay and I want to be accepted on what I do. When teams play against me, I want to feel they are playing against me, not against Len's little brother. Right now, I'm just trying to help us have the best season we can have."

He ultimately did, with the help of Venable. In early March, Venable converted a 15-foot jumper at the buzzer to put Northwestern in the state championship final four in 1987, some nine months after the death of Len. Five days later, Northwestern played for its first state title since 1968 in, poignantly, Cole Field House.

As Venable remembers, Jay could display a loose demeanor similar to Len's, often joking with his teammates before games to stay relaxed. But before the state championship final in 1987, he was quiet and reflective. Venable remembers seeing tears well in Jay's eyes in the locker room before the game and remembers Jay writing Len's Maryland No. 34 on the back of his basketball shoes. He scrawled "Len" on one shoe and "Bias" on the other.

Fueled by his brother's spirit in the arena he had dominated not long ago, Jay Bias scored a game-high 25 points and helped the team come back from an 11-point deficit in the third quarter, with 16 of his points scored after halftime. Venable remembers it as Jay's best performance of the season. Jay also grabbed 30 rebounds in the two final four games, 14 in the final.

"I gave 100 percent in the rebounding and that's my strong point," Jay said after the game, which Northwestern won 73-63. "I was trying to be like Moses Malone. I wanted every rebound."

In his last game for Northwestern, Venable scored 15 points, and was named an All-Met all-star in the D.C.-area for the second consecutive season as well as a Street & Smith All-America. Venable had dreamed of attending Maryland, but poor SAT scores kept him from receiving a scholarship to a top NCAA Division I basketball school – including James Madison University, for which he says Driesell recruited him. Venable traveled a couple of hours north to attend Allegany Community College. During his freshman year, Allegany advanced to the Round of 16 in the national junior-college tournament, with Clint averaging 18 points per game as a point guard and leading the team in steals.

Derrick Curry was also on that Northwestern state-title team. When he and Jay returned after that championship season, for their final year in school, Curry noticed a change in his classmate. "It got to the point where he lost interest in basketball for a while," he says. "His attitude completely changed our senior year. He just didn't care."

Curry remembers Len as a crybaby who took out his frustrations on an opponent by "shooting the lights out on him," he says. "But Jay would go down and elbow somebody and get thrown out of the damn game. Len used his head more than Jay. Jay had a more bad attitude overall, and it grew worse after Len died. A lot had to do with the pressure that was put on him. After Len died, everybody babied Jay. He was still a kid, but people didn't hold him accountable for things and they let him get away with a lot. Outside the home nobody would tell him, 'Jay you're wrong.' "

Northwestern struggled during Jay's senior year, finishing 10-12 and missing the state playoffs. But Jay put up big numbers, averaging 25 points – only four fewer than the year before – and 12 rebounds a game for the Wildcats. And he managed to avoid the on-court altercations that soured his junior season. His mother, Lonise, even commented to the *Washington Post*, saying she was very pleased that he was going to Allegany. "It will give him a chance to get himself together," she said. "Jay has been under a lot of pressure lately and Allegany will be good for him."

Lonise Bias added that Jay earned a 2.83 academic average during his senior year, but he failed to reach 700 on his SATs, preventing him from earning a Division I scholarship for his freshman year. He averaged 17 points and 8 rebounds per game at Allegany on a team that finished 32-4. "I study, play basketball and go to high-school games," he said in a *Baltimore Sun* story in March 1989. "It's like I'm on vacation. I love basketball. It's my food. I have to have it. It's like I'm an addict."

Bias majored in telecommunications at Allegany and earned a 2.9 grade-point average the first semester. At Allegany he and Venable strengthened their friendship. "We sat up plenty of nights and had long talks about the neighborhood and basketball, about how things were in life," Venable says. "He said 'When you leave, I don't think I'm coming back to Allegany.' He said 'I probably won't even play basketball.' If Leonard would have been there I think Jay would have gone to college for four years and might have played in the pros. I guess he didn't have that drive. Basketball wasn't important to him anymore."

Bias left Allegany after one season. When he returned home, he first worked as an assistant manager at a dining facility at the Collington Episcopal Life Center in Mitchellville, Maryland, not far from his Columbia Park home, and later at a bank. He applied to American University in the spring of 1990, but after he was denied entry due to insufficient transferable credits, he expressed interest in attending a continuing-education program at American with the hope of gaining admission in January 1991. Bias registered for an algebra class on June 28, 1990, but did not earn a grade. He did not register for the fall semester.

Basketball had become an afterthought. Perhaps he was waiting for Len to tap him on the shoulder and say "Let's go shoot some hoops" at The Rec. Lonise Bias claims that, four years after Len died, Jay was still waiting for him to walk through their front door.

During the summer of 1990, Venable noticed that Jay was not his usual self, but thought it was because he was no longer playing basketball. It was also around that time that Johnnie Walker saw something he thought he would never see: Jay walking into the Eastside Club in Southeast Washington, D.C., with Brian Tribble. "It was unbelievable," Walker says. "I just looked at them. I was thrown back."

Meanwhile, Venable was moving in a more positive direction, beginning his first year at Bowling Green University in what would be a prolific basketball career at the Ohio school. He earned all-Mid-American conference first-team honors his junior year, averaging 16.8 points and 4.6 assists per game on a team that finished 18-11 and made it to the National Invitational Tournament, losing in the first round.

Entering his senior year, Venable was a conference player of the year candidate. The season started well for the quick, 5-foot, 10-inch point guard. After a season-opening 18-point win over Akron, Bowling Green hosted fifth-ranked Michigan State, led by All-America Steve Smith, on December 1, 1990. In a game recognized as one of the most memorable wins in the history of Anderson Arena, Bowling Green won by 13 points, due in large part to Venable. He scored 24 points, hitting four 3 pointers; converted all eight of his free throws and had five assists. Venable was carried off Bowling Green's home court by his teammates as the game hero.

Four days later, before an evening game at Western Kentucky, Venable's euphoric basketball world took a stunning turn. He had just finished showering in the team hotel following a shootaround. "We had a room with connecting doors," Venable says, his voice growing somber. "Twelve guys on the team, they were watching sports on ESPN. Someone said, 'Hey, your boy just got killed.' I said, 'No, man, stop playing.' I looked at it on TV and it was like everything just messed me up, my whole body got weak. I went downstairs, called my parents on the pay phone. They told me what happened. I just walked around, went down to the lobby. I couldn't eat, couldn't sleep, the whole time we were in Western Kentucky."

Venable's voice trailed for a few moments. Tears covered his face as he recalled the dark day. "I had nothing in me," he says.

Venable considered asking for the night off, but after talking with his parents, coach and teammates, he decided to play. His performance mirrored his frame of mind. In 35 minutes of action, Venable scored just eight points, shooting 2 of 13 from the field, including 0 of 5 from three-point range. Venable rebounded to his usual basketball form three days later in Bowling Green's next game at home, scoring 21 points in a 20-point win over Butler. But the melancholy remained.

It still does. Some two decades later, Venable was engulfed by gloom as he remembered the details of Jay's death. Back in Hyattsville, Jay had gone to a jewelry store in Prince George's Plaza to check on an engagement ring he had ordered for the girlfriend he had dated throughout high school. In the store Bias saw Jerry Tyler, who accused Jay of flirting with his wife, a store clerk. The two men argued. As Bias walked away with two friends, Tyler said "C'mon outside, c'mon outside," one of the friends, Andre Campbell, said in a news report. Bias responded, "Look, I'm just purchasing a ring... all this stuff ain't necessary, man."

Campbell said that minutes later someone in a Mercedes-Benz drove up next to the car in which Jay sat in the passenger seat while waiting at a stop sign outside the mall. Someone from the car fired, killing him. Tyler was convicted of the murder. Venable noted that the store clerk who chatted with Jay attended Northwestern High School and that she and Venable's high-school girlfriend were best friends. Venable and his girlfriend had actually ridden to a Northwestern prom in the same limousine as Tyler and the clerk, who even mingled a bit with Jay at the prom.

In 1986, Venable had attended Len Bias's memorial service, leaving for a day the prestigious same Five Star Basketball Camp that Len had attended a few years earlier. When he returned to the camp, he remembered how counselors and players were prompted to tears during a moment of silence for

Bias. "I knew Leonard was famous and a lot of people cared about him and liked him," he says. "But it really didn't hit me until I came back to camp. They knew I went to the funeral; they asked all kinds of questions. I was sitting there saying these cats don't even know Leonard and they're crying and weeping. I was 'wow, it was amazing.' A lot of the kids really looked up to Leonard. We didn't think of him like everybody else did. We thought he was like one of us."

Venable cried again as he turned his thoughts to how he reacted to the death of Jay Bias. Deciding to stay with his Bowling Green team rather than return to Maryland for Jay's service, attended by 3,500 people, didn't prevent Venable from dwelling on his friend's death.

"I was wondering how Mr. and Mrs. Bias were taking it," he says. "I wanted to come home for the funeral, but I talked to Mrs. Bias, and she told me go ahead and stay in school, that everything was fine. I wish I would have been there, but I don't know how I would have taken it. All I kept thinking was, 'If I come home I'm never gonna see him anymore.' He wasn't going to be there. The last conversation I had when I was home, I said, 'Why don't you go to school, go play basketball?' I guess he didn't want to play anymore."

Venable did manage to connect with the Bias family later in his senior year at Bowling Green, making time to visit with Lonise Bias when she gave a speech at a high school near the college in Ohio. Lonise Bias pointed Venable out in the crowd as someone who grew up with Len and Jay, prompting him to stand up. "She was always giving encouraging words, [she's] a wonderful person," says Venable.

Despite losing his best friend, Venable's basketball numbers improved a bit from his junior year, to 17.4 points and 4.6 assists per game. He was not chosen as the conference's top player that season, as some had predicted, but was named to the Metro Athletic Conference second team. After leaving Bowling Green, Venable spent a few years trying to play pro basketball. He says he secured a summer-league contract with the Sacramento Kings of the NBA, and played with the team during the season on a 10-day contract. He also played in the Continental Basketball Association, the Global Basketball Association, the Atlantic Basketball Association and the World Basketball League.

Venable most recently worked in maintenance for the Maryland National Capital Park and Planning Commission in Prince George's County, before a back injury forced him out of work. He was collecting disability as of October 2011. He hopes to play basketball again someday, most likely at The Rec, where he stops by a couple of times a week to "talk to the guys."

DERRICK CURRY

Derrick Curry's burly body tests the limits of his taut shirt, his arms and shoulders suited more to a linebacker than a power forward. And they suit his musical skill well. Curry bangs on conga drums, laying down a pounding percussive base for his go-go band's up-tempo beat that sends a small crowd in The Meeting Place into a chant-along frenzy.

At about 6 feet, 1 inch tall and weighing in around 250, Curry is clearly the largest man in the band, but his bulk is mostly hidden behind the chest-high drums in the back right corner of the small stage area that's really not a stage, but rather just a place on the basement floor of this downtown

Washington, D.C., bar. In the faint light, Curry's presence is loud but at the same time inconspicuous. Like Clint Venable, Curry was a Northwestern teammate of Jay Bias who harbored dreams of playing basketball in college and the NBA. But Curry instead became an unwitting bit player as a crack cocaine dealer.

Curry has a unique perspective on the deaths of the Bias brothers: While still mourning the loss of Jay, it was the earlier death of Len that helped put him in jail. If Bias had not died the way he did, from cocaine intoxication, chances are Curry wouldn't have received a prison sentence of 19 years and 7 months in October 1993 for conspiracy and distribution of a little more than a pound of crack cocaine.

During a summer evening in 2010, after finishing his go-go sets at the Meeting Place with his band, Endurance Unlimited, Curry talked about his drug ordeal. He doesn't pretend to be above reproach; as a 19-year-old, he says, he knowingly twice traded cocaine for mobile phone parts, as a favor to his friend Norman Brown, but didn't think anything of it because, he says, he wasn't profiting from it. What he didn't know is that he was trading with undercover police.

"It wasn't mine," he says. "I ain't making no money off of it. The government made it seem like I was selling drugs. I never made a penny off of anything we did. I was naïve to the fact that you can get in trouble."

By October 1990, after a year at Pratt Junior College in Kansas, Curry was attending Prince George's Community College, trying to improve his grades so he could play Division I basketball. He hoped to play for Georgetown University, which he says had expressed interest in him while he was in high school. One day that month when his car wasn't working, he borrowed a car that belonged to Brown, a friend from his Mount Rainier, Maryland, neighborhood, near the D.C. line and down the street from the gang-infested area known as Woodridge. Brown had served a six-month sentence at a halfway house in 1987 after selling 75 grams of cocaine to undercover police and is now serving a life sentence after being convicted in April 1991 on six counts of cocaine distribution. On his way to visit a high-school teammate, Curry says, he noticed a car following him. He denies press reports that he realized it was the police.

Curry says he parked his car at a recreation center across the street from his former teammate's house and went in. While there he called Brown, who then told Curry that cocaine was in the car. When Brown asked him to retrieve the drugs from the car, Curry says he refused and left the car where it was while he walked away from the apartment. During my interview with him, Curry denied claims by police that he knew he was transporting the drugs that were found in the car he abandoned. Police later found Curry's college textbook on criminal justice and a notebook with his name on it inside the station wagon along with the cocaine.

After he was sentenced to prison, Curry felt he had disappointed his parents. His father for a time served as a high-school principal in Prince George's County and was a professor at Bowie State University and had worked hard to keep kids out of just this kind of trouble. But he was also angry – not with himself, he says, but with Brown. "I felt that he didn't come to my defense," says Curry, who went on to offer what Brown should have said to federal drug investigators: "This man ain't in no drug ring. He didn't really know what was going on." He mimicked Brown's likely thought process: "If I'm going down, then everybody's going down."

Curry missed the funeral for his high-school teammate Jay Bias because the day after Bias was killed, Curry was arrested as part of a large and lengthy investigation. He stayed out on bond for more than two years while prosecutors tried to convince him to turn state's evidence, but he refused. Following the mandatory minimum sentences established by the 1986 Anti-Drug Abuse Act passed months after Bias died, the judge handed down the nearly 20-year sentence.

Aside from a time spent in solitary confinement, Curry admits prison could have been a lot worse. He read books, earned college credits and played lots of basketball. Inmates gave him the nickname "Grandmama," a reference to former pro Larry Johnson's character in a commercial. Curry, his prison buddies felt, looked and played like Johnson. Curry says prayer and his faith in God helped him get

Derrick Curry is a drummer for the go-go band Endurance Unlimited. (courtesy of Derrick Curry)

through prison, along with an acquired awareness of his surroundings and his reputation as a good basketball player.

"I had a lot more good days than bad days," he says. "I was fortunate in a sense of my status going into prison, and my street status, and people knowing me and having that respect. People respect me as a person and basketball player. And in prison, as long as you're not gambling, owing people money, not a snitch, and not messing with the transvestites and gays, you were all right."

For a time he even shared a cell at a prison on Maryland's Eastern Shore with Brian Tribble, whom he had known since he was 12 and still considers a friend. After Len Bias died, Tribble spent time with Curry and Jay Bias, buying them basketball gear. "I think it was out of respect for my basketball," says Curry. He admits to hanging out with Tribble and Brown in the Woodridge neighborhood, but claims Tribble never brought drugs around him.

Arthur Curry knew he could not sit idly by with his son in prison, so he contacted Families Against Mandatory Minimums for help. FAMM, started in 1991 to fight the mandatory minimum sentences enacted within months of Len Bias's death and to advocate fair and proportionate sentencing laws, submitted an appeal to the commutation attorney for the U.S. Justice Department. On the morning of January 20, 2001, just hours before President Clinton left office he granted clemency to a group of prisoners that included Curry.

Curry was 31 when he got out of prison and still hoping to play professional basketball, but a bad knee curtailed his dream. With his athletic career stifled, Curry – who earned an associate's degree in business administration from Allegany Community College while he was incarcerated – chose to become a social worker soon after leaving prison. In the summer of 2011, Curry's income came from his work with the go-go band. In the past he has worked as a clinical and rehabilitation specialist and as the director of a youth mentoring program.

Curry says he has forgiven Brown and that his life imprisonment is unfair. "He didn't deserve it. He wasn't a big-time drug dealer. I'm living better now and got more stuff and money than he had when he was selling drugs."

Clearly enjoying his time as a go-go performer, Curry has been with the band for eight years despite never taking lessons. Instead, he says he learned the art by watching such legends as Milton "Go-Go Mickey" Freeman. He fine-tuned his skills in prison, where for a time he performed monthly with a band in the gymnasium. During breaks and after the show, Curry mingled comfortably with the patrons, including a few female admirers. It's no wonder Curry tries to perform a few nights a week. He may have lost his dream of playing professional basketball, but – unlike at least two of his childhood friends, Len and Jay Bias – he is very much alive.

BRIAN TRIBBLE

Brian Tribble moved through his spacious and comfortable Victorian home in northwest Washington, D.C. with the restless energy of a fired up athlete. His lean physique and his hard, chiseled face belied his age of 49.

During a two-hour meeting in April 2010, Tribble was a congenial and generally chatty host. He talked eagerly and matter-of-factly about how his life has evolved since Len Bias died, but when the conversation turned to his days with Bias he grew guarded, unsure if he wanted to cooperate with this book.

The topic of who provided the drugs to Bias on the night the basketball star died surfaced toward the end of our discussion. During a question-and-answer session on stage at the premiere of the documentary *Without Bias* in September 2009, he said, "Only two people know that. It's me and Lenny. And Len ain't here. I can easily say that Len brought the drugs into the room. That's crazy. It's never going to be known because he's not here. If the man is here to defend himself, fine; if not, it is what it is. We are trying to move on."

When asked the same question during our meeting, Tribble says more succinctly that "not everybody involved is here to defend themselves."

For the last quarter century, since partying with Bias, David Gregg and Terry Long on June 19, 1986, Tribble has been forced to defend himself against the prevailing theory that he provided the fatal cocaine. His raspy, spacy voice on the 911 call from the scene was played repeatedly on newscasts in the ensuing days, shattering Tribble's anonymity.

"I've done a lot of shit that was bad, but I became a drug dealer after [Bias died]," he says during a later phone conversation. "Before that I was just a light-skinned dude running around [the Maryland] campus."

Born on June 9, 1962, in Washington, D.C., Tribble was the youngest of four children. His mother, Loretta, was a homemaker and a religious woman. His father, Thomas, was a part-time jazz drummer who also owned a furniture and upholstery business. Tribble was considered bright and a hard worker who often offered to help neighbors with yard work and shoveling snow. A neighbor called him the "sweetheart of the neighborhood." Former teachers and school administrators described him as an above-average student who was sensitive, perceptive and prepared.

Tribble was part of an under-14 boys club team in the Woodridge section of D.C. the first time he remembers seeing Bias trying out for an under-12 team in the league, but they didn't meet. Tribble says he later played junior varsity basketball at H.D. Woodson High School but failed to make the varsity team at McKinley Tech High School in D.C, which he attended his junior and senior years.

Still, Tribble had hoped to play basketball at the University of Maryland when he entered the school in 1980 as a business administration major. Through people he knew at DeMatha High School, Tribble says, he became good friends with Maryland basketball star Adrian Branch, a DeMatha graduate who started at Maryland in 1981. He remembers playing one-on-one games against Branch in Cole Field House. "I could beat him full court because I could run him into the ground," he says proudly. "But I had no chance in a half court game."

In 1982, during his third year at Maryland, Tribble met Bias after recognizing him while walking on campus. They became close friends immediately. But while Bias would soon become a star, Tribble's goal was just to play for the school. He says he was one of eight picked to play on Maryland's junior varsity team during his junior or senior year, although Driesell says there was no junior varsity team at the time. Tribble adds that the team was unable to schedule any games. He continued to play pickup games on the Maryland campus, often against some members of the Maryland team, including Bias.

Maryland coach Lefty Driesell remembers meeting Tribble once in Cole Field House, under dubious circumstances. He thought Tribble was stealing a basketball that belonged to the team and asked Tribble if he had it in his gym bag. "He said 'no, I don't have it,' " says Driesell. "So I asked him to open the bag and there was a ball inside. I told him never to come around here again. I never saw him again."

Tribble denies he stole a ball.

In 1982, Tribble says, he was riding a scooter to American University to see if he could persuade the school's basketball coach—ironically, Gary Williams, who would later become Maryland's head coach— to let him try out for the team there. On the way, he collided with a car. He sued the driver for $1 million, claiming the accident ended his chance for a lucrative pro basketball career, and settled for $10,000. He used some of that money to buy a 1979 Mercedes-Benz 450SL.

Tribble stopped attending classes at Maryland in 1983 and moved into a $600 a month apartment a couple of miles north of College Park while reportedly operating a furniture refinishing business. Bias frequented the apartment and according to testimony by Terry Long at Tribble's trial in 1987 used cocaine there on at least one occasion. Tribble claims drugs were not "a big factor" for either of them. "He did not use drugs around me that much and I didn't do drugs that much," he says. "I knew he used it but it was infrequent."

When Bias died, Tribble's life fell into total disarray.

 He was indicted on four charges related to the death of Bias: possession of cocaine, possession with intent to distribute cocaine, distribution of cocaine and possession of PCP. Essentially, a grand jury accused Tribble of supplying the cocaine that killed Bias.

Tribble's attorney, Thomas Morrow, in a 2011 phone interview disputed claims that Tribble lived the life of a drug dealer. "He didn't have two nickels to rub together," says Morrow. "If he was a drug dealer, he was not a very good one. From the mid-1980s he lived hand-to-mouth. He was paying through the nose to keep the Mercedes. It was purely for image. Brian was not what people thought he was. Had he ever used drugs? The answer was pretty obvious. But he was not a drug dealer."

On June 4, 1987, Tribble was acquitted of all charges. After the trial, Morrow told him that he had a chance to turn his life around. The attorney remembers a sincere Tribble responding, "you've given me my life back and I'm not going to let you down." In a television interview following the trial, Tribble cautioned people against using cocaine, saying the drug "can put you through more pain than you can imagine."

On June 9, 1987, Tribble arranged for a quiet party to celebrate his 25th birthday. But word spread and a large crowd gathered. Tribble was surprised. The Bias trial had brought Tribble fame he didn't expect. "After that party, I figured I could make some money from what happened to me," he says.

Tribble made an arrangement with promoters at the East Side nightclub in Southwest D.C. to stage parties on Tuesday nights where patrons could meet him. Tribble received the full amount of the cover charge, which totaled up to $6000 each night. He also collected $1 for every picture taken in the club by a photographer he hired. "It was like my own little playground," he says of the weekly parties, which went on for about a year.

But notoriety from his role in the Bias case brought drug-dealing opportunities his way, and he took advantage of them. Law enforcement agents claim that dealers from all over the United States wanted to work with him. "People were willing to front him large quantities of cocaine and he could pay later," drug enforcement agent Veronica Baker told the *Washington Post* in 1990. "The Len Bias thing … made drug dealers have more respect for him and in his own mind, he was maybe accused wrongfully and he had beat it."

Tribble reflects on that time with regret. "How many ways can you describe how stupid I was to deal drugs?" he says. "It was a big mistake. It was all just pure greed."

Gradually, drug enforcement agencies compiled evidence. James Minor, a witness for the prosecution in a cocaine conspiracy trial against Rayful Edmond III, a prominent drug dealer in Washington, D.C., testified that Tribble was present at a District drug market area in 1988. In October 1989, DEA agents arrested two men driving Tribble's Mercedes-Benz during a cocaine sting operation in Alexandria, Virginia. Both men were convicted of possession with intent to distribute 15 kilograms of cocaine.

In late July 1990, federal agents arrested a Bahamian who carried four kilograms of cocaine on a flight from Miami to Dulles International Airport near Washington, D.C. The Bahamian told the agents that the drugs were intended for Tribble. He agreed to continue with the delivery.

On the night of Thursday, August 2, 1990, Tribble sat in his car in the parking lot of the Sheraton hotel in New Carrollton, Maryland. He was watching a drug transaction in another part of the parking lot when DEA agents moved in and arrested Daniel D. Thomas, whom Tribble was watching. Tribble sped away from the scene, but a federal agent soon rammed into Tribble's car. He fled on foot. Helicopters hovered overhead and dogs tracked scents for two hours searching for Tribble, but he got away.

A panicked Tribble called Morrow. "He was scared to death," Morrow says of the phone call. "He wanted to know what he should do. I said, 'you have to turn yourself in. You don't want to remain a fugitive.' He said 'I got away the first time, I think they want to just get me the second time.'"

Morrow, concerned that Tribble might get hurt, offered to negotiate a surrender. Just before noon on August 6, 1990, Tribble turned himself in to the U.S. Marshals Service in Baltimore. At Tribble's detention hearing, prosecutors claimed he was responsible for distributing between nine and twenty-two pounds of cocaine per month and engaged in a "consistent pattern" of drug trafficking. Further, a search of Tribble's Forestville, Maryland, home turned up paraphernalia for converting cocaine powder to crack. On August 8, Tribble was ordered held without bail and later pled guilty.

For more than three years while incarcerated, Tribble talked with authorities in drug investigations. Tribble denies he provided any information to investigators that implicated any other drug dealers. "I told them things that they already knew," he says. "It was as if the prosecutors were asking me questions to help me get a reduced sentence."

On October 15, 1993, Tribble was sentenced to 10 years and one month in prison and received credit for the time he had already served.

While incarcerated, Tribble earned a fitness certification and shortly after leaving prison, he landed a job as a trainer at a Bally's fitness center in northwest Washington, D.C. Tribble says he was fired after only about 30 days, but was never given a reason. "Maybe it was because I was Brian Tribble," he says, referring to his reputation as the person who killed Len Bias.

Tribble later found a job at a Washington Sports Club in Bethesda, where he says he worked tirelessly to build a respectable reputation. "I worked all day, seven days a week, for months, and I loved it," he says. He's now a fitness trainer with his own company, URFit2, training what he calls "high end" clients in their homes and at Fitness First in Bethesda. He boasts of perks that include free stays at clients' vacation homes in such places as Martha's Vineyard and Ventnor City in New Jersey, near Atlantic City.

At his home in April 2010, Tribble introduced me to his wife and the youngest of his three daughters, who range in age from 11 to 32. His two older daughters are from a relationship with a woman Tribble did not marry. We ended the discussion agreeing to talk later. Tribble needed to think about his involvement with the book. He did say that he thought about how to "monetize" his part of the Bias story and that he was considering writing something himself about Bias's death.

I spoke with Tribble on the phone several times in the late summer and early fall of 2011, mostly to confirm background information. During a call in August, he reiterated his interest in being paid for cooperating with this book and for a possible future book deal. "Money's the only reason I'm doing it," he says. "It's always about money, isn't it?"

During a phone call in late October, Tribble acknowledged that he was paid $30,000 to be part of the documentary *Without Bias*. During the call, he also discussed grander plans to embark on a speaking tour after publication of his book to talk about the lessons he's learned from his part in the Bias death. "I want to teach people that choices have consequences," he says. "I hope that somebody doesn't make the choices I've made. I know I'm at an age where I feel like, hopefully, I can help somebody."

LONISE AND JAMES BIAS

So many times we're ready to throw in the towel. Life's too hard, I can't make it, I can't go on. But I stand here as a witness today, understanding that what my family went through was not for us. It was to stand up in such a time as this to let people know that you can make it. The best is yet to come.

–*Lonise Bias speaking on January 14, 2011 in Williamsport, Pennsylvania.*

For the past 25 years, many have marveled as Lonise Bias has turned personal grief into a catalyst for change, transforming herself from a middle-class Christian mom into a national icon so that others can benefit from her unfathomable loss. Within weeks of the famous death of her eldest son, Len, she began speaking out against drug use, and the murder a few years later of Jay only fueled her mission. Even a quarter century later, Lonise Bias still preaches passionately to all who will listen, promoting the power to overcome even to those who don't remember or think they don't care.

Of the several hundred who attended the speech at the Pennsylvania College of Technology, most were students not yet born when Len Bias died. The first three who entered the ACC Auditorium on the compact campus to hear Bias deliver her "Living Beyond the Dream: A Message of Hope for Families, Communities and the Nation" speech on Martin Luther King, Jr.'s birthday admitted they were there only because a teacher required it. When asked if they knew who Len Bias was, all three said no. Even for a story as huge as the death of Len Bias, 25 years is a long time.

Lonise Bias walked into the auditorium about a half hour before she was scheduled to begin her presentation and appeared uneasy as the crowd slowly ambled in. She sat alone and quiet for about a half hour in the front row facing the stage in the seat farthest on the right, a seemingly reluctant or fatigued warrior. Any trepidation Bias may have felt appeared to vanish as she began to speak. Anticipating that most in the crowd needed a tutorial about her story, she started her speech with a video recapping her journey from inconspicuous mother to in-demand public speaker following the death of Len.

In the video, ESPN basketball analyst Dick Vitale said Len's game was even better suited for the quicker play of the NBA, with its transition game and the 24-second clock, than for college basketball. "He would have been a star," he said.

- - - - - - - - - -

Lonise Bias gave birth to Len, her first child, on November 18, 1963, in Washington, D.C. The Bias family moved to Columbia Park in 1975. John Ware, a retired pharmacist who grew up in Washington, D.C., and played two years of college football, has lived in the house across the street since 1970, and described Columbia Park as a quiet, Christian neighborhood where people rarely walked up and down the streets. "You didn't have people bothering you," he says. "I think they were comfortable while they were here."

Ware says that his wife, Ada, and three children were good friends with the Bias family and that his oldest son, Byron, was close in age to Len; his younger son, Steven, was the same age as Jay; and his daughter, Tanya, was the same age as Michelle, the only Bias daughter. "We always waved to each other, spoke and chatted when we could," he says of the two families.

Ware says that although they visited each other's houses only a handful of times, the Biases were so fond of his family that they invited them to attend the wedding of Eric, the youngest of the Bias sons, whom they called "The Fridge." Len and Jay Bias played basketball in Ware's backyard, shooting at a basket nailed to a tree. In Ware's eyes, Len showed a highly competitive spirit that stood out from that of the other boys.

"Kids that age playing basketball, they throw it up, maybe it goes in, maybe it does not," says Ware. "[Len] wanted the ball to go in every time he shot the ball. I knew then that he was going to be a basketball player."

Ware also recalls glaring differences between the brothers. Len, he says, was a respectful young man who would always speak to Ware and his wife. He never made that connection with Jay who, he says, was less affable, less approachable than Len. "He was off with his boys," says Ware.

Although Lonise Bias has become the more public parent, James Bias also had a strong role in the family, with the physical presence and mindset to influence his sons in athletics. He played basketball and lifted weights recreationally, and, while serving in the U.S. military, he was known to run up to 10 miles a day. Brian Waller, Len's good friend and neighbor who spent many days at the Bias home, remembers James as a man dedicated to the well-being of his family. "James Bias got up and went to work," Waller says. "He made sure things were as they should be in his household. I don't know why that wasn't enough for Leonard in the end to be the man his father was. It's sort of a mystery."

Ware called James Bias a good disciplinarian and someone who showed a lot of interest in his children, a "real family man," he says. "They spent a lot of time with their kids."

Johnnie Walker, a mentor for both Len Bias and Brian Waller and who was close the Bias family, remembers a solid fondness between Len and his father and says that one reason Len decided to play basketball at Maryland was to stay close to his family. "He had a great respect for his father," says Walker.

James rarely needed to solidify his status as the man of the house, but Waller remembers a rare physically hostile moment between father and son when Len was a 10th grader. Waller and Len were in the Bias driveway when Len "said something smart to his father," says Waller, who then mimicked James sending a hard punch to Len's chest. "He couldn't catch his breath. He let the air out of his chest. From that day forward, I never saw him act out to his father. I never saw him do that to his father again."

The Bias family didn't dote on Len over his basketball success and didn't talk about basketball unless Len wanted to. Most of the time, Len tried to be a fun older brother to his two younger brothers. "He came here [the basement] and rassled all over the place [with Jay and Eric]," said James in a 1987 *Washington Post* story. "On the sofa. Chasin' around the house. He didn't seem the same person on the basketball court: forceful, aggressive, trying to force his will on others."

For Father's Day in 1986, two days before the NBA draft, Len gave his father a barbecue grill. The day was full of fun, crazy activity. Lonise Bias said in the *Washington Post* story they were "having a ball." When Len came home from Boston the night before he died, according to print and broadcast reports, he greeted his jubilant family with hugs. "I did it, I did it," he said. Michelle remembers her excited brother thanking their dad for everything.

Len began handing out Reebok shoes to the family from a big box. "Frosty," as Len Bias was nicknamed, had turned into a summertime Santa Claus. Sitting in a chair, he held his dog and told him "We goin' to Boston, we goin' to Boston, me an' you, we goin' to Boston," Michelle said in *Without Bias*. He tried to wait for his mom to return home before he went out to visit friends in College Park, but grew impatient and departed. Lonise's feelings of unease began months before Len died, in the form of premonitions that foretold a mysterious death in her family, as she explained in *Without Bias*. As she watched her son during the NBA draft broadcast, her anxiety grew stronger. Something held her back from screaming for joy and reveling in the moment.

When the phone rang at 6:35 a.m. on June 19, Lonise remembers awakening to bright sunlight as her son's Maryland teammate, Keith Gatlin, told her that Len had had a seizure and was on his way to the hospital. Here's how James Bias remembered the call, as he stated in *Without Bias*. "Who is it? And she said 'What? What are you saying?' And so, I'm saying 'What is it, who is it? Who's calling?' And she said, 'It's Keith, he said that Frosty' – we called him Frosty – 'Frosty had a seizure.' And I'm saying, 'A seizure? What is he talking about? What do you mean, what kind of seizure?

Where is he?' And she said 'They said he's at the hospital.' "

Michelle, too, woke up to a ringing phone. Her aunt was screaming that Frosty was dead. Michelle sat on her parents' bed and started screaming. When Eric awoke, Michelle told him that people were saying that "something must be wrong, [that] Frosty is dead," she said in *Without Bias*.

En route to the hospital, Lonise asked God to save her son, but God had already made up his mind, telling her Len was gone, that "this is done." When she arrived at the hospital, she calmly asked a nurse if Len had died. The nurse said no, that he was hooked up to machines that were keeping him alive. She asked if he was breathing on his own and the nurse replied, "We're breathing for him." Lonise said that he was gone, but the nurse insisted he was still alive. A short time later, Lonise Bias drew close to her lifeless son as he lay on a bed. She rubbed his head and his face, then bent over and kissed him goodbye.

As the traumatic day evolved and word spread about Len's death, chaos engulfed the Bias family. Television cameras and production trucks lined up in front of the Bias home on Columbia Avenue, and they would remain there for weeks. Cars flooded the streets. Flocks of people cried. Hordes of media overtook the neighborhood, trying to capture the rapidly evolving emotions.

But the worst had not yet arrived for the grieving mother. "The hardest thing for me, even harder than looking at Len's body, was before they took him to the church for viewing, when the stretch [limo] pulled up in front of our home," she said in the *Washington Post*. "That super stretch. That tore me up."

July 3, 1986

Dear Mr. and Mrs. Bias:

Nancy and I understand, as parents, the terrible void which Len's death has left. While there are no words which can ease the pain of this loss, our thoughts and heartfelt condolences are with you. Len is now in Our Lord's safekeeping, and we pray that this knowledge will be a source of consolation.

With our deep sympathy,

Sincerely,

RONALD REAGAN

President Reagan sent condolences to the Bias family after Len's death. (*Ronald Reagan Library*)

Michael Jordan was the first person to send flowers. They were peonies. Another flower arrangement came from Larry Bird. The Biases received a letter from President Ronald Reagan and heads of state. But condolences, even high-powered ones, can only go so far. About a year later, she said in the *Washington Post*, "There are times, when I see his picture in the living room, that I shake my head and say: 'Where is Leonard? What happened?' It seems as though everything has moved so fast."

In the months immediately after Len died, James acted like any father would, with a mix of grief, anger, confusion and resolve. During a memorial service for Len a few days after he died, James spotted Len's two most prominent coaches, Bob Wagner and Lefty Driesell, and pointedly told both of them that they killed his son.

Almost a year later, he sat in a red director's chair Len had received at the 1985 Maryland basketball dinner, near a wall filled with Len's trophies and mementos in the Bias house. "I think there's going to be some things revealed that'll be shocking to a whole bunch of people," he said then in the *Washington Post*. "Eventually. It's going to be revealed. It'll get out. It has to. And when they do get out, lots of eyebrows will be raised and people will say: 'Why? How did this come about?' I don't know if the real Len Bias story will ever be revealed. … Nobody has come forth and said: 'I've seen the drugs Len Bias used.' Cocaine or anything else. Nobody."

But Tribble had already told Walker, two days after Bias died, that he had used cocaine with Len a few months earlier. And within weeks of James Bias's words, two of Len's former teammates, David Gregg and Terry Long, would provide evidence under oath that Bias had been a recreational cocaine user. Long and Gregg admitted during testimony in Brian Tribble's trial that they had both used cocaine repeatedly with Len.

"The biggest problem for me was looking at Leonard's possessions, all piled up in the bedroom," James Bias said in the same interview. "All of his stuff brought from the university. Every time I go in there, I can see his things. His own personal effects. Looking at basketball, something that's got nothing to do [in a father-son way] with Len, doesn't bother me one bit. Looking at his picture; looking at his personal things. That's the tough part of it. They say time heals all wounds. And I think in this case, possibly, it will be the same. But you never outlive it, because there's always these question marks. What really happened to Len Bias?"

What happened to his second son, Jay, some 54 months after Len died, is not in doubt.

At a press conference on his front lawn on December 6, 1990, two days after Jerry Tyler shot Jay to death, James Bias promised to campaign against gun violence. He said that any man who kills should also be killed. "I don't care if you got upset and pulled a gun …" he said. "I got a headache, I'm not shooting anybody." He also said that anyone who sells guns is as much a murderer as the person who pulled the trigger because "they are providing the instrument of death."

The next day, just hours before he would attend Jay's funeral, James testified before a panel on Capitol Hill organized by the Educational Fund to Stop Gun Violence. Escorted by activist Jesse Jackson, he told the panel that he couldn't bring his son back but that he can influence the court system, and that's what he had to do. The pair promised to form a coalition to fight for gun control and educate youths on alternatives to violence. But Joshua Horwitz, the executive director of the Educational Fund to Stop Gun Violence who attended the panel, claims Jackson never formed a gun-specific group and could not recall James Bias helping develop a national campaign against gun violence.

- - - - - - - - - -

On June 18, 1987, the Bias family, representing Len's estate, filed a $27 million lawsuit alleging fraud and negligence by Lee Fentress, Bias's agent, and Advantage International, the company that represented Bias in negotiations with the Boston Celtics and Reebok. The Biases' attorney, Wayne Curry, claimed that filing the lawsuit so close to the anniversary of Len's death was pure coincidence and blamed the delay in part on a long criminal investigation and trial of Brian Tribble on drug charges related to Len's death.

The lawsuit claimed that poor management of Bias's account by Fentress and Advantage prevented the family from receiving a potential life-insurance payment. The Bias family believed that Advantage had secured a $1 million policy on Bias, saying that Fentress on separate occasions in April 1986 told James and Lonise Bias that it existed. The Biases claimed in the lawsuit that they did not buy life insurance because Fentress had already purchased it. Fentress denied recommending life insurance because it was against company policy to purchase life insurance for its unmarried athletic clients as young as Bias because it was considered a poor investment.

The suit, which asked for $2.6 million from Reebok, also claimed that Paul Fireman, the president of Reebok International at the time, told James and Len Bias that an agreement had been made between Reebok and Len Bias. The company denied the existence of a contract and Joanne Borzakian Ouellette, who worked for Reebok at the time, confirmed in 2010 that no contract existed.

The suit claimed that Bias was to be paid $325,000 per year for five years by Reebok, with the first payment of $162,500 due on June 18, 1986. The suit also claimed that Fentress told James and Len Bias that an agreement with Reebok had been made. The lawsuit also sought $1 million in damages from Fidelity Security Insurance Co. for an alleged breach of contract. In April 1985 the Biases purchased a $1 million disability insurance policy with Fidelity that included an accidental rider.

First a district court and then an appeals court threw out the lawsuit. The lower courts determined that Fentress and Advantage were not liable for failing to get life insurance because as a cocaine user Bias was "uninsurable." The district court said that no insurer in 1986 would have issued such a "jumbo" policy to a cocaine user unless he lied about his use of drugs – which would have made the policy void. An appeals court upheld that ruling.

The lower courts also denied a claim by the Biases that the contract between Reebok and Bias was signed on June 18, saying that it could not have been signed because it would have to have been approved by the company's legal department. The Biases took their case to the U.S. Supreme Court. On November 5, 1990, it refused to hear the Bias appeal. A month later, Jay Bias was killed.

- - - - - - - - - -

When Len died, I prayed to God. I did not want to live. Four years later, Jay died. I prayed to God again and guess what? Here I am alive and well today. I could not see anything but darkness when Len died. And then when Jay died – the same hospital the same bad news all over again – I didn't think I could make it. And my two remaining children; I can remember going into my bedroom when Jay died and I called them and I screamed and I cried and told God how unfair it was for me to have to carry this burden and what was going to happen to my two remaining children, they buried two brothers. How are they going to make it?

—Lonise Bias speaking on January 14, 2011 in Williamsport, Pennsylvania

Lonise Bias gave her first speech after Len's death on July 26, 1986, at a church in Hillcrest

Heights, Maryland, just southeast of Washington, D.C., and about 10 miles from the Bias home in Columbia Park. A young female friend of Len's invited her to speak after she appeared on The 700 Club, a television show syndicated nationally on the Christian Broadcasting Network. The show's staff had been impressed with Bias's eulogy at Len's memorial service.

Before appearing on The 700 Club, Bias's speaking background had been limited to grade-school ceremonies and church talks. But she quickly adjusted to her new role as a motivational speaker, giving hundreds of speeches within the first year of Len's death to young people, college students and business groups.

On December 3, 1986, Bias returned to the University of Maryland campus for the first time since the death of Len to speak in front of some 150 students about drug use and abuse. Bob Wade was among those in the audience. "God had to take something special to save a generation," she said that day. "Somebody has got to get out and say something. I believe God is using me. I'm basically a sower of seeds. I tell people what is right and what is wrong. Maybe some will get the message."

By the December 3 event in College Park, Bias had appeared at 60 speaking engagements. The work was so steady that she decided to leave her job as an assistant manager in the customer-service department of the National Bank of Washington, although a *Washington Post* report about her speech said she received only payment for airfare for her speaking engagements and that a friend helped set her schedule. After the College Park speech, Bias told a reporter that after a speech in Connecticut an eighth-grade girl folded a small piece of paper into her hand that read, "I have used drugs, and no one knows but you. I will never use them again after hearing you."

During one stretch leading up to the first anniversary of Len's death, Lonise spoke on a Friday at the Mayflower Hotel in Washington, D.C., at a seminar sponsored by the Psychiatric Institute Foundation called "Cocaine: New Strategies in Treatment and Prevention" and at a church the same day. On Saturday she appeared in Baltimore and Camp Springs, Maryland. On Sunday and Monday she was in Missouri, on Wednesday and Thursday in Connecticut. Two days later, she made an appearance in Raleigh, North Carolina.

"I never write anything on paper," she said in a 1987 *Washington Post* story. "It all comes from the heart. I never know what I'll say till I get there."

Since becoming a motivational speaker and consultant, Bias has accumulated a client list that includes the White House Office of National Drug Control Policy as well as the Drug Enforcement Agency, the Department of State, and the U.S. Office of Personnel Management, according to the website lonisebias.org. She has spoken to military groups, students of all ages, corporate groups, faith-based groups and the National Basketball Association. Bias, who received an honorary Doctor of Education degree from Anna Maria College in Massachusetts in May 1990 and prefers to use the honorific, has been listed with at least a half dozen speakers groups, including the American Entertainment International Speakers Bureau and Speakers.com. AEI hires her for a few events per year at a fee that does not exceed $10,000 to speak to groups that include schools, churches and teachers, colleges and Fortune 500 companies. Speakers.com promotes Bias's fee as ranging from $5,000 to $10,000.

Mark Castel, the president of AEI, says he has been setting up speeches with Bias for some 20 years and raves about her as a client. "As an agent, I'm looking for people who are going to say she's a great speaker, and that's what you're looking for," he says "We've never gotten less than an excellent rating from her. You have people on the stage who are phony baloney. She's not like that. She's very gracious about everything in this business. When we bring an event to someone, I like to hear one word, and she always says, 'Yes. I'll do it.' " Castel says that Bias has also donated her time to speak.

Bias has also listed her services on two separate websites that promote her personal business. On bspeaks.com, Bias listed nine events in 2010 on her upcoming-events calendar. She also promotes her certification as a teen and family and life coach. Speeches have taken place at a high-school graduation ceremony in Upper Marlboro, Maryland, a Methodist church in Temple Hills, Maryland, and Youth Opportunities Upheld, a child-welfare and behavioral-health organization in Worcester, Massachusetts. Lonisebias.org promotes The Abundant Life Resources A More Excellent Way, LLC, which listed nine events at which Bias was scheduled to speak in 2009. The group stresses the well-being of youth, family, community and the workplace and offers help organizing workshops and retreats, among other services.

In McHenry, Illinois, on April 19, 2011, Bias was the keynote speaker at the Town Against Tragedy held at McHenry High School, which focused on the theme of tragedy and loss among young people in McHenry. Some 1,700 people packed the school's auditorium to hear Bias repeat her mantra that young people are "reachable, teachable, lovable and savable." Bias made appearances at two middle schools earlier that day to help promote the event at the high school. She was paid $7,000 for all three appearances, which included her travel expenses. Terry Fitzgibbons, assistant principal at McHenry High School, says Bias was well worth the investment. "She brought a unique and energetic style," he says. "She was very approachable by young people and parents. It was truly a once-in-a-lifetime opportunity to meet her."

The video presented at the beginning of her speech in Williamsport in early 2011 included a still image of a pensive Len Bias looking into the distance, with the words "Our kids are reachable, teachable, loveable and savable" written to the left. It ended with another still frame, this one of a heavy mass of clouds filtering the sun in the sky with the words "the best is yet to come."

After the video ended, awkward silence filled the room. The audience seemed confused about how to react. Bias knew what to do to elicit a response. "Can I get some love?" she said, prompting a flurry of appreciative applause. Within minutes, Bias had commanded the attention of the crowd, made up mostly of college students in their late teens and early 20s. She told them that she "loved each and every one" of them. "God took the love I had for my sons Len and Jay and multiplied it for mankind. I understand here today that my family and I drank from the bitter cup for you to bring words of encouragement and wisdom. I love you all."

"Learn to feel good in your skin," she later preached, urging her listeners to ignore the many messages that they shouldn't be satisfied with who they are. "Know that you're spiritually made. Know that you're beautiful, you are the gift. Get to know yourself."

Bias says she "cares absolutely nothing about what anyone in here thinks about me today. We are so jacked up and twisted about what people think about us. When you can appreciate yourself, love yourself, know that you are not perfect, know that you don't have it all together."

Halfway through the speech, which lasted about three-quarters of an hour, most in attendance had looked up from their phones, stopped their texting and seemed engaged, infused with Bias's pastor-like passion. During one high-energy passage, Bias recounted how she, pregnant with her only daughter, was riding the bus home from work in 1968 after King's assassination, looking out the windows to see chaos and burning buildings as race riots consumed Washington, D.C, and thought the world was coming to an end.

"He spoke about everybody being one," she said, referring to Dr. King. "He was a blessed seed that went down into the earth to bring forth life, and life has come forth with the unique understanding that there is no progress or change without struggle. He was the beautiful, precious sacrifice that went down to bring forth life. And the best is still yet to come."

The final words of Lonise Bias's speech asked for introspection: "Where are you going? How are you going to build? If I die today or tomorrow will I have left a legacy? How will people remember you? How? How?"

After the speech, Bias greeted about two dozen listeners who waited in line to speak with her, thanking them for attending. One young man told her that he needed to hear her speech because he was going through "something." The young man's problems, which he explained to her, seemed trivial at best compared to what Bias has endured, but she showed compassion for his dilemma. "Man up, man up," Bias said with preachy enthusiasm. The young man looked into a video camera recording the interaction and says, "I need to man up and stop crying. She made me feel strong, though. I'm inspired."

A group of young women approached Bias and repeatedly thanked her for the speech.

"Did you get anything out of it?" Bias asked the group. "Yes, yes," one woman said eagerly. After Bias signed a few autographs, William Astore approached and started talking about his passion for the Boston Celtics. Astore, a professor of history at Pennsylvania College of Technology who grew up a Celtics fan in Brockton, Massachusetts, is about the age Len would have been had he lived. Astore told Bias that he wished her son could have done something great for the team, and how sad he was when Len died. "I never stopped to think what his family was going through," he says, compassion in his voice. "And I never thought I would meet Len's mother."

In a conversation later, Astore told me, "At that time, cocaine use was glamorous, part of the high life, the good life," he says of 1986. "His death brought home to me, 'no, it's not that way at all.' [Dying] could have happened to me."

Astore required the 20 students in his class on the Holocaust to attend the Bias speech, hoping that her speech would show them an example of someone who had turned her back on hate. "I teach a very grim, depressing, tragic subject," he says. "One of the reasons the Germans and Hitler killed the Jews was hatred and a lack of acceptance. Lonise's message of getting beyond hate, not succumbing to it, [even] self-hatred, and her experience trying to get over what happened to her and losing her son, I wanted our students to realize that along with a message of tragedy there is a message of hope. The message was inspiring, and a correction to all the notions out there that tend to make you feel bad about yourself."

During the speech, Bias proudly stated that both of her surviving children, Michelle and Eric, are married and have provided five beautiful grandchildren. But it was clear she still maintains a relationship with Len that cannot compare to any of her children.

After the auditorium cleared, a photographer asked Bias to pose in front of a freeze frame from the NBC feature that was projected at the beginning of her speech. She stood on the stage silhouetted in darkness and facing the image that showed Len at the NBA draft, wearing the iconic white-pin-striped suit that symbolized his dapper style and now represents a tragedy frozen in time. A headshot of his younger brother, Jay, head turned slightly to the left, looks in Len's direction from behind him. Bias spread her arms wide toward the image, as if asking her sons for inspiration and strength to help her maintain a mission of spreading her message of acceptance, perseverance and strength amid adversity.

Chapter 6
The Celtics

The revelers at the Reebok reception for Celtics stars Danny Ainge and Dennis Johnson in the early evening on June 18, 1986 had good reason to relish the recent fortnight. Ten days earlier, the two honorees had helped the Boston Celtics win their third NBA title in six seasons, and 16th overall. Then, just the day before, the team had made Len Bias its top pick and the second overall in the NBA draft, promising more to cheer about for years to come.

Ainge and Johnson were two of the marquee athletes on Reebok's pro basketball sponsorship roster, and Reebok, based just outside of Boston, wanted to honor the title they helped Boston win and to show its appreciation for their work promoting the Reebok brand. Joanne Borzakian, at the time an associate marketing manager for Reebok's basketball division, helped manage the accounts for the pair and attended the party. A recent graduate of Bentley College in Waltham, just west of Boston, Borzakian had been working in what she called her dream job for about a year. Her family had held Celtics season tickets since 1974, and she went to games with her father, Bob; her mother, Gladys; and her brother, Robert.

In the late morning of June 18, Borzakian met Bias at Logan Airport in Boston to escort the player to Reebok's headquarters in nearby Avon after his short flight from New York. Beginning at about noon, Bias met with Borzakian and other members of the Reebok staff along with his father, James, and his agent, Lee Fentress of Advantage International, who had years earlier helped negotiate a Reebok sponsorship deal for Bias's college coach. They discussed ways for Bias to become part of their basketball sponsorship program, in which players would make personal appearances in the Boston community to promote the burgeoning basketball shoe brand.

"We wanted to sign a new young talent, and he was our number-one choice at the time," says Borzakian Ouellette, who was married after Bias died. "We wanted him to meet the powers that be and see if it was a good fit. We didn't just sign an athlete to attach a name to a shoe. Our athletes had done 120 appearances a year collectively."

Bias had planned to return home to Landover immediately after the meetings at Reebok headquarters, but as the day wound down Borzakian's boss at Reebok suggested she ask Bias if he wanted to attend the reception for Ainge and Johnson at the Royal Sonesta Hotel in Cambridge. She presented the idea to Bias, who agreed, but only after Borzakian promised to make sure he would get home that night.

Borzakian Ouellette worked for 16 years at Reebok, advancing to the position of global marketing director for NBA and NCAA basketball. During that time, she worked with such marquee players as Shaquille O'Neal and Dominique Wilkins. She remembers Bias as quiet and polite throughout the time they spent together. "This was not Shaquille O'Neal," she says. "O'Neal had a presence, a personality, and was lots of fun." Bias, she says, was not especially gregarious at the reception, but "neither was he looking at his watch to get out of there."

Some 70 people, mostly Boston-area sports retailers, attended the reception for Ainge and Johnson, and they responded with a strong ovation as the veterans entered the room. When Bias walked in, the crowd grew even more excited, says Borzakian Ouellette.

"Everybody was ooohing and aaahing, saying 'This is great!'"

Ainge, Johnson and Bias posed for pictures, and Reebok president Paul Fireman introduced Bias as the newest member of their family. Borzakian Ouellette remembers that Bias was the quietest of the three while posing for pictures and interacting with guests. "When it was time for him to leave, I told him a limousine would take him to the airport. He said, 'I'm glad to be going home. I can't wait to see my mother.'"

Bias flew back to the Washington, D.C., area about 9:30 p.m. Within 12 hours, he would be dead. It would be more than two decades before the Celtics would replicate the 10 days of euphoria they felt from the day they won the NBA title on June 8 until that reception on June 18.

"The elation and feeling of accomplishment was the consequence of a long-term plan," says Jan Volk, the Celtics general manager from 1984 to 1997. "The plan was to make ourselves as good as we could be. This was a loss that couldn't be made up by simply working harder. It was a void that could not be filled in a normal course of time."

Ainge, now the Celtics president of basketball operations but then still a player, got a sense of Bias's potential by playing with him during the summer of 1985 at a camp in Marshfield, 30 miles southeast of Boston. "He was perfect for us," Ainge said in the *Boston Globe* in 2003, looking back on what would have been Bias's 40th birthday. "I was never so excited. With Kevin McHale, Robert [Parish], and Larry [Bird], he would give us the perfect rotation. I looked at it as a great fit for him and the franchise."

It was after his sophomore year at Maryland, when he attended the Red Auerbach Basketball School camp, that the Celtics embraced the concept of Bias joining the team. Auerbach, the Celtics president, began the camps in 1960 for players at the junior-high-school level. College and Celtics players worked as counselors, with the understanding that they would scrimmage twice a day. Volk described the games as "captain's practices," where the players with the most authority on the Celtics would manage the games.

Some of the Celtics top players, including Bird, attended the camps that Bias attended; in the past, Hall of Famers such as John Havlicek and Bill Russell had also showcased their skills. Brian Waller, Bias's childhood friend, remembers Bias boasting after his first camp about how he "had his way" when matched up against Cedric Maxwell, a seven-year NBA veteran and the 1981 NBA Finals most valuable player, during a game on the first day. At the start of a game the next day, Waller says, Bias took note that no one wanted to guard him: When teammates reminded Maxwell that he had guarded Bias the day before, he responded, "Someone else guard him tonight."

Volk, who was part of the Celtics management team that drafted Bias, saw him play for the first time at the camps. "I was very impressed with his ability to get his own shot and shoot effectively with range," says Volk. "You could see that he belonged there with those pros. He was flat-out mean on the floor. Larry played against him and was ecstatic about him playing in Boston."

Waller claims that when Bias left the camp after his sophomore season, Auerbach invited him into his office to tell him that he would do everything possible to make him a Celtic. After the Celtics won the No. 2 pick in the lottery in May, 1986, Bias became their prime target. The Celtics had obtained the lottery selection after trading Gerald Henderson, a starter from the 1981 Celtics NBA title team, to the Seattle Supersonics in 1984 for its first pick in the 1986 draft. Media reports predicted that the Philadelphia 76ers would make North Carolina center Brad Daugherty the top pick in the draft, with the Celtics picking Bias second unless they decided to select a center and grab either Chris Washburn of N. C. State or William Bedford of Memphis State.

The Celtics scouting report put Bias in a rare category, concluding that he was a bigger Michael Jordan with a better outside shot, although he didn't drive to the basket quite as well while dribbling. Shortly before the draft, Bias tried to ease his anxieties about his NBA destination with a direct plea to Volk when the Celtics executive dropped him off at the airport to head back home after a series of interviews with the team. "He said goodbye and then looked me straight in the eye and said 'Please draft me,' " says Volk, who tried to be vaguely reassuring without giving any guarantees because he knew anything could happen at the last minute. Still, he says, "I knew if we had the first pick, he's who we would have taken."

As the team did with all its prospective draftees, the Celtics conducted a background check on Bias. It revealed no concerns, but he might still have been their top pick even if the team had discovered he had drugs. "There were absolutely no red flags; everything came up good," says Volk.

"There was no indication that he was even a recreational drug user. And at that point in time, recreational drug use was an issue, but it was not terribly troublesome. If we had found that there was recreational use, we would have explored it more. Had we been aware of recreational drug use, it might not have made any difference because of how that was factored in the equation at that time."

The Celtics were not the only group to discuss drug use with Bias. In what was standard procedure for their clients entering the NBA, Jeff Austin, an assistant to Fentress, met with Bias about two weeks before the draft to discuss NBA drug rules. "He was very dismissive, [insisting] that he did not use drugs," says Austin, now the head of basketball operations for Octagon, a sports marketing and management firm. "I believed him. I had no reason not to believe him. I didn't question him at all."

By draft day on June 17, the Celtics and most others who knew Bias felt little if any concern that drugs were a problem for the young player. But that didn't mean there were no lingering worries. When Volk left his office the day before the draft, he felt confident that Philadelphia would pick Daugherty and the Celtics would select Bias. It helped the Celtics that the 76ers had some concerns about Bias. Pat Williams, who was the 76ers' general manager at the time, remembers how his chief scout, Jack McMahon, felt uncomfortable about Bias and never brought him to Philadelphia for pre-draft interviews.

"He said 'There's something about Len that bothers me,' " says Williams, the Orlando Magic founder and senior vice president. "He had scouted him in the ACC, came back, and said 'There's no need to bring him in, we're not going to consider him.' I thought many times about that quote from Jack." McMahon died in late 1989.

But the night before the draft, Philadelphia traded its top pick to Cleveland in exchange for forward Roy Hinson, creating what Volk called a "night of considerable uncertainty." And Bias clearly was a target of many teams: Washington Bullets general manager Bob Ferry said Bias was the only player in the draft "who excited all of us." But Volk felt reassured about picking Bias after Cleveland general manager Harry Weltman told him the morning of the draft that the Cavaliers were interested in picking Daugherty.

Bias wasn't sure that his dream to become a Celtic would finally come true until after Cleveland made Daugherty the first pick and a Celtics representative asked him as he sat behind Boston's table, "Are you packed for Boston?" After NBA Commissioner David Stern announced Bias as Boston's pick, the crowd roared. The newest Celtic uncoiled his long, lean frame from his arena seat, walking slowly as he approached the stage, smiling. Someone handed him a Celtics cap. Cameras flashed as he shook Stern's hand. A couple of minutes later, during his first comments in a television interview, Bias was asked by former NBA star Rick Barry why he wanted to play for the Celtics.

"They're a good team and they got, uh, good, uh, supporting players," he said sheepishly, stammering a bit as he toyed with the Celtics cap. "I can go up there and sit on the bench and whether I go in and play or not, and I learn a lot from, ah, the players there or learn a lot from playing myself."

Barry asked him if he could accept the role of being a benchwarmer for a while. Bias chuckled and said, "I guess I'm gonna have to." Asked where he needed to improve, Bias said, "Well, I think I need to improve more on my ball-handling and my all-around play."

When Barry made some closing comments at the end of the interview, Bias smiled before peering to the side and biting his lip. Later, he said the first thing he wanted to buy was a Mercedes-Benz automobile. As for the Celtics, they felt they already had their prize. "He's going to be a star some-day, no question about it," Auerbach said in an interview from Boston. "He gives us a lot of support. He can play some guard, he can play some forward, he can play a power forward, a quick forward. He is the best athlete, in my opinion, in the whole draft, and he's going to really help this ball club. … He'll get his playing time. … We've had guys sit around for a while. Except in this particular case, he's gonna play. In fact, he's ready to play now. Larry Bird said if we drafted this kid, he'd even come to rookie camp. He's very high on the kid. He's the guy we wanted, and we got him."

Bias seemed to accept a reserve role as a Celtics rookie. "I'm ready to take the role of a learner now," he said in the *Boston Globe* the day of the draft. "I can learn from great players here."

And the Celtics offered an array of talent who could have served as tested tutors. Bird, entering his eighth season, was a seven-time All-Star forward, a three-time league MVP and the MVP of the 1984 and 1986 NBA finals. Center Bill Walton, a league MVP in 1978, was entering his 10th – and what would be his final – NBA season. Forward McHale, a two-time All-Star and Sixth Man of the Year award-winner, was entering his seventh NBA season. Robert Parish, a six-time All-Star, was entering his 11th season. Auerbach coached Boston's nine NBA championship teams in the 1950s and 1960s. All are members of the Naismith Memorial Basketball Hall of Fame.

At Maryland, Bias had developed into a dangerous offensive weapon from the perimeter facing the basket, especially from the corners, and a lethal scoring weapon around the basket. Assignments to guard such top college players as Ralph Sampson, Jordan and Clyde Drexler sharpened his defensive skills. His leaping ability and overall athleticism helped create an area of intimidation near the basket.

Now, he was the ideal complement to an aging frontcourt. At 28, McHale was the youngest, while the most senior was Walton at 33. With Bias, the Celtics appeared primed to begin another period of domination. It seemed unimaginable that they could repeat their feat of eight consecutive NBA titles from 1959 to 1967, but with Bias serving a relief role for the veteran frontcourt players, at least a couple more NBA titles in the '80s seemed realistic. Volk saw Bias as a main component in extending the team's generational success. "We had a mature team that had been very successful for five or six years, which in the NBA is a generation," says Volk. "Most teams turn over in five years. We were looking to try to transition that core group into the next generation of successful Celtics teams."

After the draft, Bias boarded a shuttle flight to Boston to begin negotiations with the Celtics and Reebok. Media reports the next day claimed that Bias had agreed to sign a contract with Reebok, one stating it was a $1.6-million, five-year endorsement deal. During the hectic day, Bias found time to place a courtesy call to Driesell. "He said, 'I just want to thank you for everything you've done for me,' " says Driesell. " 'I just want to let you know that I signed a million-dollar contract with Reebok.'"

Perhaps in his youthful enthusiasm, Bias overstated his situation. "There might have been numbers discussed, but there was nothing on paper. There was no deal in place." Borzakian Ouellette says.

According to a *Washington Post* story, while returning from Boston the day after the draft, Fentress advised Bias to be patient during the contract negotiations with the Celtics and said he would seek a three- or four-year deal worth close to $1 million a year. The Celtics, however, had exceeded the league's salary payroll cap and were looking at signing Bias to a contract that paid him the league minimum.

"Lee had not accepted the possibility that the most we could offer was the minimum," says Volk. "Neither of us had a lot of flexibility. Bias could not sign with anyone else because we had exclusive signing rights to him for a year. And we weren't going to trade the top five players, or Walton, (Jerry) Sichting or (Scott) Wedman."

Like many associated with Len Bias who were abruptly awakened early on the morning of June 19, 1986, Volk thought he was immersed in a bad dream when his phone rang. A producer from a Boston-area television station asked Volk to confirm what he felt was a baffling report. "He said, 'I'm sure this is a cruel hoax. There's a wire story coming across that Len Bias has had a heart attack.' I said, 'That's ridiculous.'"

More phone calls followed. The producer called back a short while later, saying he had called Bias's agent and that Fentress hung up on him after saying all he had heard was that Bias had suffered a heart attack. Volk then called Don Gaston, the majority owner of the Celtics at the time, who expressed concern about Bias's safety, basketball be damned. A call by Volk to Auerbach confirmed the dreadful news. "He said 'He's gone,'" says Volk. "Red was absolutely devastated."

Auerbach found out that Bias had died from Washington, D.C.-area sportscaster James Brown, a former basketball player at DeMatha High School and Harvard University, when he called at about 9 a.m. Moments later, Auerbach got a call from Driesell, confirming the horrific news. Later in the day, Auerbach learned another bit of shocking news from Driesell: that cocaine was found in Bias's blood.

"This makes me sick all over, it makes me sick all over," Auerbach said late on the day Bias died, in a *Boston Globe* report. "It's unbelievable. We tested him [for drugs], and San Francisco [the Golden State Warriors] tested him. There never was any trace of drugs. Lefty told me, 'I swear on my life, I hope to die if this kid ever used drugs before.'"

Talking in 2010, Volk said he didn't expect the effect of Bias's death on the team to be felt for a while. "I remember saying, as horrible as this is, we're really going to feel this for a very, very long time, but probably not for a year or two. I was wrong. It affected us almost immediately."

The spirit of Len Bias first haunted Jan Volk a few months after Bias died. On Opening Night for the 1986 NBA season in November, when the Celtics raised their 1985-86 championship banner and when Bias would have made his Celtics regular season debut had he lived, Volk found an unused plane ticket with Bias's name on it under a cushion of a sofa in his office.

- - - - - - - - - -

At 10 a.m. on June 19, Williams was set to announce that he was joining a group from Central Florida attempting to land an NBA franchise for Orlando. A few minutes before the start, Williams was asked by a television reporter if he had heard about Bias. "I said 'Yeah, he went to Boston.' The reporter said 'No, he died this morning.' "

The immediate impact was understandably emotional, even from those who only knew of Bias. ESPN.com writer Bill Simmons was a 16-year-old Celtics fan in Stamford, Connecticut, when Bias died. He wrote in a 2001 column that he spent the first few hours in denial, wondering if Bias really had died and hoping that he could still be revived. He then spent three hours walking up and down Wyndover Lane, looking for an answer.

Matt Ribaudo watched Bias play at Cole Field House about 15 times while a young boy in Westminster, Maryland (about 45 minutes from College Park) and became an instant fan. During one game, against N.C. State, he was able to move up close to the court and the ball ended up in his hands when it went out of bounds. A referee approached to retrieve it. "He comes over and says, 'You got something for me?' " says Ribaudo. "I said 'I want to give it to Len Bias.' " The referee would have none of it, and Ribaudo missed out on his dream of meeting the player. "My world consisted of Larry Bird and Len Bias," he says. "Len Bias was right there with GI Joe and Superman. He was a superhero."

Ribaudo's family had moved to Stamford, Connecticut, by the time of the 1986 NBA draft. The night before, the restless 7-year-old told his mom that whoever drafted Bias would be his favorite team, so he became a Celtics fan by default. It was about 9:15 a.m. on June 19 when Ribaudo's mother began screaming for him to come downstairs. At first he thought he was in trouble for doing something wrong, but it was worse than that: She had just heard of Bias's death while watching the *Phil Donahue Show*. After she gave him the news, Ribaudo sat at the base of his stairs and cried. When his mother tried to comfort him, he ran outside and sought refuge first in his tree house, and later, he wrote in a June 2010 blog entry on a CLNSradio.com, a New England-based sports website, spent what felt like hours alone on a swing set. He says he is still in denial about Bias's death.

"I can't describe my emotions and can't tell you just how much this affects me," he says. "There is nothing else in my life that has affected me like that. It affects everything I've done. I've never done cocaine. To me he was a God-like figure." Ribaudo owns a lasting tribute to his hero: a framed picture of the iconic *Sports Illustrated* cover that featured Bias after he died. Its headline: "Death of a Dream."

- - - - - - - - - -

Throughout a 90-minute phone conversation, part-time basketball coach Pete DiGiulio said it again and again: If Len Bias had not died, he would not have become an anti-drug crusader. If Bias had played for the Celtics, perhaps helping the team continue a championship run for another decade, DiGiulio would likely have been focusing his energy on rooting for his beloved team and teaching ball-handling skills at basketball camps. Instead, DiGiulio – in addition to his full-time job as a prevention specialist with the Revere public schools in Massachusetts – speaks to thousands of young athletes each year at dozens of camps, colleges, elementary schools and high schools about drugs, and has ever since late June 1986.

After the Celtics drafted Bias, DiGiulio shared the elation of his fellow fans. "The mood in Boston was that we've found somebody to replace Larry Bird," he says. "The future of the Celtics looked bright. Red Auerbach did it again. He found a diamond."

When Bias died two days later, DiGiulio says he and others fell into a sports depression that reminded him of how a Yankee-fan friend reacted after the team's all-star catcher Thurman Munson, considered the heart and soul of the team, died in a plane crash in August 1979. "We thought 'How could that happen?'" he says. "I'm not naïve. I've dealt with drugs, found dead kids, counseled kids. That was just hard to believe."

A 1973 graduate of Boston College, DiGiulio had worked as a coach at basketball camps, coached high-school teams and talked to kids about drugs at various schools throughout the mid-1980s. But less than a week after Bias's death, he approached his friend Jim O'Brien, then the new men's basketball coach at Boston College, and offered to talk at O'Brien's camp exclusively about the perils of drugs. Camps already had special instructors for shooting, ball-handling and other skills, DiGiulio figured, so why not focus on something different?

O'Brien agreed to be DiGiulio's first client. His second was the Championship Basketball School on Cape Cod. After he accepted a position as an assistant men's basketball coach at Babson College in 1986, he spoke about drugs at that camp as well. The next summer he added a camp at Boston University. DiGiulio built his client base by adding high-school camps and schools.

DiGiulio says he speaks 40 times a year, sometimes through a grant program administered by the NCAA. DiGiulio titles his presentations "The Power of Know," a twist on the "Just Say No" anti-drug campaign promoted by former first lady Nancy Reagan during a U.S. anti-drug campaign in the 1980s.

" 'Just Say No' went out with Nancy Reagan," says DiGiulio. "I say yes to the alternatives of doing drugs. I talk about the power that everybody has. We work, we exercise; we cheat and kill for power. We have the power to know, to start learning billions of bits of information when we're little. Some of that is about drugs."

A former touring comedian, DiGiulio approaches his talks from a different perspective than those who have experienced addiction. His motto is "Don't be scared, be prepared." DiGiulio's approach allows him to relate better to teenagers, most of whom are not addicted to drugs or alcohol but might use them.

Alexis Mastronardi, the associate athletic director of Emmanuel College in Boston, was a student in DiGiulio's health class at Beachmont Elementary School in Revere in the early 1980s. When she was planning to bring in someone to talk about drugs to the school's freshman athletes in 2001, she remembered his style and thought it would work well. DiGiulio has spoken to Emmanuel's student athletes each year since. "He's extremely charismatic and energetic and he really grabs the athletes' attention," says Mastronardi. "He's diving on the floor, jumping around and yelling. It's funny and amusing but, at the same time, they're learning something. The best way they learn something is by having fun."

Throughout his Emmanuel presentations, DiGiulio chews gum. Mastronardi's favorite trick is when he spits it on the floor and then rubs it into the dirt of a grimy radiator or the bottom of his shoe before offering it to students. "He'll say 'Anyone want to eat this?'" says Mastronardi. "Some of the kids are horrified."

After one young woman took the gum into her mouth during a presentation at a basketball camp at Rutgers, the girl next to her vomited. The gum-chewing antics send a message of health awareness and the knowledge about taking risks. "They won't chew that gum, but there's a joint going around at a party and it's got saliva and a piece of Doritos on it and they take a hit from that joint," he says.

Some students who feel they've heard it all about drugs and alcohol, DiGiulio admits, are reluctant to sit through his presentation and have walked out. At Curry College in Milton, a Boston suburb, he remembers one burly football player in the early 1990s voicing his displeasure, bolstered by profanities, about having to sit through yet another talk about drugs.

"He says, 'How long is this thing going to last because I've heard this already and I don't want to listen to it again,'" says DiGiulio. "He sat right next to the door and as soon as I was done, everybody left but he's sitting there as I'm packing up my stuff. I said, 'I thought you were in a hurry to get out of here.' He said, 'Man, after listening to you, I've got a lot of thinking to do.'"

For his efforts, the Freedoms Foundation of Valley Forge named DiGiulio its George Washington Honor Medal Winner for demonstrating responsible citizenship, free enterprise, education and long-term civic accomplishment. "I have friends who knew me when I was working at camps, being crazy, always the entertainer," says DiGiulio, who acknowledges drinking beer but says he has never taken drugs. "When they first heard I was doing lectures about drugs, they started laughing. They say things like, 'You really think those kids are going to listen to you?' I'm not sure I save lives, but I think I leave impressions on a lot of minds and they take what they want. I'll never know what my success rate is, but I'm sure it's above zero."

DiGiulio's compensation ranges from a restaurant gift certificate for speaking to an elementary school class to a few hundred dollars from a college athletic department. It's not money that motivates him, he says, it's his audience. He relishes the times they respond with a standing ovation. It happened with an all-black audience at a Rutgers University Basketball camp in the mid-1990s. He says a student approached him after his talk and said he had never heard anyone talk about drugs in such a way.

DiGiulio embraces the times he learns new things from his audience. At the same camp, someone asked him why he didn't talk about bullets. DiGiulio replied he prefers to avoid the topic of gangs in his speeches. No, the person said, it's a new way to take drugs. Some users melt wax around the drug of choice and insert the "bullet" into their rectum. DiGiulio soon included the item as part of his display of drug paraphernalia at his speeches.

DeGiulio talks fondly of the time a man approached him following a presentation at Grafton High School, about 50 minutes southwest of Boston just off the Massachusetts Turnpike. "I'm in the parking lot behind the school, and it's dark," he says. "I'm a city kid. When I saw him coming up behind me, I clenched my fist, was ready to go. But he said he was a custodian. He said, 'I've been clean for 21 years and have been going to meetings every week. But that was the most impressive talk I've ever heard because you're honest.' He said, 'Kid, you can't lose with honesty.' That was one of the most heartfelt comments I've ever heard."

- - - - - - - - - -

The 1985-86 Celtics were arguably one of the best teams in NBA history, compiling a 67-15 record, notching the second-most wins in a season in team history and winning their third consecutive division title on the way to becoming NBA champions. In 1986-87, the Celtics were considered strong favorites to win their fourth NBA title in seven seasons and almost did, winning their division again before losing to the Detroit Pistons 4-2 in the NBA finals.

The Celtics could not request compensation or other redress from the NBA for the loss of Bias. In that respect, the death of a player is no different than an injury. In the next few seasons, with Bias offering spells of relief, the Celtics frontcourt could have avoided the heavy minutes that were starting to take a toll on their aging bodies. At age 29, McHale played through a broken foot bone for the last three months of the 1986-87 season, limiting his time on the court and the Celtics' chances to repeat as NBA champions. Bird, after bone-spur surgery to his heels, played only six games during the 1988-89 season. Boston won 42 games that season, its lowest total in 10 years. Walton played 80 games for Boston on the 1986 championship team, but an ankle injury forced him out of all but 10 games the season after Bias's death.

The Celtics managed a 29-5 start in 1990-91, but Bird ended up missing 22 games due to the chronic back problems that had bothered him to varying degrees for a few years, and Boston lost in the Eastern Conference semi-finals. During his final season, 1991-92, Bird missed 37 games after off-season back surgery.

The leading scorer for the Celtics in 1992 was Reggie Lewis, the Northeastern University star who was the team's top selection in the 1987 draft, the year after the Celtics chose Bias. During his rookie year in 1987-88, Lewis appeared in 49 games, starting none, as the Celtics that year showed lingering signs of superiority and advanced to the Eastern Conference finals. But it was truly a team in transition. Not only was the fearsome frontcourt of Bird, McHale, Robert Parish and Walton easing past their prime, point guard Dennis Johnson completed his 12th NBA season.

To fortify its backcourt, the Celtics selected guard Brian Shaw in the 1988 draft, but Lewis's role became more significant after Shaw chose to play in Europe during the 1989-90 season. In the 1989 draft, the Celtics picked 6-foot, 10-inch Michael Smith of Brigham Young, the team's leading scorer and a Western Athletic Conference Player of the Year. Smith thought the Warriors would select him and that the Celtics would draft guard Tim Hardaway, who became a three-time NBA All-Star and won a gold medal.

Volk later said that Smith was not the player the Celtics had hoped he would be, but added that the Celtics did not pick Hardaway because they had drafted Shaw the previous year and, based on a commitment from his agent, thought they were going to sign free agent Larry Drew. The Celtics were so sure they had secured a deal with Drew that they sent someone to pick him up at the airport. But Drew never appeared, instead choosing to stay with the Lakers for more money.

While the Celtics were losing their luster, the Bias legacy was quickly growing in Boston. A report in the *Boston Globe* in late June 1990 referred to a new curse in the great sports city, of Celtics fans sitting on their stools, shaking their heads and muttering, "It's the curse of Len Bias. Ever since then, nothing has gone right."

Eerily, the most-famous sports curse in Boston history reared its head just months after Bias's death in 1986 when Red Sox first baseman Bill Buckner muffed a routine ground ball in game six of the World Series, helping the Mets win the game and, one game later, the series. "The Curse of the Bambino," dating back to the sale of Babe Ruth to the Yankees after the 1919 season, would live until the Sox finally won the World Series in 2004 – their first since 1918.

The Bias curse crippled the Celtics quickly. Walton's foot and ankle problems ended his career in 1987. Forward Scott Wedman's 15-year career, the last five with the Celtics, ended with only six appearances during the 1986-87 season due to heel problems. McHale endured foot surgery to repair stress fractures. Bird missed all but six games during the 1988-89 season after surgery to remove bone spurs. Coach K.C. Jones, who led the Celtics to NBA titles in 1984 and 1986, resigned at the end of the 1988 season.

Shaw played in every game for the Celtics as a rookie in the 1988-89 season and averaged 8.6 points and 5.8 assists a game. But he chose to play in Italy the following year before reluctantly returning to Boston for the 1990-91 season. In early 1990, he asked out of his contract to return to Italy but the Celtics refused. Shaw lost an appeal to void the contract. He was traded to the Miami Heat in January 1991.

Smith, the top draft pick in 1989, started the season on the injured reserve list with back and shin problems. "It's kind of spooky, really," former Celtic great Bob Cousy said in a 1990 *Boston Globe* story that recounted the misfortunes of the Celtics after Bias died. "I'm not superstitious, but when things go cold, for some strange reason, they can go cold for a long, long time. It really makes you wonder."

Not everyone subscribed to the theory. "A curse? Oh sure, we ought to get that witch from Salem to snap the spell," said Tommy Heinsohn in the same *Globe* story. Heinsohn is a former Celtics player and coach, and current broadcaster. "The Red Sox had her at one time, to exorcise the ball club. I think that's a lot of baloney. There are reasons why teams falter. Red's philosophy has always been to keep the nucleus of the team together for as long as possible. That way, you develop chemistry, and have people, from a technical standpoint, who can offset each other's weaknesses. But it's increasingly difficult to put that nucleus together, never mind keep it together."

Although the Celtics started the 1990s strong, vaulting out to a 29-5 record during the 1990-91 season, things took a turn for the worse when Bird hurt his back in practice. The team soldiered on to finish the season 56-26, then lost in the second round of the playoffs to the Pistons. Reggie Lewis was the team's third-leading scorer that season, behind Bird and McHale, and would lead the team in scoring the next two seasons as team captain.

When the beloved Lewis died of a heart attack while playing a pickup game at Brandeis University in late July 1993, it was in some ways a more severe blow to the team than the death of Bias: By then, Lewis was considered one of the most dangerous shooting guards in the league, behind only Michael Jordan. Lewis had decided to keep playing basketball despite being diagnosed with cardiomyopathy, a thickening of the heart muscle, after he collapsed during a playoff game earlier in the year. The condition can cause death during strenuous exercise. The team of cardiologists suggested that he stop playing basketball, but the player sought a second opinion, and another doctor identified a fainting condition made worse during periods of stress. Lewis's death certificate issued in November 1993 listed a virus that inflamed and scarred his heart and led to the cardiac arrest that killed him. But two other doctors who examined Lewis's heart during the autopsy discounted the virus theory and claim they discovered scarring that can be attributed to cocaine damage. No undisputed reason for his death has ever emerged.

There is no dispute that Lewis had become an endearing symbol of the Celtics franchise, his popularity enhanced by a reputation for supporting the Celtics community. "He was the star of our team," says Volk. "Keep in mind Len Bias had never played in a game for us. [The death of] Reggie was more difficult in a sense because he was part of our family. And there was some forewarning with a longer story to tell."

Steve Bulpett wrote about the death of Bias for the *Boston Herald,* where he has covered the Celtics for nearly three decades. The day Bias was drafted in 1986, Bulpett flew on the same airplane from New York to Boston as Bias. A couple of days later, he traveled to College Park to report on the player's death. He remembers after a long day of exhaustive reporting telling himself that Bias's death was the worst thing he would ever have to write about while covering the Celtics.

"I spoke too soon," says Bulpett. "Bias's death was a shock, but Lewis's death was more traumatic not only because he had played for the Celtics but because he played for Northeastern. He was part of the community. Bias to Celtics fans was a ghost. Lewis was the guy they lived with for years."

After Lewis died, Celtics Director of Basketball Operations Dave Gavitt wanted to rebuild the team, but the team's owners did not agree and replaced him with M. L. Carr, who admitted in a *Boston Globe* story in 2006 that he wasn't trying to lose but that he also never increased the talent to give the team a better chance to win more often. Carr had hoped the team's poor performances would have put the Celtics in a strong position to take Tim Duncan as the top pick in the 1997 NBA draft.

The season after Lewis died, the Celtics finished 32-50, its worst record since the 1978-79 team that won only 29 games. Through the 2001 season, the Celtics never won more than 36 games in a season, and employed four different coaches. They recorded losing records for eight consecutive seasons. The 1996-97 team coached by Carr won only 15 games, the lowest total in the team's history. Dee Brown, a sixth-year guard, said in a *Boston Globe* story that people called the Celtics a "laughingstock. We had no direction."

A year after leading Kentucky to the NCAA championship, Rick Pitino in 1997 accepted a 10-year contract to coach the Celtics. The organization was hoping for some good fortune in the 1997 NBA draft lottery, where a top pick could lead to Duncan. But the Celtics earned the third and sixth picks, with the Spurs getting No. 1. With the No. 3 pick, Boston took point guard Chauncey Billups; with No. 6 it chose forward Ron Mercer. Neither lasted long with the team: Billups was traded to Toronto midway through his first season, while Mercer was traded to Denver two years later.

Carr says Pitino wanted to offer the Spurs anything to trade for the No. 1 pick. "He'd have had to offer the State House, the John Hancock Building and the tolls from the Mass. Turnpike," Carr said in the *Boston Globe*. "And that might still have not gotten it done."

Pitino's time with the Celtics could be considered nothing but disastrous, with three losing seasons – including 19 wins in 1998-99, the second-lowest total in Boston history – and a 12-22 record in the 2000-01 season before he was replaced by Jim O'Brien.

With third-year player Paul Pierce leading the team in scoring for the second consecutive year, the Celtics put together an impressive turnaround in O'Brien's first year as head coach, winning 49 games in the regular season and advancing to the Eastern Conference finals. But the Celtics failed to maintain that momentum and managed just two winning seasons until its magical turnaround when it won the NBA title in the 2007-08 season, just one year after winning only 24 games.

The Celtics have returned to the heights they knew so well before the death of Bias. If there was a curse, it appears to have been broken. Like Red Sox fans since 2004, Celtics fans no longer look to the past to explain every play, every game, every season that falls short of perfection. But it is impossible to forget the Bias death in Boston. Bulpett talks to school children in the Boston area a couple of times a year about how focusing on academics will expand their career options. During his talks, he mentions the superlative talents of current NBA stars Kobe Bryant and LeBron James. But the story that most penetrates the eager minds of the youngsters is the one that tells of Bias's tragic death and how drugs can destroy even the strongest among us. He uses Bias's story to stress how some decisions do not offer a second chance.

"They can't relate to Len Bias; to them he's a mythic figure," says Bulpett. "But they do seem to get it. I'm surprised. The teachers are surprised. Principals assign the students to write a thank you note, and I'm surprised about how many bring up that part."

Chapter 7

The Nation

Dorothy Gaines was a nurse and PTA mom when police raided her home in Mobile, Alabama, in August 1993, looking for drugs. She claims she didn't know that her then-boyfriend, who was living with her at the time, was involved as a courier for a drug dealer. No evidence was found that Gaines herself had sold or even possessed drugs. The state of Alabama dropped its case against her, but federal prosecutors charged her with drug conspiracy. Gaines received a sentence of 19 years and 7 months, leaving behind three children – including a son just 9 years old – and two grandchildren. Her oldest daughter was forced to leave college to care for her siblings and raise her two children.

Thousands of low-level cocaine dealers, possessors and users – and more than a few people like Gaines, who were simply unlucky or unwise in their choice of associates – received lengthy prison sentences over the last 25 years as a result of anti-drug legislation passed in the late 1980s that require mandatory minimum sentences for drug offenses. Hundreds of thousands of lives, like those of Gaines's children, were disrupted. The federal prison population has soared, from 36,000 in 1986 to 215,000 today, at a cost of about $27,000 per inmate. More than half of all federal prisoners are there for drug offenses; many had either a minor criminal record before their conviction or no record at all. The Federal Bureau of Prisons is nearly 40 percent over capacity.

And it can all be traced back to the death of Len Bias.

- - - - - - - - - -

Political gatherings in the nation's capital often feature glitz and glamour and include diplomats and dignitaries. The event on the seventh floor of this downtown Washington, D.C., office building may have been held just a block from the White House, but it felt worlds away. In a room the size of a small coffee shop, about 50 people celebrated a victory two decades and many ruined lives in the making.

If there were political undertones, they were muted. Today was a day for tales of gratitude, relief and exhilaration. Hosted by the Crack the Disparity Coalition in early September 2010, the protagonists on this feel-good day included a few directors and supporters of nonprofit advocacy groups and a handful of ex-convicts whose lives had been turned upside-down by the Anti-Drug Abuse Act of 1986, passed in direct response to the death of Bias.

One of them was Gaines, who spent six years in prison before her sentence was commuted by President Clinton on December 22, 2000, and has become an advocate for sentencing reform. Gaines won release from prison with the help of such groups as the Families Against Mandatory Minimums, the Criminal Justice Policy Foundation and the Drug Policy Foundation (now the Drug Policy Alliance), all formed after the death of Bias to promote fair sentencing and compassion for deserving drug offenders. Now she was among those who spoke to the energized crowd in the offices of the Open Society Policy Center, one of several advocacy groups that work toward sentencing reform. Gaines, a tall and husky woman whose passion and energy for her cause is evident as she speaks, encouraged the listeners at the reception to continue the fight against unfair prison sentences. "Those of you who have loved ones in [jail] I tell you to tell the young men and women in there, 'Stop watching *The Young and the Restless*,' she says, referring to the daytime soap opera. "Everybody there is young and restless. Get in the law library. There is a case in there that we can fight. When I went to prison, the girls would tell me, 'You've got 20 years, you might as well just sit there and do it because you can't fight the feds.' But that bothered me."

Gaines fought federal drug laws and won, and her fight for freedom has not ended. She spoke in a shaky voice, fighting back tears, as she thought of her 26-year-old son Phillip, who had been in prison for 18 months after a conviction for possession of crack cocaine. Gaines says Phillip's problems are directly related to her incarceration. He started using drugs at the age of 10, a year after Gaines went to prison, and has tried to kill himself repeatedly. "Now I fight to get my son out of prison," she says. "Crack has caused him to do some things that have sent him away to prison."

Gaines's story resonated profoundly with her audience, including Karen Garrison, who won the early release of a son, Lawrence, in 2009 after he served nine years of a 15-year sentence for conspiracy to distribute powder and crack cocaine. Her other son, Lamont, was given 19 years and was released to a halfway house in mid-October 2011. Lawrence and Lamont Garrison, identical twins, were arrested a month before they were to graduate in 1998 from Howard University with dreams of becoming lawyers. The owner of an auto-body shop was arrested as part of a drug operation and implicated the Garrisons so he could get a reduced sentence, saying he provided kilograms of crack cocaine weekly to the Garrisons. Other witnesses supported the claims by the auto-body shop owner.

Investigators found no drugs or drug paraphernalia on the twins or in their mother's house, where they lived. The boys owed thousands of dollars in college loans, indicating they did not have excess cash despite the claims they were dealing cocaine. The twins could not afford to hire attorneys; they were appointed lawyers who often fell asleep during their court proceedings, says Karen Garrison. She further claims that the lawyers failed to gather information and witnesses that would have easily dismantled the government's case against her sons. Still, the Garrisons also lost an appeal of their case. At the time of their arrest, the boys worked as full-time juvenile counselors in Maryland. They were convicted of conspiracy to distribute powder and crack cocaine and were sentenced in 1998. Neither had a prior conviction.

- - - - - - - - - -

Eric E. Sterling, a federal sentencing reform advocate, may have seemed an unlikely guest at the ceremony. For a decade, from 1979 to 1989, he was counsel to the U.S. House of Representatives Committee on the Judiciary, and was also a principal aide in developing the Comprehensive Crime Control Act of 1984 and the Anti-Drug Abuse Acts of 1986 and 1988. In 1989 he switched roles from federal policy wonk to consumer advocate when he became president of the Criminal Justice Policy Foundation, a private, nonprofit group that promotes education about criminal justice problems.

He admits now that passing the anti-drug bills was a mistake. "The legacy of this legislation should be whether or not it has succeeded in making the United States a safer, healthier place for its citizens," says Sterling, who has become an advocate for sentencing reform. "From my perspective, it has not. It failed. I did not think at that time that mandatory sentencing was a good idea. But the members of Congress and the Judiciary committee were my clients and that was my assignment. I had certain kinds of concerns and reservations about that kind of approach. This weighs on me a great deal."

The Anti-Drug Abuse Act of 1986 reestablished mandatory minimum sentences for first-time drug offenders that had been removed from federal law in 1970. It stated that a person manufacturing or distributing at least 500 grams of powder cocaine faced a five-year mandatory minimum sentence, with a maximum 40 years, and those manufacturing or distributing at least 5,000 grams of powder cocaine received a 10-year minimum sentence, with a maximum of life imprisonment. A person manufacturing or distributing at least 5 grams of crack cocaine received the five-year mandatory minimum while those manufacturing or distributing at least 50 grams of that form of the drug received the minimum 10-year sentence. For sentences longer than the minimum, there was no hope of parole; it had been abolished in the Comprehensive Crime Control Act of 1984. By comparison, someone would have to possess 100 grams of heroin or 100 kilos of marijuana to receive the same five-year sentence with no parole as someone found with 5 grams of crack cocaine.

There would be more legislative action against drug abuse by Congress. The 1988 Anti-Drug Abuse Act passed on November 18 applied the mandatory sentences of the 1986 act to anyone who was a member of a drug-trafficking conspiracy. Under the law, if a defendant worked as a doorman to a crack house but never sold, used or purchased the drug, he was liable for all the crack sold during the time the group operated the crack house, even before and after he worked as a doorman. Within six years of passage of the conspiracy amendment in 1988, the number of drug cases in federal prisons increased by 300 percent. From 1986 to 1998, that number increased 450 percent.

Willie Mays Aikens, who is best known as the first player to hit a pair of home runs in two games of the same World Series in 1980 for the victorious Kansas City Royals, was at the celebration, as well. An abuser of drugs and alcohol, he sought help and entered a rehabilitation center in 1983. Aikens stayed clean and sober for several years, but in 1994 received a prison sentence of 20 years and 8 months for selling crack cocaine to an undercover officer. After changes in the federal sentencing guidelines for crack-cocaine offenses, he was released in June 2008. Aikens didn't address the crowd, but the presence of someone who had known such fame and success was a reminder that undue sentencing for drug convictions cut a wide swath through society.

During a later phone conversation, Aikens acknowledged that he deserved to serve time in prison for his crimes but called his 14-year sentence "overkill. It took me two or three years to come to my senses," he says. "I needed time away from what I was doing. It didn't take 14 years for me to look at my lifestyle and make a change in it."

Typical of most who serve such long prison sentences, Aikens suffered collateral personal damage. His daughters were 5 and 6 years old when he entered prison in 1994. "I missed all those days with them growing up," he says. "And I missed time with my sister and my mom. It's time I lost that I can never get back."

Aikens has truly been humbled by his experience as a drug and alcohol abuser and a prisoner. When we spoke on the phone, he referred proudly to a job he held at the age of 55 with a construction company that leveled the asphalt surface surrounding manhole covers on the streets of Kansas City. "I enjoyed it," he says. "I never looked at it as work. I looked at it as a workout." However, he was laid off from the job in August 2010.

Aikens's luck changed a few months later. In February 2011, the Royals hired him as a full-time minor league coach to work as a hitting instructor with rookie league teams from Surprise, Arizona; Idaho Falls, Idaho; and Burlington, North Carolina. Since leaving prison, he has spoken to about a dozen groups at churches, schools, sporting events and prisons to help people change their lives. Aikens's story is being published by Triumph Books and is scheduled to be released in April 2012.

Aikens was playing professional baseball in Mexico in 1986 and says he didn't know about Bias's death until the early 1990s. "I might have heard about it, but it went in one ear and came out the other," he says.

- - - - - - - - - -

At the time of Bias's death, scrutiny of drug use among athletes by groups who monitor major sports in the United States was escalating, although the University of Maryland had been testing its athletes since 1980. J.J. Bush, an athletic trainer at Maryland since 1972, started the program in conjunction with the university's health center. Athletes were tested when a number given to each athlete was called. "One person might get tested four times in one year," says Bush. "Some might not at all. It was strictly random, and it's still random."

But, Bush added, coaches could request an athlete be tested if they suspected he or she might be abusing drugs. If any athlete at Maryland tested positive, the school's athletic director, the health center director and the team's coach would have been notified.

The NCAA began mandatory drug testing at all of its 73 championship events and 19 post-season football games in the fall of 1986. An athlete who tested positive for any of the 200 banned drugs was ruled ineligible for future championship competitions for at least 90 days. The testing plan, which was announced in the summer of 1985, proved ambitious but lacked punch. Still, the test survived, and now mandatory tests are given before the start of postseason play for all NCAA sports as well as being conducted year-round.

The NBA and the National Basketball Players Association established its first drug policy in 1983. It mandated the suspension or expulsion of players convicted of using or selling the following drugs: amphetamine and its analogs (including, but not limited to, methamphetamine and MDMA), cocaine, LSD, opiates (heroin, codeine, morphine) and phencyclidine (PCP). The league added marijuana and steroids to its banned list in 1999. The NBA added performance-enhancing drugs, including DHEA, in 2002 and ephedrine in 2004.

As of 2010, the NBA can permanently expel a player from the league if he tests positive for any of the banned substances after conferring with the National Basketball Players Association. A player can apply for readmission to the league each time he has been expelled. NBA players are tested randomly four times during the season. A player who voluntarily enters the league's substance-abuse program is tested randomly more often. Once a player enters the substance-abuse program three times, he is expelled from the league and then can apply for readmission.

"Our program is threefold," says Robert Gadson, the director of security and agent administration for the NBPA. "It's educational, punitive and rehabilitative, and is designed to assist players who have an issue with banned substances." Gadson added that cocaine ceased to be an issue with NBA players sometime in the late 1990s. Marijuana and performance-enhancing drugs are of most concern now.

- - - - - - - - - -

It was in direct reaction to the death of Len Bias from cocaine intoxication that the U.S. Congress passed the Anti-Drug Abuse Act of 1986 on October 17, less than four months after his death. Perhaps the most profound portion of the sweeping legislation involved increased penalties for drug possession and trafficking of cocaine and most other federal drug offenses, sending tens of thousands of first-time offenders – mostly low-income blacks – to prison with sentences approaching 25 years.

"The death of Bias was the thing that put it over the top to pull this together," says Scott Green, a special adviser on crime and drug issues for the Senate Judiciary Committee from 1980 to 1990. During that time Green was a top aide to then-Senator Joseph Biden, who became chairman of the committee in 1986. "It was a tipping point. The attention and scare and shock provided by somebody with that kind of talent, a young guy at the top of the world, the fact that drugs took him away that quickly. Was it an overreaction? Probably. But a lot of good things came out of it."

For instance, the law established enhanced penalties for an adult who helped any person under the age of 21 violate the Controlled Substances Act, which was passed in 1970. It gave the Department of Justice the authority to make grants to state and local law-enforcement agencies for narcotics assistance. It authorized $241 million in 1987 for the prevention, treatment and rehabilitation of drug and alcohol addicts, including a special allotment to at-risk youth and veterans, and created the Drug Free Schools and Communities Act.

Robert DuPont, M.D., was the president of the American Council of Drug Education when Bias died and had already established himself as a leading authority on drug abuse and prevention. From 1973 to 1978, he was the first director of the National Institute on Drug Abuse. Dupont is the President of the Institute for Behavior and Health Incorporated, which promotes strategies to reduce the demand for illegal drugs. He claims the death of Bias was the most important date related to drug abuse in the United States since the founding of Alcoholics Anonymous in June 1935.

"It changed the basis on which everyone was thinking about drug abuse," he says. "It focused the national attention on drug abuse like no other event has. It brought it home to everybody. Len Bias was an American prince, and he was at the height of his fame. He was a man who had everything. The way drugs had been thought about up to then was it had to do with disadvantaged, poor people who didn't have good families or an education. Bias was the antithesis of that. He came from a wonderful family, had tremendous support. He was sought-after. He was magic. It surely didn't have to do with him being depressed, being poor, uneducated, all those stereotypes. One stereotype was that he was black, but he was not disadvantaged in any way."

DuPont also claims that the death of Bias played a large role in establishing drug-testing in the workplace. On January 4, 1987, an Amtrak train crash in Chase, Maryland, killed 14 people after the train operator ignored warning lights to slow down. The operator tested positive for marijuana while operating the train, helping compel Congress to authorize mandatory random drug-testing for all employees in safety-sensitive jobs in industries regulated by the Department of Transportation.

"The combination of those two events [the Bias death and the Amtrak crash] created the modern effort at workplace drug-testing," says DuPont. "If there had been the crash without the Bias death, the country was not ready for it."

Further, in 1988, Congress passed the Drug-Free Workplace Act, which requires some federal contractors and all federal grantees to agree that they will carry out policies to create drug-free workplaces as a precondition of receiving a contract or grant from a federal agency.

Drug use among some teenagers slowed down dramatically after Bias died, according to figures from the Office of National Drug Control Policy. The number of high-school seniors who said they used cocaine in a 30-day span had increased from 1.9 percent in 1975 to 6.7 percent in 1985. The number of high-school seniors using cocaine from 1985 to 1992 fell to 1.3 percent. Of all federal legislation passed as a result of the death of Len Bias, none was more significant than the 1986 Anti-Drug Abuse Act, which increased fines and imposed mandatory life prison sentences for convictions of certain high-level drug traffickers. It established a mandatory 15 years in prison for those committing drug-trafficking offenses while armed. Further, the law established money-laundering as a federal offense as it relates to profit motive offenses such as drug-trafficking, racketeering and arms-exporting.

The Anti-Drug Abuse Act of 1986 affected foreign policy as well. Under certain conditions, it suspended or eliminated U.S. financial assistance to illicit drug-producing and transit countries. The Anti-Drug Abuse Act of 1988, which complemented the 1986 law, established the White House

Office of National Drug Control Policy, whose director is referred to as the "Drug Czar." It also reduced U.S. assistance by at least 50 percent to major illicit drug-producing and transit countries unless the President proves to Congress that such a country is cooperating with the United States or is taking adequate steps on its own to remedy the problem.

"Up to that point, I don't think that the State Department spent a lot of time dealing with the drug issue," says Green. "It wasn't a major priority. This infused the drug issue into their overall policy-making."

The political roots of the Anti-Drug Abuse Act stretch back to the late 1960s, when drug use became fashionable among young, white middle-class Americans, many of whom used protests and rebellion as settings for their drug abuse, and when heroin addiction was a major problem in the U.S. military in Vietnam. President Nixon in a special message to Congress identified drug abuse as a "serious national threat" following a steep rise in drug-related juvenile arrests and street crimes between 1960 and 1967. He declared a "war on drugs" in 1971 and called drug abuse "public enemy No. 1 in the United States." Two years later, Nixon created the Drug Enforcement Administration to better streamline the efforts of federal agencies working against drug abuse.

In February 1975, President Ford released the White Paper on Drug Abuse that named heroin, amphetamines and mixed barbiturates as drugs of serious concern. Cocaine became more of a concern in November 1975 after Colombian police seized 600 kilos of the drug from a small plane in Cali. Drug traffickers in that country responded by killing 40 people in one weekend, signaling the new power of Colombia's cocaine industry with headquarters in Medellin.

Newsweek published a story on cocaine in May 1977 that some critics claimed glamorized the drug. The story reported that "some party givers pass it around along with the canapés on silver trays ... the user experiences a feeling of potency, of confidence, of energy."

Around this time, cocaine started affecting the careers of NBA players, including David Thompson, considered by many to be the most explosive and dynamic player in basketball history. Michael Jordan called him his favorite player while he was growing up. Thompson was known to have a 44-inch vertical jump, a couple of inches more than Bias. He was a two-time NCAA Player of the Year who led N.C. State to a national title in 1974.

Thompson, who grew up with 10 siblings in a shack near Charlotte, North Carolina, made an early impact on the league with the Denver Nuggets. He averaged at least 25 points a game in each of his first three seasons and scored 73 points, a career high, in the last game of the 1977-78 season.

But when he began to use cocaine the next season, his problems began. Feeling pressure from a five-year, $4 million contract that made him the highest paid athlete in the history of team sports, Thompson started showing up late for practices or missing them entirely. As his cocaine and alcohol use escalated, his play became less consistent. A knee injury limited him to 39 games during the 1979-80 season, and although he finished the following season with a 25.5 points per game average, he never again averaged even 16 points a game in any of his final three NBA seasons.

Sensitive and soft-spoken, Thompson acknowledged trouble expressing his emotions. His NBA career ended in March 1984 following a loss to the Philadelphia 76ers after he hurt his knee when pushed down a flight of stairs during a fight at the Studio 54 nightclub in New York City. Thompson admitted to being excessively drunk at the time. He was forced to retire and soon after declared bankruptcy. "I would try to stop completely, but I just didn't have the willpower," Thompson told the *Seattle Post-Intelligencer* toward the end of his career.

In the mid-1990s he referred to the misconceptions about cocaine in an article in *Slam*: "In the '70s, we were socializing too much. A lot of guys were goin' to the clubs, doin' cocaine. We didn't realize the dangers of drug 'n' alcohol abuse. It was before celebrities began dyin' from it. Len Bias. John Belushi. It was a misconception that cocaine was the elite drug. The rich man's drug. It was thought to be safe, nonaddictive 'n' undetectable if used in the right amounts. No one had an inkling of an idea as to how cunning, how powerful its addiction is. It wasn't just a thing. It was an NBA thing. John Lucas. Walter Davis. A lot of guys were battlin' drug or alcohol abuse. I think it's now seen for what it is – an epidemic. I'd never seen marijuana, cocaine or anything like it until I got in the pros. I was a 20-year-old millionaire. I felt I was invincible. I was wrong."

If a party host wanted to project an image of being cool and hip in the 1980s, he provided cocaine along with the chips and dip. The drug was relatively cheap and seemingly everywhere. Cocaine, processed from a naturally occurring alkaloid in the leaves of the coca plant, stimulates the central nervous system and suppresses the appetite. If you wanted to enhance your awareness or alertness, you snorted a line of cocaine. By the mid-1980s, the problems associated with cocaine use had surpassed those associated with marijuana in the United States. The White House tried to step up its initiative with the drug problem when First Lady Nancy Reagan started her "Just Say No" anti-drug campaign in 1984 to encourage children to avoid recreational drugs.

John Brown, the owner of RJ Bentley's Restaurant, remembers the omnipresence of cocaine in the 1980s. "Unfortunately, during that time, cocaine was perceived as very much of a social, non-addictive, fun drug," he says. "But you could wipe your hand across every toilet tank cover in every bar and there would be a white residue. Guys would go into a bathroom and snort it on the top of the toilet tank. Certainly it was nothing we condoned or promoted but if you were living in the real world, it was there. You'd see and you knew people who'd do it. You'd go to any restaurant in D.C. and people were doing it. It was considered harmless in a lot of ways"

Tom Cash, a Drug Enforcement Administration Special Agent from 1973 to 1995, worked for seven years in Miami as a special agent in charge of the Miami, Florida, field division, which included operations in the Caribbean and Latin America. "Cocaine was described by some as the perfect recreational drug," he says. "That was total bullshit. That was because the effects of cocaine were relatively unknown. It was a socially acceptable drug. You'd go to somebody's house and you would say, 'I'd like to have a vodka tonic, a screwdriver and some cocaine.' "

Quintin Dailey had developed a connection to Bias before either player let cocaine drastically alter their lives. Dailey, a Baltimore native, was an All-America guard at the University of San Francisco who averaged 25.2 points a game during his senior year. Dailey helped show Bias around the campus when Bias visited the University of San Francisco on one of his few recruiting trips in 1982. Bias started playing for Maryland the same year that Dailey began his 10-year NBA career while serving three years' probation for assaulting a female student during his senior year at San Francisco. Dailey says the incident led to his abusing cocaine.

"A lot of it had to do with the stress of dealing with the case," he says. "I started using quite a bit. I was getting booed every place I went. All the negativity that took place with me made me go into a shell. That is the way I thought I would handle it. You get with some certain people who worship you as a player. You meet a certain crowd, something pops up and you try it and you like it and you try it again. The next thing you know is you purchase it."

At the time he was playing, Dailey recalls that the NBA wouldn't test a player unless a problem was suspected. "There was not a policy that tested very random and made you worry about losing your job," he says. "They didn't want people to know they had the problem in the NBA. If you don't admit it, very seldom did you have testing."

Dr. Jack Ramsay, an ESPN basketball analyst and an NBA coach from 1966 through 1988, says the drug policy early on focused on rehabilitation. "There was a period of time when drugs were a problem in the NBA. It was during the David Thompson era. I was very concerned and the league was very concerned. They had a very good policy as far as I could tell. You could report it if you had a problem and you would get treatment and there would be no repercussions."

Dailey, who died of hypertensive cardiovascular disease in November 2010, violated the NBA's drug policy twice during his NBA career. He said in the summer of 2010 that he had been clean and sober since February 1986, some four months before Bias died. After Bias's death, Dailey says the NBA started paying more attention to a player's activities off the court. Some teams even started hiring people to investigate the backgrounds of players they were considering drafting. One was Chris Wallace, now the general manager and executive vice president of the Memphis Grizzlies. The Portland Trail Blazers hired Wallace in December 1986 to monitor the off-court activities of active and potential players. Wallace worked for the Trail Blazers for three years before performing the same duties for at least five other NBA teams.

"Teams at that point started to get a little concerned about what they may not know," he says. "It was the combination of Bias's death and the fact the some players had issues out of that draft."

"That draft," in 1986, included Chris Washburn, the No. 3 pick out of N.C. State; William Bedford, the No. 6 pick for the Phoenix Suns; and No. 7 pick Roy Tarpley of the Dallas Mavericks. All were eventually expelled from the NBA for repeated violations of the league's drug policy. Pat Williams, the 76ers' general manager at the time, called the 1986 draft the "drug draft." He says, "That [draft] turned out to be a nightmare. There was so much underachievement, so many ruined careers. You kept hearing things about all these big guys. You had all these rumors. Washburn, Tarpley, Bedford, all had a chance to be great players. There was this little cloud around them."

During a radio interview in 2010 that discussed his drug past, Washburn identified the city of Oakland, the home base for his team the Golden State Warriors, as "Coakland," a reference to the high availability of cocaine in that city. Washburn, who claims that Bias introduced him to the drug in April 1986, says that Bias's death persuaded him to only briefly interrupt his cocaine use. "It did shake me up for a while, but it didn't really affect me that much," he says. "I probably didn't start back (using cocaine) until toward the end of August in training camp. Coaches started putting on the heat, and I started staying up late at night."

As his drug use increased, Washburn struggled with maintaining an inconspicuous presence. He was easy to recognize, driving in a Mercedes-Benz to what he described as the most dangerous places in California at 2:30 in the morning searching for cocaine. Due in large part to his drug use, Washburn played in only 72 games for three teams in four years before he was expelled from the league after failing a third drug test in 1989.

"In the beginning, I could do it and go to games," he says. "I didn't think I had a problem. But then I started being late to everything. I would show up 15 minutes before game time, and I should have been there 90 minutes before then. When I bought the drug, the stronger it was, the better it was. I'd say, 'I've got the Len Bias, the killer drug.' It was supposed to be the best stuff. I had to go through 15 years with it and another 10 to get myself together."

When Horace Balmer became the head of security in the National Basketball Association in 1985, he says,f drugs were already a major concern in the NBA, at a level he would rate at 10 on a scale of 1 to 10. It was a result of the drug problems faced by such players as Thompson, Lucas and Dailey; Marvin Barnes, a former Providence University All-America who played in the American Basketball Association and the NBA from 1974 to 1980 before an addiction to cocaine helped end his career; and Micheal Ray Richardson, banned for life by the NBA in 1986 after he failed his third drug test.

Balmer spent 20 years as a New York City police officer. He brags that he was death on drug users. "If a guy was using drugs in the NBA, you did not want to see me in the locker room," he says. "When I was interviewed for the job, I was told that we would try and eradicate drugs in the NBA. The concern was very high. My job was to protect the NBA, to visit and talk to as many people in drugs as I could. Dealers, treatment centers, guys in jail, nonathletes. I wanted to know, how did you hook the athletes, what was the first thing you did to him?"

Soon after he joined the NBA, Balmer talked with incoming rookies at the league orientation program about the temptations and perils they faced, including drug abuse. He recounted some of the selling points people would use to lure athletes to cocaine. "They said it was better than heroin, and you could not get addicted to it," he says. "They thought it would not hurt the body and that is was recreational. They were told it would get you nice and high and don't worry about it. It won't hurt you. Athletes were told by people selling it that you can use the drug during the off-season and you can walk away from it anytime you wanted to, you won't become addicted to it. If you went to a fabulous party, they'd put it out just like they'd put out liquor. Cocaine had become the Hollywood drug. A bowl of cocaine was at every party you went to."

Women would try to attract high-salaried athletes as regular drug customers by getting them hooked on cocaine. "One athlete, a boxer, was turned on by a beautiful girl," says Balmer, who retired from the NBA in 2004 but returned to the league in 2010 as a consultant. "She would put cocaine in his mouth when they kissed to get him hooked and [the boxer] would become a customer."

The night of the 1986 NBA draft at the Felt Forum in New York City, after the Celtics made Bias the No. 2 overall pick, Balmer escorted Bias to his car. "He was the happiest man I saw in my life," he says, remembering Bias flashing a big smile. "I never thought he was going to die [two days later]. I had never heard anything bad about him, never heard about Len using drugs recreationally. I would have gotten it through the grapevine. Nobody knew that Bias was gonna die but the fact that he died, it became another part of the program. It shocked everybody."

Balmer feels the legacy of Bias's death more greatly affected lives beyond the NBA than within the NBA. "A lot of kids who had the opportunity to use drugs chose not to use drugs," he says. "It was an eye-opener. He didn't die in vain. Because of his death, a lot of people in this country began to make drugs a target."

- - - - - - - - - -

After Bias died, the U.S. Congress, motivated by political and practical matters, quickly moved into reaction mode, prompted to act in part by the Comprehensive Crime Control Act of 1984 that established the United States Sentencing Commission to provide guidelines for federal judges as they handed out sentences. The act overhauled the federal sentencing system and revised bail for drug and organized crime defendants, among others. Passage of the bill helped the Republicans gain 19 seats in the House of Representatives and President Reagan toward a comfortable reelection in 1984.

Following the 1984 election, the Democrats still held a 71-seat advantage in the House, and its speaker, Thomas P. "Tip" O'Neill, seized the moment to fortify his party's anti-drug abuse position. Sterling saw the O'Neill-led response to the Bias death as part of prime political maneuvering.

"It was a Democratic initiative to flank the Republicans," says Sterling. "The Democrats had lost the Senate in the 1980 elections, and they knew historically that the president's party does not do well in Senate elections six years after a president wins. The Democrats were hungry to take the Senate back. They had controlled the House and Senate since the early 1950s. They thought, 'What can we do to restore the natural order? We need to take the initiative.' "

O'Neill was first elected to Congress in 1953 to represent a district of Massachusetts that includes Boston, succeeding John F. Kennedy when he was elected to the U.S. Senate. By the time O'Neill retired, he was revered by Democrats as one of the most beloved politicians in Massachusetts history. Soon after he was elected, O'Neill developed a reputation as an outspoken liberal. Growing up, O'Neill played basketball in part because his school couldn't afford the cost of an ice-hockey team. In an early sign of his leadership abilities, he was selected captain of his high-school team. He also displayed a consistently passionate position toward the Celtics, fed by the conquests of the vintage teams in the 1950s and 1960s that won 11 NBA titles and were led by such Hall of Fame players as Bob Cousy, Bill Russell and John Havlicek. Through 1986, the Celtics had won 16 NBA titles.

"He didn't have season tickets because he could not afford them," says O'Neill's son, Tom, a former Massachusetts lieutenant governor who now operates a government relations firm in Boston. "My father loved the Celtics and Red Auerbach. And he knew Len Bias was going to be a terrific ballplayer. He saw Bias as the third or fourth iteration of the Celtics greatness in the middle of the century during the Cousy years."

The impact of the young ballplayer's death was a topic often brought up at family weekend dinners. "My father felt the passing of Len Bias on a couple different levels," he says. "He felt the impact on the team and on Len's family and the Celtics fans and that it wasn't a lone incident. This type of thing could happen to anybody."

The death of Bias also resonated in another, more poignant way. Tip O'Neill's son Michael had shown signs of addictions to alcohol and drugs since the early 1980s. Tom described his brother as a smart man who couldn't shake his addictions. Michael left his family, lived in different apartments and was "basically homeless," says Tom. Michael died in 1997 at the age of 44, three weeks after being hit by two cars in one day while he was wandering the streets. "He was a diehard Celtics fan," says Tom. "He saw [Bias's death] as a sign to change his way of life. But as so many in that situation, they just can't fight through their addiction."

Michael's drug use was a motivator for Tip to pass the bill. "Len's death had an impact on my father because of his greatness, but my brother's problems with drugs had much more of an impact," Tom O'Neill says. He ended a phone interview by expressing gratitude for the time to reflect. "Boy, I certainly did not expect to talk about my brother today," he said, before pausing briefly to collect himself. "Thank you."

Tip O'Neill witnessed how powerfully Bias's death affected his constituents and heard from congressional colleagues, especially after they returned from spending the July Fourth holidays in their home districts, about the widespread concern of their constituents about not only Bias's death but concern over deaths from cocaine in general.

O'Neill had decided to retire at the end of his term, which expired in January 1987, so it does not appear that he was trying to score personal political points by pushing for the new anti-drug act. Still, O'Neill worked hard for its passage and certainly saw the potential political benefits for his party. He knew the House and Senate needed to approve the bill by early October for the Democrats to claim credit in the November elections for an anti-drug program.

Republicans used this urgency to add amendments they felt Democrats would resist, but many Democrats voted for them because they wanted to appear tough on drugs before the election. The Republicans re-established harsh mandatory minimum sentences that had been repealed in 1970 to reinforce a "tough on drugs" position. All anti-drug bills reported by the many House committees were bundled together into a single Anti-Drug Abuse Act of 1986 introduced after Labor Day. It passed the House and Senate after a few days of debate.

"It caught President Reagan and the Republicans by surprise," says Green. "It gave the Democrats a position on a crime and drug issues that traditionally they had been soft on. And the original Reagan approach was to make cuts in programs. Agencies that supported drug treatment and education had taken some hits. It was an opportunity to increase those budgets."

No Congressional hearings were held to review the effects of mandatory minimum sentences, although some hearings were held to discuss other pieces of the bill. "No experts on the relevant issues, no judges, no one from the Bureau of Prisons, or from any other office in the government, provided advice on the idea before it was rushed through the committee and into law," says Sterling. "Only a few comments were received on an informal basis."

Passage of the bill certainly did not hinder advancement by Democrats in Congress in the 1986 elections. They gained five seats back in the House, increasing their advantage in the chamber to 81. In the Senate, Democrats gained eight seats to score a 55-45 advantage.

The anti-drug theme played a part in the outcome of 1988 congressional elections. Representative Tom Foley, a Democrat from Washington State, took over as Speaker of the House in 1989, continuing a stretch of Democratic speakers that started in 1955 and ended in 1995. Foley had sponsored the 1988 Anti-Drug Abuse Act.

"It was a much more cynical exercise than it was in 1986," says Sterling. "Earlier there was the sense that this was politically shrewd but there was also the sense that with the death of Bias that this was a terribly dangerous drug. And especially, crack use was getting worse and a bill would be good for the Democrats politically. They saw the outcome in 1986 from the Anti-Drug Abuse Act and wanted to replicate it in the next election, hoping for the same kind of benefit."

The Democrats maintained their 10-seat advantage in the Senate and gained three more seats in the House while the Republicans, with the election of George H.W. Bush, held on to the presidency.

- - - - - - - - - -

The federal government had hoped that mandatory minimums would result in more prosecutions of high-level drug offenders. But federal agents found they lost a bargaining chip to plea down low-level offenders in exchange for information about the leaders of drug deals. "The mandatory minimums didn't help our investigations," says Cash. "Federal agents weren't for mandatory minimums. The mandatory minimums were never engaged at the federal level. States picked it up. You can't get anyone to cooperate when you're looking at 10 years."

Someone who possessed five grams of crack cocaine received the same five-year mandatory minimum sentence as someone who distributed 500 grams of powder cocaine. Inner-city blacks favored crack cocaine while white suburbanites preferred powder cocaine, so the penalties created racially discriminatory results with their harsh sentences for first-time offenses. Most of those who received the minimum mandatory sentences were low-level offenders who were young, male and black. Through his work, Sterling found that one of four defendants of powder cocaine-related crimes is white while for crack cocaine there are 10 black federal defendants for every one white federal defendant. He calculated near the turn of the 21st century that on a years-in-prison-per-gram-of-cocaine basis, a low-level crack offender is punished 300 times worse than a high-level powder cocaine trafficker.

"What primarily has caused the disproportionate racial disparity is the Drug Enforcement Agency and the Justice Department focusing on low-level street dealers of crack cocaine involving blacks," he says. "If they had focused on the high-level offenders, such as those who manufacture or import cocaine, no one would complain about the racial disparity."

Until 2010, crack cocaine was the only drug where possession of more than five grams with no intent to distribute was treated the same as drug-trafficking. Possession of any other drug as a first-time offense is a misdemeanor that does not require a prison sentence. The maximum term of imprisonment is one year.

In 2007, African Americans accounted for only 18 percent of crack cocaine users in the U.S., but 83 percent of those receiving federal sentences for crack cocaine offenses. They also received disproportionately harsher sentences for comparable offenses by white defendants. "Mandatory sentencing was pandering to the public," says Cash. "We'll put them all in jail. The only way you defeat drug-trafficking is to reduce the demand. Nobody wants to do that, has the balls to do that, and we have missed the message every day."

In a 1991 report, the U.S. Sentencing Commission, which establishes sentencing policies and practices for federal courts, criticized mandatory minimums, saying that all defense lawyers and nearly half of the prosecutors asked about mandatory minimums had serious problems with them. Jeffrey Harding works as a defense attorney in Upper Marlboro, Maryland. He's also been a prosecutor, serving as assistant state's attorney for Prince George's County from 1984 until 1991. Harding was the lead prosecutor in the case against Brian Tribble, who was charged with crimes related to the death of Bias.

"As a defense attorney, I think the mandatory minimums are draconian, uncalled for and ineffective in their purpose and have been a total failure," he says. "As a prosecutor, I didn't like it because it took away from the judge the ability to fairly sentence a defendant. It armed a prosecutor with too much power in those cases."

Harding did see some benefit from mandatory minimums as a prosecutor. He uses as an example police arresting someone for selling crack on a street corner. While conducting a background check, police find a prior conviction of possession with the intent to distribute cocaine. The person faces a minimum sentence of 10 years without parole.

"So now we say to him, 'We can either do that or you can sit down in the room and talk with us and tell us who you got it from, and you'll wear a wire for us' " says Harding. "Before the mandatory minimums, these guys would [not cooperate]. It gave and still gives the police and the prosecutor a great deal of leverage over the defendant. It helped police and the prosecution to go up the ladder of narcotics distribution to get the next highest guy. That's probably the only benefit."

In a 1995 study, the U.S. Sentencing Commission reported that only 11 percent of federal drug-trafficking defendants were major traffickers. The commission suggested amendments to equalize the penalties for crack and powder cocaine possession and distribution at the current powder trigger points. But Congress rejected the recommendations, and President Clinton signed the legislation that stifled the commission's effort to equalize crack and powder cocaine sentencing under the guidelines.

By 2005, the diligent work by those advocating sentencing reform for low-level drug offenders started to reap benefits. Members of Congress forged a bipartisan effort that supported a bill to eliminate the cocaine-sentencing disparity. They included House Republicans Mike Castle and Ron Paul as well as House Democrats Charles Rangel, Sheila Jackson Lee, Maxine Waters and Bobby Scott. In the Senate, Republicans Jeff Sessions and Orrin Hatch joined Democrats Joseph Biden and Richard Durbin. Interestingly, Biden had led the Senate Democrats in passage of the 1986 Anti-Drug Abuse Act.

Momentum continued to shift toward reducing mandatory minimum sentences when Congress in 2008 allowed a recommendation by the U.S. Sentencing Commission to reduce prison-sentencing guidelines for some crack cocaine criminals by more closely tracking the 1986 law. The hard work by advocates of fair sentencing paid off dramatically on August 3, 2010, when President Obama signed the Fair Sentencing Act of 2010, which reduced the mandatory-minimum-sentencing disparity of the trigger quantities for crack cocaine and powder cocaine from 100-to-1 to 18-to-1. Those convicted of distributing at least 28 grams of crack now receive the minimum five-year sentence, while distributors of at least 280 grams of crack will receive a minimum 10-year sentence. The previous amounts were 5 grams and 50 grams, respectively.

The legislation also eliminated a mandatory minimum for simple possession of crack cocaine. The U.S. Sentencing Commission in July 2011 made crack penalties retroactive and since Nov. 1, 2011, inmates have been able to request reduced sentences.

In a huge turnaround from the 1980s, a bipartisan coalition of lawmakers supported the Fair Sentencing Act, which passed the Senate by unanimous consent, meaning the chamber was able to approve it quickly without a vote, reflecting its strong support. The House passed the bill by voice vote, reflecting its near-unanimous support.

Representative Daniel Lungren of California, one of the authors of the 1986 Anti-Drug Abuse Act while a member of the House Judiciary Committee, supported the Fair Sentencing Act. In a statement in July 2010 during House debate for the act's passage, Lungren admitted that Congress in 1986 had little reason to approve the 100-1 disparity in mandatory minimum sentencing, saying that the bill initially came out of committee with a 20-1 ratio. "We didn't really have an evidentiary basis for it, but that's what we did, thinking we were doing the right thing at the time."

He added: "Certainly, one of the sad ironies in this entire episode is that a bill which was characterized by some as a response to the crack epidemic in African American communities has led to racial sentencing disparities which simply cannot be ignored in any reasoned discussion of this issue. When African Americans, low-level crack defendants, represent 10 times the number of low-level white crack defendants, I don't think we can simply close our eyes."

- - - - - - - - - -

Kemba Smith, an only child, grew up in a protective, upper-middle-class home in Richmond, Virginia. Smith symbolizes the plight suffered by many first-time offenders of cocaine crimes since the death of Len Bias.

Smith was a debutante but overly critical of herself in some ways – her nose was too big, her legs were too skinny. Her life changed dramatically in 1991 soon after she met Peter Hall when she was a freshman struggling to establish a comfortable identity at Hampton University in Virginia. Hall, from New York, was eight years older than Smith, who was impressed by his charm, self-confidence and sense of adventure. Smith was further impressed by Hall's well-appointed, tri-level apartment that included three televisions in one room and a sophisticated music system. At the time, few people, including Smith, knew that Hall faced arrest warrants for buying cars under false names and for selling drugs.

In the summer of 1991, Hall beat and choked Smith after he said he saw her holding hands with another man. For Smith, that incident began a nine-year odyssey that included cross-country travels providing emotional and at times logistical support for a drug dealer and murderer. She was repeatedly beaten, and endured brief spells of poverty that included homelessness.

Smith was not the only female college student who had been lured in by Hall to serve as his drug mule. On his behalf, they carried large quantities of cocaine across state lines, obtained vehicles and secured apartments in their names. Federal drug agents labeled Hall and his brother leaders of a violent drug ring that dealt up to $4 million in cocaine between New York and Virginia from 1989 to 1993.

Smith finally had enough of her halting life with Hall by the summer of 1994 after they relocated from San Diego to Seattle, where the two had no money and spent nights sleeping in bus stations. Smith also discovered she was pregnant with Hall's child. She turned herself into police in August that year after finally breaking away from Hall and returning to her parents' home in Richmond.

Even in the comforts of her parents' house, Smith was still under Hall's power, more than once giving false testimony to police about him. But Smith eventually tired of living a life of lies, and on October 1, 1994, she told her father she was ready to tell the truth. Two days later, Smith found out from her lawyers that Hall had been killed in Seattle by a gunshot wound to the head. A few days later, Smith pleaded guilty to federal charges of conspiracy to distribute cocaine, lying to federal authorities and conspiracy to launder drug money. Smith admits it was a mistake to stay with

Hall and to lie to investigators.

Smith says one woman involved with Hall cooperated with the government against the drug dealer before he was killed and was placed in the witness protection program. Smith, her friends and her family had hoped that her confession would prompt similar leniency from prosecutors. They were mistaken. The government chose to keep Smith, who was seven months pregnant, in jail until sentencing. While in jail, Smith gave birth to a son, William Armani Smith.

At her sentencing hearing on April 20, Smith's attorney, William Robinson, Jr., said Smith did not deny the actions that led to the charges. But he claimed she was not of her "own" mind while committing the crimes. He added that her actions were consistent with those of a battered woman and that she was under coercion or duress, which under federal guidelines would allow the judge to apply a lower mandatory sentence. Prosecutors, however, claimed that she was aware of the drug organization's activities and aided and abetted the conspiracy. After U.S. District Judge Richard B. Kellam handed down a sentence of 24.5 years, Smith cried as she was led back to a holding cell. Her parents, Gus and Odessa, wept as they walked out of the courtroom. During an interview in September 2010, Smith admits to having used marijuana but claims she never used any of the drugs she helped Hall sell. She also admits that she knew early on in the relationship that Hall was a drug dealer.

Kemba Smith (*provided by Kemba Smith*)

"I take full responsibility for the choices that I made," she says. "That Kemba still had issues with picking the right guy, had self-esteem issues. I still don't like for everyone to know me as the girl who went to prison and made those stupid choices. I missed out on plenty of opportunities. Number one is the six and a half years of raising my son. I wish I could get that back."

Smith's was not the only life affected. Gus, an accountant, and Odessa, a schoolteacher, depleted their life savings paying for Kemba's legal fees and traveling to visit her during stays in federal prisons in San Francisco and Connecticut. They were forced to file for bankruptcy twice. Gus and Odessa raised Kemba's son, William, while she was in prison. "That was a tremendous emotional undertaking for us and for her," Gus says. "That's a completely different dynamic to know that your grandson is the son of a drug dealer."

Smith spent six years in prison before President Clinton commuted her sentence on December 22, 2000, the same day as Dorothy Gaines. U.S. Representative Bobby Scott of Virginia was one of the first people to help the Smiths, who are his constituents. "You can rationally say that she broke the law, but not of any significance," Scott said in an interview in his Capitol Hill office. "She was an accomplice. She got caught with whatever the guy was dealing. That is so insulting to suggest that that sentence made any sense. The policy makes no sense."

Groups that helped Smith felt the same way. The NAACP Legal Defense Fund offered free legal assistance starting in 1996. Families Against Mandatory Minimums helped mobilize support for Smith's commutation by Clinton. Smith talked gratefully about her new life as a national symbol of unfair sentencing practices. She travels the country speaking about her past and has published a book titled called *Poster Child, The Kemba Smith Story*. Smith is married, and has a baby girl who was 5 months old when we spoke.

"I now know what it's like having a newborn to come home to, and I know what I was missing," she says.

In mid-September 2010, Smith traveled to Washington, D.C., to be a guest on a panel that discussed new opportunities to end old policies related to mandatory minimums. The panel was organized by the Congressional Black Caucus and included Representative Maxine Waters of California, a caucus member.

Bronze-skinned and pretty, Smith moved with a controlled grace, her lean athletic build a steadying presence. "I care about those that I left behind in federal prison, who had 10, 15, 20 years, 30 years," she said with a calm purpose. "Two women I know have life sentences and are still in there. I feel I am one of the fortunate ones when I know their stories are similar to mine. First-time nonviolent drug offenders to be sentenced to 24.5 years in prison is ridiculous. We need to have a discussion for sensible drug policy."

At the end of the presentation, while Smith answered questions, she encountered hostility from a homeless spectator who yelled, "If you used, you abused," a reference to her connection to Hall. Smith responded calmly, saying she respected the person's opinion. She emphatically stated that she had never used the cocaine Hall sold. After the session ended, Smith talked with the spectator. "He was passing judgment on his own personal experience," she says. "I tried not to show my frustration. Everybody's entitled to his or her opinion. I leave myself open to people blurting things out. Once a 14-year-old girl gave me the [middle] finger."

Smith attended one year of law school at Howard University after her release from prison and hopes to resume her legal studies. She has started a foundation to promote good decision-making and to help people develop, among other things, a sense of identity and family. "One of my friends said, 'Kemba, you're always trying to go out and save the world,' " she says. "But I wanted to have the things every woman dreams of, even though I didn't think it would happen. I'm fortunate that with my situation there has been some good. God has allowed blessings and given me favor to be able to speak about the situation and use it as an education tool for young people."

Smith relishes how her life has evolved, but wonders if the wisdom she has gained through her tribulations has been worth the journey. "For the average person," she says, "there wouldn't have been anything good about it."

Gus and Odessa Smith remain close to their daughter, and travel to support her cause. They attended the Crack the Disparity Coalition event in Washington, D.C., in September 2010 – the same event at which Gaines spoke – to represent their daughter, who was honored with a plaque for her support of the Fair Sentencing Act.

Afterward, in a small, comfortable room down the hall from where the ceremony had taken place, Gus and Odessa spoke somberly about how Kemba's troubles had affected their lives. They talked about how they spent their savings traveling to California and then to Connecticut to visit Kemba in jail, and to support her legal efforts. They discussed with discomfort how prison authorities ignored them when Kemba gave birth to their only grandchild just weeks after she had been placed in prison, how Kemba had lain in a prison bed for 45 minutes after giving birth, her hands and feet handcuffed to the bed as two armed officers stood in the room. "They were concerned she might escape," Odessa says quietly. "Where was she going to go? She just had a baby." The hospital administrator soon came to Kemba's aid, placing her in a more comfortable room next door, where Kemba and her parents were able to spend some time with the baby and only one of Kemba's hands was cuffed to the bed.

Gus remembered an emotional service the first time he attended a Baptist church in Washington, D.C., during the time Kemba was incarcerated that helped him accept the gritty reality of his family's challenges. "The minister talked about how God uses some people to do his work," says Gus.

"Some people live [to be] 125 and never accomplish what God sent them here to do. Some people at 25 get it all done."

The minister's comments made Gus think of Kemba and about the thousands of kids and teachers who wrote her letters while she was incarcerated. Some encouraged her to stay strong and expressed sympathy for her situation. Others told her about a brother or mother who was in jail. Some girls asked for advice, wondering what they should do about a young man who was not good for them.

Some wondered how she could be so stupid. "I didn't take offense to it," says Kemba. "It's great that they think that way. Hopefully their life journey won't cause them to sway in their beliefs. I was just like them, but something happened to me."

She advised them not to do what she did and end up in jail. She told them to get a good education and to keep their lives on the right path. And she wrote every one of them back. "She talked to them, helped them out from behind bars," says Gus. "I thought about what she was doing and what God had instilled in her to get done. I started crying and couldn't stop. [The minister] said the Lord has allowed this to happen to make a difference in the law, which it did, and make a difference in other people's lives."

The minister told Gus after the service that she knew who Gus was when he walked into the church, that she kept a copy of a magazine story written about Kemba in her nightstand, and that she prayed for her every night.

"From that point on, I knew this was God's work," says Gus. "Kemba was the poster child."

Chapter 8

Michael Leonard Bias

Tina Maynard remembers well the first time she saw Len Bias play basketball. As a 13-year-old in 1982, the Annapolis eighth grader went to watch a Maryland state semi-final playoff game between Bias's Northwestern High School team and Annapolis High School. A rallying point was Ted Watson, a star player on the Annapolis team and the brother of her friend Rena Watson. But once the game began, Maynard's attention turned to another player on the court. Len Bias, who showcased his lean and powerful athleticism during the game, helped lead Northwestern to a 16-point victory. "I was young," Maynard says of her instant crush. "He was tall and he was the star ball player."

"She was fascinated with [Bias]," Watson says. "That was the type of girl she was. She liked athletes."

Maynard and Bias finally met at a party in the fall of 1985, just as Bias was beginning his senior year at Maryland. Within weeks, Maynard says, she was pregnant by him. Michael Leonard Bias was born in the summer of 1986, some two weeks after Bias died. A DNA test has never been done, and the Bias family has not responded to requests for interviews. But Derrick Curry, a friend of the Bias family and a teammate of Jay Bias at Northwestern High School, says someone close to the family told him about five years ago that they know Len has a son.

Maynard talked about Bias for about 10 hours during several visits to the Annapolis townhome she rents and during a series of phone calls. She spoke of Bias and his surroundings during the 10 months she says they knew each other with authority, and her family members and friends support many of her recollections.

As she sat during the first visit on a humid afternoon in July 2011 with her sons Marlon, 18, and Martez, 16, and some of their friends, Maynard proudly showed me a neat scrapbook of Bias's press clippings and pictures going back to when she was in high school. She offered a picture of Bias standing in front of a car, in slacks and a dress shirt, posed with his arms behind his back. She says Bias wrote the following note on the back of the picture: "to my young love, stay sweet, and ... the one with your cute a_ _ self (joke), Love ya, Lenny ..."

Maynard met Bias after Watson, a friend since childhood, began attending the University of Maryland. Early in September 1985, Maynard went to visit Watson at her room on campus. "Here's an opportunity to meet Len," she thought. Maynard had been staying in Watson's room for a couple of days before going with her to a botany class. Maynard was pleasantly surprised to see Bias sitting in the classroom, but they did not speak. The next night, a Sat-

Tina Maynard and her granddaughter, Taniya, at her home in Annapolis, Maryland. *(by Dave Ungrady)*

urday, Maynard and Watson attended a party at a sorority, thinking that Bias might show up. Watson and Maynard had been enjoying the lively music and large crowd for about an hour when Bias made an entrance worthy of his status on campus.

"You could tell he was the star," Watson says. "He had an entourage of guys. Some people were whispering, 'Len Bias is here.' Some guys were like, 'Len, Len. Mr. Bias,' trying to get his attention." Maynard acted like a giddy school girl when she first spotted him. "She said, 'There he is, there he is,' " says Watson. "She grabbed my arm and took me over to him."

Watson, who knew Bias through a friend of her basketball-playing brother but did not share

Maynard's level of interest, kept the introduction simple. "I said, 'Len Bias, this is Tina Maynard. Tina Maynard, this is Len Bias,'" she says. "And then I walked away. Five minutes later, they left. I didn't hear from her for two weeks."

When Maynard finally returned to Watson's room, says Watson, "She's smiling, laughing. She says, 'I had the best time.' I was fussing with her, saying 'No one knew where you were. You could have been killed.' Her mother was about to call the state police. I just threw my hands up and walked away. It was very much out of character for her to do that."

During the two weeks, Maynard says she was with Bias much of the time before her mother ordered her back home and back in school. Maynard adds she spent much of her time that school year on the Maryland campus, often in Len's suite. She says she knew that Len was romantically involved with other women. "I never thought that he was only dating me," she says. "I was not bothered by it at all."

Len Bias poses for a picture for Tina Maynard before they went out to a movie. (provided by Tina Maynard)

Maynard claims she witnessed Bias, David Gregg and Terry Long consume cocaine in the Leonardtown apartments where they lived. She says that during the time she knew Bias, he would use cocaine consistently. "I wouldn't say he was addicted to it, he just liked using it," she says. "It was not new to him. I'm not trying to talk bad about him. He was human. I just wish people would be honest with everything."

When Maynard told Bias she was pregnant with his child, she says he asked if she was certain. After she started crying, she says he asked what was wrong. "I said 'I'm so young.' He said, 'You're going to be OK.' He could have been, 'Well, it ain't my baby.' But he didn't say that."

Maynard says she spent about as much time with Bias as she did at home while she was pregnant. Maryland players Jeff Baxter, John Johnson and Speedy Jones, who lived in the Leonardtown suite with Bias in 1985-86, could not recall Maynard nor did they know at the time that he was going to be a father. Other teammates, including Keith Gatlin and Long, as well as Bias's former Maryland coach, Lefty Driesell, said even recently that they were not aware of Bias fathering a child.

However, Phil Nevin, a freshman center on the Maryland team that year who also lived with

Bias, says he does remember Maynard spending time at the suite. When told during a phone conversation that a woman claimed to have given birth to Len's child, Nevin asked, without being told her name, "Was it Athenia? Tina? I remember."

"Was she light-skinned?" he was asked.

"Yes, that's her," he says. "I saw her occasionally."

Maynard claims she was not bothered that Bias never promised to support the child, but she thinks that if he had lived, he would have taken care of him. "I think things would have been a lot different for me," she says. "He would have said something to his mother. He was a good person. He had a good heart. Len and I had a lot of good times together. He was good to me. We went to the movies, we went to the clubs, we ate together. He was always joking."

Maynard claims that Bias called her on the day he was drafted by the Celtics on June 17, 1986, three days before the baby was due to be born. She says he asked how the baby was doing and if she saw him on television. "I said, 'Yes, I did.' " she says. "I asked him when he was coming home. He said, 'I'll see you later.' "

It would be the last time they spoke. Maynard says her sister, Gayle, called early on the morning of June 19 to tell her that Bias was dead. Maynard says she was so annoyed at the statement that she hung up the phone. Her sister then called back and told Maynard to turn on the television. She says Long hugged her at Bias's memorial service, rubbed her bulging belly, cried, and wished her good luck. Long did not recall that moment.

Maynard, 18 at the time, gave birth to Michael Leonard Bias in Baltimore two weeks late, on July 3 at 9:45 p.m. The father named on the birth certificate is Leonard Kenneth Bias. When Maynard picked up a copy of the birth certificate at the Anne Arundel County records office in late July 2011, she appeared annoyed. "His middle name is not Kenneth," she says. "It's Kevin. I'm going to have to get that changed." A clerk provided Maynard with a phone number of a county office that could help her with the change. A few minutes later, Maynard recounted how she and Bias used to tease each other about their middle names. "I said 'Kevin, that's such a simple name,' " says Maynard, as she smiled coyly. "He said, 'Beatrice, that's an old lady's name.' We had fun with that."

Michael Bias was a few months old when Maynard moved to California to make a fresh start. Before she left for the West Coast, she says, she tried to introduce her son to the Bias family. Within a few weeks of Michael Bias's birth, Maynard says, her mother called the Bias family to let them know they had a grandson. Maynard says she visited them at their home along with her mother, another sister and her uncle, Joseph "Zastrow" Simms. Maynard didn't make the call herself because she was concerned about how the Bias family would react to the news and unsure if Lonise Bias knew that Len had fathered a child. And Maynard was concerned about the perception that she was trying to take advantage of Bias's fame. "People would think I was a gold digger," she says.

Maynard remembers the gathering lasting a few hours and that Len's siblings – Michelle, Jay and Eric – came and went. She remembers seeing a color portrait of Len, which had been on display during the funeral, hanging on the wall. She claims that Lonise and James Bias held the baby throughout much of the meeting, and that James cried often during the visit. She remembers that

Michael Bias's birth certificate *(picture by Dave Ungrady)*

James asked why two casts covered Michael's feet. When Maynard said the baby had club feet, James told her that Len also had club feet, she says. Maynard also remembers Lonise Bias telling her that many women had called her to say they were the mothers of children by Len, but that Maynard was the first one to come to the house with a baby. Maynard says she responded by saying she was willing to have a DNA test done to confirm that Michael was Len's son, but she says Lonise did not respond.

Simms, Maynard's uncle, brought a streetwise perspective and his own notoriety to the gathering. Simms and his childhood friend, Roger "Pip" Moyer, who is white, grew up playing basketball together in the segregated streets of Annapolis in the 1940s; by the late 1960s, Simms was a self-described petty criminal who was serving time in jail and Moyer was the mayor of the city. When race riots spread across the United States in April 1968 in the wake of Dr. Martin Luther King's assassination, Moyer furloughed Simms from prison and the two boyhood friends walked the streets of Annapolis to show unity between whites and blacks. Their solidarity helped calm the city and their story was made into a documentary, *Pip and Zastrow: An American Friendship*, released in 2005.

Zastrow remembers the meeting between the families as mostly uncomfortable. "I wasn't expecting her to run out and say, 'Here's my son's child,' " he says of Lonise Bias. "And I wasn't expecting the cold and aloofness that I got."

Maynard says the Bias family showed little interest in Michael after that day. She says she saw Lonise Bias speak three times, once along with Simms at a church in Annapolis, while she was home visiting from California. They brought Michael along so Lonise Bias could see the young boy. A nervous Maynard asked Simms to take Michael to greet Lonise

Michael Bias played basketball for his high school team. (*provided by Tina Maynard*); Michael Bias's mug shot (*Anne Arundel County police*).

after her speech. Simms recalled the brief encounter. "She didn't completely ignore me, but it wasn't that great of a meeting," he says. "It was no better than 30 seconds."

- - - - - - - - - -

Michael Leonard Bias potentially represents the most intimate element of the mixed legacy of Len Bias, a connection that extends beyond a similar bloodline and shared genes. The life of Michael Bias, like that of Len Bias, has been greatly affected by drugs, which have contributed to Michael Bias accumulating a lengthy criminal record and living a misdirected life. He spoke calmly as he sat in a chair on the secured side of the visitors area at the Anne Arundel County Detention Center during a conversation in July 2011. Through a window, his face looked eager as he talked about Len Bias as his father. Michael made it clear that the most important thing he wants from the Bias family is recognition.

"I want to meet the other side of my family," he says. "They owe me an open conversation. It's like a missing piece in the puzzle in my life."

That missing piece has compelled Michael, says Maynard, to live an unfulfilled life. He has spent much of his adulthood so far incarcerated for crimes that range from driving without a license in 2004 to an incident in February 2008 when he was charged with armed robbery and reckless endangerment. He was sentenced to probation on the condition that he enter therapy. Michael says that he wants to try to enter a therapy program for the second time. "Everything has been a struggle, financially, emotionally," he says. "It's been a tough break for me all my life. It's been a jinx from when I was born because he died."

He was 11 or 12, Michael says, when his mother told him about the high-profile life of Len Bias, and he learned more as he paged through his mother's scrapbook, then more still from friends and family over the years. "Every day I tell people I'm his son," he says. "At first, it was like, 'Damn, really?' They said, 'For real?'"

Michael says he started to sell drugs – crack and powder cocaine, marijuana and ecstasy – when he was 14, and that he hasn't spent a full year at home since he was 13. Through his late teen years, he stayed at youth reform facilities. "I believe in my heart Michael would have been a different person if [the Bias family] had acknowledged him," says Maynard.

Michael looks a bit like the man he believes is his father, with a lean, muscular build. "I don't have his body, but I have his cut," he says. But Michael appears to have inherited little of Len Bias's supreme athleticism. He played basketball and football as a youth, and was a speedy running back and basketball player at Anne Arundel High School and the reform school, Bowling Brook Preparatory Academy, where he earned his General Educational Development degree. But he possessed marginal talents and a fraction of Len's will and determination to be a great athlete.

Michael has struggled with holding on to jobs, in part due to his criminal record. His aunt, Sheila, (she asked that her last name not be used), Tina's oldest sister, says she has felt a close bond with Michael since the day he was born and for a time talked with him every day. She recalls an interview he secured for a job at a department store in the spring of 2010 when he was out on parole. Michael tried to impress his interviewer, getting a haircut and buying new clothes. He was excited about joining the work force and talked about saving money and renting an efficiency apartment. "Then they got around to asking him if he had a criminal background," Sheila says. "And he told them that he did, and he didn't get the job. That broke his spirit. He wanted to work and do the right thing."

On November 13, 2010, Michael was involved in an incident that led to a conviction of second-degree assault. He was sentenced to three years in jail and five years' probation and in November 2011 was serving time in a correctional facility in Jessup, Maryland.

During our conversation in July 2011, Michael said he wants to be a rap artist. His eyes widened with surprise when I mentioned that rap producer Yo Gotti's name was attached to a recently released compilation of songs under the title "Len Bias Story." (A member of Gotti's group later told me that a deejay mixed the songs without Gotti's knowledge.)

"Yo Gotti? I'm a big fan," he says. "All of us in here are Yo Gotti fans. He's real street. I got so much respect for Gotti. He has a bit of an attitude from years of distress, being lied to."

Michael called himself "a street dude who raps." A few hours after I talked with him, his brother Marlon queued up a song Michael and his brother Marcus had produced and played it through the big-screen television that dominated the living room of Maynard's house. The repetitive, percussive beat formed the base that supported the following lyrics, which referred to the area where Michael grew up.

Copeland niggas we keep it real

I'm allergic to fake [people]

I need my Benadryl.

- - - - - - - - - -

About halfway through our first conversation, Tina Maynard sat on the couch, talking fondly of the 10 months she knew Bias and the frustration she feels with the Bias family. Two-year-old Taniya, the daughter of her son Marcus, 20, grew restless. Taniya repeatedly picked things up and threw them down, prompting Maynard to calmly and constantly remind her to put the items down gently. At age 43, Maynard, the mother of four boys, is raising Taniya. Maynard used the example of raising a grandchild to question the absence of the Bias family in Michael's life, and she wondered why Lonise Bias and her family have for the most part ignored him. "Why don't you acknowledge your grandson? That's what I would want to ask her," she says.

Does she think it will happen? "No," she says. "It hasn't thus far. Michael's 25 now. He's a man."

Maynard says she has never asked the Bias family for money to support Michael and doesn't plan to do so. "The fact that she did not acknowledge my son is her loss," she says of Lonise Bias. "He's always been loved by his mother."

AFTERWORD

The toughest speed workout I endured as a middle-distance runner on the Maryland track team was called the "Murphy." Our coach, Stan Pitts, learned the workout from a Duke quarter-miler during an Atlantic Coast Conference meet in the early 1970s. Impressed with Mr. Murphy's ability to finish strong, Pitts thought the workout could help his runners.

The Murphy forced us to respond while under severe fatigue. It called for a reverse ladder of intervals, from 800 meters to 600 to 400 to 300, all run at close to full effort. At the beginning of the workout, in between each interval and at the end, we ran two 200-meter sprints, in faster speeds as the workout progressed. Thankfully, we ran the workout only a few times a season. It left runners gasping and limp – sometimes both.

Once, we ran a double Murphy on an invigorating, early spring day, progressing down from the 800 and back up again on the old Byrd Stadium track. We endured the Murphy by gutting it out, plowing forward with our heads down and focusing on the mission, knowing that once it was over we would be better runners for having done it.

At times while working on this book, I felt as if I was immersed in a double Murphy. When each new challenge arose, I kept my head down, intent on resolving each predicament and quelling each quandary. I have tried to write as complete and comprehensive a narrative on the complex and mixed legacy of Len Bias as I possibly could.

In late 2009, during a phone conversation, Dick Dull randomly asked when I would write his book, saying that his story has never been told. Just give me the word and we'll do it, I replied.

Dull, for the most part, has avoided commenting on the tragedy publicly or discussing its impact personally. So in 2010, when the time finally arrived, the first person I called was Dull, who as Maryland's athletic director when Bias died was dramatically affected by the death.

Dull was an assistant track coach at the school when I was a member of the team in the late 1970s. As did most of my teammates, I grew very fond of Dull. He was a trusted confidant to many of us and helped guide me through some personal challenges, offering wise advice with compassion and patience. While an assistant athletic director he even helped me get a job selling football season tickets after my junior year during the summer of 1979.

When Dull expressed willingness in early 2010 to cooperate with the writing of this book, I felt invigorated about the project. I trusted his perspective and wisdom and felt he would talk with intelligent, measured introspection about how the Bias death affected his life. Dull had never talked expansively on the subject. "It's about time the real story was told," he said to me during a phone conversation. Dull's affirmative response made me feel that this project would not be too difficult, and it convinced me, perhaps too hastily, to move forward.

But after we had several discussions on how to proceed, Dull surprised me with an email in May 2010, saying he would not participate, that he needed to continue to put "this saga behind [me]." I was disappointed, but I understood his decision. I knew from brief discussions I had with Dull during the late 1980s and into the 1990s how difficult the transition was for him after Bias died. Dull and I did have a lengthy discussion about the Bias death in 2003 for my first book about Maryland athletics, *Tales from the Maryland Terrapins*, and those comments are used in this book.

After Dull changed his mind, I realized that perhaps it would be more difficult to convince people to talk about Bias than I had originally thought. That realization proved true. The death of Bias still strikes raw nerves some 25 years later. Many people most affected prefer to remain silent on the topic, or talk guardedly about it. An exception was the documentary *Without Bias,* which, unlike this book, featured the cooperation and blessings of the Bias family. And at least one person, Brian Tribble, says he was paid to participate in the documentary.

There would be more disappointments. Tribble chose not to meet again after our first meeting in April 2010 after I refused his request for payment and because he hopes to write his own book. We did have several discussions later by phone to confirm information.

Kirk Fraser, the director of *Without Bias,* stunned me by graciously offering access to interviews on tape, background materials and pictures that he had gathered while making the documentary. He also offered to help connect me with Lonise Bias, who had failed to respond to my repeated requests through emails, phone calls and letters for an interview. I left the meeting feeling as if I had scored a major victory. I had already talked with a couple of Bias's teammates and some of his friends but felt the book would not be complete without talking to members of the Bias family. I never received the materials from Fraser and he stopped returning my calls and emails.

Trying to persuade the Bias family to talk proved futile. Just a few months into starting the book, I obtained the phone number for Eric Bias, the lone remaining son and youngest child of James and Lonise Bias. A friend of Eric gave me the number on the condition that I not reveal the source. I reluctantly agreed, feeling that I was running out of options to reach the family. In most cases, these kinds of arrangements end badly, and this one did.

When I talked to Eric, the first thing he asked me was how I acquired his number. I told him I had promised to keep the person's identity private. Understandably annoyed, Bias asked me if I expected him to talk to me without telling him how I obtained the number. I told him I understood his position, but I did not want to violate the promise. He said that if I told him who gave me his number, he would talk. I refused. I asked the source three times to allow me to reveal his identity, but failed to receive permission. Eric Bias and I have not talked since.

I figured the only way I would be able to arrange a meeting with Lonise and James Bias was to approach Lonise after one of her speeches. I attended Lonise Bias's speech in Williamsport, Pennsylvania, after seeing a Google alert on the event. I requested access through the host school's media office to explain the book to her, arriving an hour early in the hope that she would talk with me before the presentation. She refused. After the speech, people randomly waited in line to talk with Bias. Not wanting to ambush Bias, I asked a school representative if I could join the group. They said no.

Lonise asked at least one of Len's teammates not to talk extensively for this book. Speedy Jones, a senior on the team when Len died, still feels a strong connection to Lonise. After talking with me for about 30 minutes, he said he needed to check with her to ensure that it was OK to talk more about Len and his legacy. About a month later, Jones told me that Lonise Bias requested he not talk more about her son, but left it up to him. He honored her request.

There were some pleasant surprises. Johnnie Walker, a Bias mentor who has talked little about him, initially refused my requests for an interview. But after I stopped by to visit him at his job at Dunbar High School in Washington, D.C., and we talked further, he agreed to discuss Len. We met twice at the home of Brian Waller, one of Len's closest friends. The three of us talked deeply for five hours about Len's life and the impact of his death.

John Johnson, a rising sophomore on the Maryland team when Bias died, chose to talk at length about his teammate for the first time, saying he wanted to honor Bias's memory. We talked comfortably for three hours at RJ Bentley's Restaurant in College Park.

And I was honored when Stanley Plumly, the Poet Laureate of Maryland and a former college basketball player who heads the creative writing department at the university, agreed to write the foreword. I met Stanley through my wife, Sharon, who is good friends with Stanley's wife, Margaret.

I secured the only interview with Michael Leonard Bias, who claims to be Len Bias's son. At the time, he was incarcerated at a detention center in Annapolis. We talked for about an hour.

The Washington Metropolitan Basketball Hall of Fame announced on October 4, 2011, that it will induct Bias. The day after the announcement, the hall's founder, Bob Geoghan, sent an email asking if I would present Bias's award. I eagerly agreed to his humbling request. Geoghan explained that he asked me to present the award because of a story I wrote in the *Washington Post* on June 19, 2011 – 25 years to the day Len died – suggesting that the University of Maryland pick Bias to be in its Hall of Fame. Geoghan said it helped convince him to select Bias for the Washington Metro Hall.

Those and other small triumphs have eased concerns I felt about writing this book. Would people think that I was exploiting a tragedy for my own benefit? I'm sure some will. But as a former Maryland athlete, I felt extra pressure and responsibility to present the story as a fair and accurate accounting of the impact of Bias's life. I tried to tell the story through the impressions and observations of those who knew him best in life and those who were most affected by his death. I hope I have humanized his story. I purposefully have tried to avoid perspective or opinion. This story is stong enough to stand on its own.

I felt that the fact I was a former athlete at Maryland would help me secure interviews, and it worked in some cases. But it did not persuade David Gregg and Terry Long, two of the more important characters in the Bias tragedy, to agree to extensive interviews. Long turned down my request during a phone call, but did confirm some information during a couple of other very brief calls. My communication with Gregg was more dubious. When I reached someone I believed to be Gregg on what I was told by a friend was his cell-phone number, a voice awfully similar to Gregg's said he was not there. I asked who was speaking. The person identified himself as Jim Johnson and promised that he would relay a message to Gregg. I never received a call back. Gregg, through his attorney, later refused to talk.

After I finished the dreaded Murphy workouts, a sense of weary relief always enveloped me. I feel the same after having completed this book. As a young writer decades ago, I remember reading a comment from a prominent writer that sometimes writing can hurt. Unlike the Murphy, the pain of completing an arduous writing project is more mental than physical.

In running, a grueling workout or a difficult race often brings satisfaction, even if a win is elusive. Similarly, it's rewarding to complete this book, although I realize so much more could have been written. The story of Len Bias's legacy is far-reaching, beyond even what is presented in this book, and likely one that will continue to resound for another quarter century.

ACKNOWLEDGEMENTS

To write this book, I relied on archived records and comments from many who experienced and still vividly remember the death of Len Bias and how it affected their lives.

I communicated with the following people, mostly by phone or in person but also by email and text message. They include: teammates Dave Dickerson, Derrick Lewis, Keith Gatlin, Jeff Baxter, Speedy Jones, John Johnson, Greg Nared, Derrick Lewis, Bryan Palmer, Phil Nevin, Terry Long and Jeff Adkins; friends Brian Tribble, Derrick Curry, Bob Wagner, Johnnie Walker, Brian Waller, Mike Morrison, Charles Payne, Clint Venable, Ernie Graham, Myriam Leger and John Ware.

Former Maryland athletic officials, coaches, athletes and managers as well as university personnel include Dick Dull, Lefty Driesell, Bobby Ross, Keith Booth, Chuck Walsh, Jack Zane, Gerald Gurney, Sue Tyler, Michael Lipitz, Azizuddin Abdur-Ra'oof, Ferrell Edmunds, Jim Kehoe, Jim Dietsch, Jack Jackson, Chris Weller, John Lucas, Len Elmore, Bonnie Bernstein, Bob Nelligan, John McHugh, Bill Goodman, Stan Pitts, Jack Jackson, Bill McHugh, J.J. Bush, Joe Krivak, Frank Costello, Jim Spiro, Dr. John Slaughter, Wendy Whittemore, Dr. J. Robert Dorfman, Dottie Warren and Kenny Beaver.

Former and current NBA players, coaches, and employees include: Quintin Dailey, Chris Washburn, William Bedford, Scott Wedman, Dr. Jack Ramsay, Chris Wallace, Robert Gadson and Horace Balmer.

Joanne Borzakian Ouellette, formerly of Reebok, and former Celtics general manager Jan Volk provided insight into Len Bias's brief time in Boston. Others who cooperated include: ACC Barn-storming organizer Mike Sumners, sports agent Jeff Austin, Duke basketball coach Mike Krzyzewski, Mark Castel of AEI speakers bureau, college professor William Astore and former Massachusetts Lieutenant Governor Tom O'Neill.

Also: Kemba Smith, Gus Smith, Odessa Smith, attorneys Thomas Morrow, Jeffrey Harding and Wayne Curry, former high school coach Morgan Wootten, Matt Ribaudo, Pete DiGiulio, Willie Mays Aikens, Dorothy Gaines, Karen Garrison, Scott Green, Dr. Robert DuPont, Tom Cash, Orlando Magic Sr. Vice President Pat Williams, U.S. Representative Bobby Scott. Tina Maynard, Rena Watson, Ted Watson, Joseph "Zastrow" Simms, Michael Leonard Bias, Eli Cohen, Mike Cogburn, John Brown, Greg Abel, Brian Straus, Alexis Mastronardi and Rick Walker.

I'd also like to thank those who provided professional guidance. They include authors and journalists Jeffrey Marx and Christine Brennan; book editor Sian Hunter, and Steve Kurkjian, a Pulitzer Prize winning investigative reporter for the *Boston Globe*.

Many helped guide me in the process to find the right people with whom to talk. They include Chris Ramsay and Paul Grant of ESPN.com, Mike Foss of ESPN, Butch Stearns of the PulseNet-work, Steve Bulpett of the *Boston Herald*, George Washington University men's basketball coach Mike Lonergan, communications specialist Meredith Geisler, Mark Blevins and Scott Witt at Bearden High School in Tennessee, my former college track and field teammate Greg Robertson, Bob Thompson, a friend of Terry Long, John Jackson at Duke University athletics communica-tions, Nkechi Taifa of the Open Society Institute-DC, Eric Sterling of the Criminal Justice Policy Foundation and Joshua Horwitz of the Educational Fund to Stop Gun Violence.

Anne Turkos and Jason Speck and their staff at the University Archives office at the Univer-sity of Maryland provided assistance with historical research and securing images. And a big thanks to Doug Dull of the University of Maryland Athletics Communications office for doing the same and providing guidance. Also, thanks to Ray Wilson of the Ronald Reagan Library for his help locating a letter the president sent to the Bias family.

A story such as this is well documented. I referred to archived materials from the following publications: the *Washington Post,* the *Baltimore Sun,* the *Los Angeles Times,* the *Seattle Post-In-telligencer,* the *Miami Herald,* the *Newark Star-Ledger,* the *York Daily Record,* the *Calgary Her-ald,* the *Charlotte Observer,* the *Associated Press*, *United Press International, Newsweek Magazine, Sports Illustrated Magazine, Slam Magazine* and *Essence Magazine*. Books used as resources include *Lenny, Lefty & the Chancellor: The Len Bias Tragedy and the Search for Re-form*; *Never Too Young to Die: The Death of Len Bias*; *Tales from the Maryland Terrapins: A Collection of the Greatest Stories Ever Told* and *Legends of Maryland Basketball*. The documen-tary *Without Bias* was used as a resource.

Special thanks to editor Barbara Huebner, whose attention to detail, concern for nuance, dogged persistence on getting it right, and undying commitment to the end result helped keep me on track. It's no surprise she's won a Pulitzer Prize for editing.

Much gratitude to the book's designer, Jeff Thoreson, a University of Maryland graduate and a seasoned journalist who has proven to be a patient colleague in all the work we've done together over the last two decades. To copy editor Kevin Fay, I appreciate your attention to detail and enthusiasm for the project. Matt Dewhurst and Kathy Leidich did great work transcribing dozen of hours of taped interviews. Shannon Sykes provided design services.

A note on style: those who I communicated with directly and are quoted are attributed with "says." Quotes from archived materials or dated events are attributed with "said."

I appreciate all those who agreed to talk with me for this book, especially teammates and friends of Len Bias who still struggle to remember his life and the way he died. This book could not have been completed without your courage, cooperation and commitment to Len's legacy.

by dave ungrady

Unlucky
A Season of Struggle in Minor League Professional Soccer

Tales From the Maryland Terrapins
A Collection of the Greatest Stories Ever Told

Legends of Maryland Basketball

daveungrady.com

facebook.com/lenbiaslegacybook

twitter: lenbiasbook; djungrady

Dave Ungrady is the author of three other books: *Unlucky: A Season of Struggle in Minor League Professional Soccer*; the best-selling *Tales from the Maryland Terrapins: A Collection of the Greatest Stories Ever Told*; and *Legends of Maryland Basketball*. Dave is a contributing writer to the *New York Times*. His work has also appeared in the *Washington Post* and *Sport Magazine* and on NBC, CNN, ESPN and Voice of America.

Dave was an all-ACC and all-IC4A middle distance runner on the University of Maryland track team, which he captained in 1980. He also played for the school's soccer team and is a proud member of Maryland's M-Club. Dave was recently inducted into the Notre Dame High School (Trenton, N.J.) Athletic Hall of Fame. He lives in Northern Virginia with his wife, Sharon, and son, Cayden.

Made in the USA
Middletown, DE
20 October 2018